写作不过如此

刘晓艳 主编

中国宇航出版社
·北京·

图书在版编目（CIP）数据

写作不过如此 / 刘晓艳主编 . -- 北京 : 中国宇航出版社，2022.9（2022.10重印）
ISBN 978-7-5159-2102-0

Ⅰ. ①写… Ⅱ. ①刘… Ⅲ. ①英语－写作－研究生－入学考试－自学参考资料 Ⅳ. ①H319.36

中国版本图书馆 CIP 数据核字（2022）第 146443 号

策划编辑：冯佳佳　　装帧设计：张圆惠　沈沫含
责任编辑：冯佳佳　　责任校对：甄薇薇

出版发行　中国宇航出版社
社　址　北京市阜成路8号　邮　编　100830
（010）68768548
网　址　www.caphbook.com
经　销　新华书店
发行部　（010）68767386　（010）68371900
（010）68767382　（010）88100613（传真）
零售店　读者服务部　（010）68371105
承　印　北京天恒嘉业印刷有限公司

版　次　2022年9月第1版
2022年10月第2次印刷
规　格　787×1092
开　本　1/16
印　张　17
字　数　450千字
书　号　ISBN 978-7-5159-2102-0
定　价　56.80元

前言

说到考研英语写作，考生从来只求模板，认为平时不需要准备，只需要考前背一个模板就搞定了。再加上一些考研老师对模板大肆吹捧，导致考生提起写作，立刻想到模板，模板的作用也就被神化了。而本书的目的就是告诉考生，没有模板，大家同样可以很轻松地写出高分作文，甚至是满分作文。

模板就是适用于大多数作文题型的固定格式，这导致考生的作文雷同率至少达到 80%，模板的这一缺点很明显。不是说模板本身不好，而是用的人多了就不好了。模板的另一大缺点是内容空洞，论述无力，只说一些假大空的话。试想一下，对于孝敬父母、自信、养宠物、污染等话题都适用的模板，内容又该是怎样的空洞呢？

那作文有指导思想吗？具体如何写作呢？怎么使内容生动具体、针对性强呢？基于此，笔者创作了本书。

本书分为七章。第一章从考研英语写作概述入手，对考研英语大纲作文部分进行解读，使考生对考研英语写作的特点及基本写作技巧有一个总体的认识。而后列举了真题及样文，告诉考生高分作文的特点及考生在写作中常犯的错误。这样，考生会对考研英语写作有一个更直观的认识。

本书第二至五章，按照构成作文的四个层次——**词汇、句型、段落、篇章**具体展开论述。首先讲写作必备的分类表达；然后由词汇讲到句型，包括句型的改写和扩写；紧接着讲段落的编排及论述方式；最后由段到篇，讲考研英语写作话题的各种类型及常见表达。本书内容层层深入，环环相扣，逻辑清楚，对于基础相对较差，短期内想搞定考研英语写作的考生尤为适用。基础较好的考生可以按照这个思路对个人写作能力做进一步的整合和提升。

通过前五章的具体讲解及论述，相信考生会对考研英语写作有一个准确的把握。第六章汇总了常见的考研英语应用文写作及短文写作的话题，并给出了相应的参考范文，希望可以满足考生的备考之需。顺此思路，第七章第一节按话题分析了考生的作文，供大家反观自己，力求避免出现相似的错误；第二节和第三节在帮助考生一一列举历年考研英语写作真题的同时，还给出了参考范文，考生可以据此“小试牛刀”，看一看自己的收获如何。

本书的最后，另附写作经典 100 句，供各位考生参考学习。

最后，希望本书能为考生的考研英语写作带来实际的帮助。只要是你有能力去做的事就一定要去做，不要给自己留下任何遗憾，希望你在考研的路上，无所畏惧，拼尽全力！

刘晓艳

目 录

第一章
考研英语写作概述

一、考研英语大纲对写作的要求

《全国硕士研究生招生考试英语考试大纲（非英语专业）》要求考生具备以下写作技能：考生应能写不同类型的应用文，包括私人和公务信函、备忘录、报告等，以及一般描述性、叙述性、说明性或议论性的文章。写作时，考生应能：

① 做到语法、拼写、标点正确，用词恰当；

② 遵循文章的特定文体格式；

③ 合理组织文章结构，使其内容统一、连贯；

④ 根据写作目的和特定读者，选用恰当语域。

二、考研英语写作试卷结构

全国硕士研究生招生考试英语试卷（一）的第三部分，英语试卷（二）的第四部分为写作。该部分主要考查考生的书面表达能力，分别占 30 分和 25 分，试卷共 100 分。

1. 英语（一）

A 节：考生根据所给情景写出约 100 词（标点符号不计算在内，下同）的应用性短文，包括私人和公务信函、备忘录、报告等。共 10 分。

B 节：考生根据提示信息写出一篇 160 ～ 200 词的短文。提示信息的形式有主题句、写作提纲、规定情景、图、表等。共 20 分。

2. 英语（二）

A 节：考生根据所给情景写出约 100 词的应用性短文，包括私人和公务信函、备忘录、报告等。共 10 分。

B 节：要求考生根据规定的情景或给出的提纲，写出一篇 150 词左右的英语说明文或议论文。提供情景的形式为图画、图表或文字。共 15 分。

三、考研英语写作评分标准

1. 评分原则和方法

① A 节作文的评分重点在于信息点的覆盖、内容的组织、语言的准确性、格式与语域的恰当。语域是指书面表达和口语表达中根据不同的交际对象而采用的话语方式，包括正式、一般和非正式的话语。对语法结构和词汇多样性的要求将根据具体试题做调整。允许在作文中使用提示语中出现过的个别关键词或词组，但使用提示语中出现过的句子会被扣分。

B 节作文的评分重点在于内容的完整性、文章的连贯性、语法结构和词汇的多样性及语言的准确性。

② 评分时，先根据文章的内容和语言确定其所属档次，然后按该档次的要求来给分。

③ 英语（一）和英语（二）A 节作文的字数要求都是 100 词左右。B 节作文的字数要求，英语（一）是 160 ~ 200 词，英语（二）是 150 词左右。文章长度不符合要求的，会被酌情扣分。

④ 拼写与标点符号是反映语言准确性的一个方面。评分时，视其对交际的影响程度予以考虑。英、美拼写及词汇用法均可接受。

⑤ 如书写较差，以致影响读者理解，分数被降低一个档次。

2. 一般评分标准

<table>
<tr><td colspan="2">第五档</td><td rowspan="3">很好地完成了试题规定的任务：
· 包含所有内容要点；
· 使用丰富的语法结构和词汇；
· 语言自然流畅，基本没有语法错误；
· 有效地采用了多种衔接手法，文字连贯，层次清晰；
· 格式与语域恰当贴切
对目标读者完全产生了预期的效果</td></tr>
<tr><td>A节</td><td>（9~10分）</td></tr>
<tr><td>B节</td><td>英语（一）
（17~20分）
英语（二）
（13~15分）</td></tr>
<tr><td colspan="2">第四档</td><td rowspan="3">较好地完成了试题规定的任务：
· 包含所有内容要点，允许漏掉一个或两个次重点；
· 使用较丰富的语法结构和词汇；
· 语言基本准确，只有在试图使用较复杂结构或较高级词汇时才出现个别错误；
· 采用了适当的衔接手法，层次较清晰，组织较严密；
· 格式与语域较恰当
对目标读者产生了预期的效果</td></tr>
<tr><td>A节</td><td>（7~8分）</td></tr>
<tr><td>B节</td><td>英语（一）
（13~16分）
英语（二）
（10~12分）</td></tr>
<tr><td colspan="2">第三档</td><td rowspan="3">基本完成了试题规定的任务：
· 虽漏掉一些内容，但包含多数内容要点；
· 所使用的语法结构和词汇能满足任务的需求；
· 存在一些语法及词汇错误，但不影响整体理解；
· 采用了简单的衔接手法，内容基本连贯，层次基本清晰；
· 格式与语域基本合理
对目标读者基本产生了预期的效果</td></tr>
<tr><td>A节</td><td>（5~6分）</td></tr>
<tr><td>B节</td><td>英语（一）
（9~12分）
英语（二）
（7~9分）</td></tr>
<tr><td colspan="2">第二档</td><td rowspan="3">未能按要求完成试题规定的任务：
· 漏掉或未能有效阐述一些内容要点，写了一些无关的内容；
· 语法结构单调，词汇使用有限；
· 存在较多语法结构或词汇方面的错误，影响了对写作内容的理解；
· 未采用恰当的衔接手法，内容缺乏连贯性；
· 格式与语域不恰当
未能清楚地把信息传达给读者</td></tr>
<tr><td>A节</td><td>（3~4分）</td></tr>
<tr><td>B节</td><td>英语（一）
（5~8分）
英语（二）
（4~6分）</td></tr>
</table>

（续表）

<table>
<tr><td colspan="2">第一档</td><td rowspan="3">未完成试题规定的任务：
· 明显遗漏主要内容，且有许多不相关的内容；
· 语法结构和词汇的使用单调、重复；
· 语言错误多，有碍读者对内容的理解，语言运用能力差；
· 未使用任何衔接手法，内容不连贯，缺少组织、分段；
· 无格式与语域概念
未能把信息传达给读者</td></tr>
<tr><td>A节</td><td>（1～2分）</td></tr>
<tr><td>B节</td><td>英语（一）
（1～4分）
英语（二）
（1～3分）</td></tr>
<tr><td colspan="2">零档（0分）</td><td>所传达的信息或所使用的语言太少，无法评价；内容与要求无关或无法辨认</td></tr>
</table>

3. 考研英语写作满分标志

根据前面的评分标准可知，考研英语写作高分作文需要满足两个原则。

黄金原则一：书写工整，字迹清晰，卷面整洁。

黄金原则二：语言第一，结构第二，内容第三。

（1）语言第一

语言指的就是单词和语法，考研英语写作中，单词和语法需要做到正确、准确、多变。

① 单词正确很容易做到。生活中，一个普通英国人常用的单词在 1 500 个左右，这就意味着，初中要掌握的 1 500 个单词必须会正确拼写。很多学生的问题仍在于总想写自己想写的词汇，一旦不会写，就傻眼了。比如：

从照片上看，这是一个内心善良的女人。

如果会写“善良”(goodness/kindness) 的英文，就很简单了；如果不会写，就换成自己会的词汇啊——美丽、诚实、友好均可以。为什么非得写“善良”呢？评卷老师只能看到你写得是否正确，不太考虑你心里在想些什么，对吗？

② 单词准确就没有那么容易把握了。比如：

你的皮肤真好啊！

皮肤好，具体地说，什么样的皮肤算是好皮肤呢？首先考虑 smooth（光滑的），其次 fair，healthy 也可以，这就是准确。又如：

你真是一位好老师啊！

好老师，具体地说，什么样的老师算是好老师呢？ responsible 可以，sincere 也可以，honest 同样可以，这就是单词准确。

所以如果想做到单词准确，你就需要有一定的单词量。你必须记单词，同时增加阅读量。写作想得高分，只靠 good，bad 是不行的。

③ 单词多变这个很容易理解，我们写作文通常使用太多重复的单词了。比如，这么多年我们发现考生作文第一段的首句通常都是“With the development of society”，然后是“Some people think that... Other people think that... I think that...”。所以作文中，不但要求单词正确、准确，还要注意一句话当中尽量不要有重复的单词，全文单词也不要有太多重复。这里的 think 可换成 consider，hold，regard，deem，believe 等。用名词 view，attitude，perspective 等相关表达代替也是可以的。

④ 语法正确比较容易做到，下面句子中会有讲解，切记的是：写不来长难句就尽量写简单句，正确最重要。

⑤ 语法多变的要求是一篇文章中连续三到四个句子的句式最好不要雷同。比如：

都说我如水多变，可知我清澈不变。

I am claimed changeable like water. However, my clarity keeps the same.

第一句话用了被动语态，转折词后的句子换成了主动语态。

（2）结构第二

① 除了告示类文章外，考研英语写作基本上还是三段式结构，并且三段比例最好坚持4∶5∶4，比例要适当。

② 句子和句子之间要多用逻辑关系词，使文章逻辑关系明显。比如：

这个男人看起来很帅，我决定嫁给他。

虽然这句话用中文说起来没有逻辑关系词也通顺，但是用英文表达必须加逻辑关系词。

那就是：The man looks handsome. Therefore, I decide to marry him.

逻辑关系词可以分为四大类：并列连词、连接副词、从属连词、介词和限定词。

并列连词：连接两个独立的句子而构成一个并列句。在第一个分句后必须用逗号。比如：

1）Drumsticks may taste delicious, but I dislike them.

2）I dislike drumsticks, so I seldom eat them.

连接副词：用于连接两个句子，使之构成一个并列句，表示两个分句之间的关系。注意用连接副词时标点比较特殊：在第一个分句后用分号，连接副词后要加逗号。比如：

I dislike drumsticks; consequently, I seldom eat them.

连接副词或短语可以位于简单句句首、句中或句尾。在句首时，只在连接副词后加逗号；在句中时，则在连接副词前、后都加逗号，但如果只是连接一个词，逗号可以省略；在句尾时，则在连接副词前加逗号。比如：

1）On the other hand, drumsticks taste delicious.

2）Drumsticks, on the other hand, taste delicious.

3）Drumsticks taste delicious, on the other hand.

有些并列连词和连接副词具有相同的意义，请参见下列表格。

连词	副词、介词短语	逻辑关系
and	similarly, equally, likewise, at the same time, in the meanwhile	平行关系
not only... but also...	furthermore, moreover, besides, also, in addition, additionally, then, subsequently	递进关系
but, yet, while, whereas	however, nevertheless, conversely, unexpectedly, unfortunately, on the contrary, by contrast	转折关系
or	otherwise	选择关系
so	consequently, therefore, thus, accordingly, hence, as a result	因果关系

从属连词：引导从句同主句相接构成复合句。从句的位置可在主句前，也可在主句后。当状语从句出现在主句之前时，常常要带逗号，但状语从句在主句之后，则不需要用逗号把它与主句分开。比如：

1）Although I decide to quit, I still want to stay there.

2) I still want to stay there although I decide to quit.

3) I still want to stay there because I don't give up my dream.

4) Because the cost of education has been rising, many students have financial problems.

5) Many foreign students suffer from culture shock when they come to the United States.

介词和限定词：在标点符号方面没有特定的要求。常用的介词词组有 because of，due to，in spite of；常用的限定词有 another，final 等。比如：

Because of your sudden appearance, I felt quite nervous.

③ 转承词的功能和意义。我们在写作中，要学会运用转承词来增强文章的连贯性，增强语言的表达力。我们根据转承词本身的意思和段落连接所需要的逻辑意义，将其大体分为以下几类，可供写作时参考。

表递进

too 也	not only... but also... 不仅……而且……
increasingly 越来越多地	to make matters worse 更糟糕的是
also 亦，也	besides 加之，更，还有
another 另一，别的	in addition 加之，又，另外
furthermore 而且	more importantly 更为重要的是
moreover 况且，并且，此外	most importantly 最为重要的是
additionally 另外	what's more 加之，此外

表举例

to name only a few 仅举几例	incidentally 附带地，顺便说一句
and so on 等等	for one thing 一方面，一则
a case in point 恰当的实例；佐证	namely 即，就是
in essence 本质上；大体上	such as the following 比如
for another thing 另一方面，再则	that is (to say) 这就是说，即
for example/instance 比如	to illustrate 举例说
by way of example 比如，举例来说	as an illustration 作为例证
as an example 作为例子	in illustration of 作为……的例证

表比较与对照

compare with 与……相比	present a striking contrast to 和……形成显著的对比
than 比	in any event 无论怎样
as 和……一样	in the same way 以同样的方式
all (just) the same 完全一样；仍然	contrary to 与……相反
in general 一般，大体上	conversely 相反地
likewise 同样地	different from 和……不同
nevertheless 仍然；不过	whereas 然而，但是，尽管
yet 还，仍旧，依然	similarly 相同地
by contrast 相反地；出乎预料地	to the contrary 相反
in contrast with/to 和……相比	

（续表）

notwithstanding 尽管，还是	on the other hand 从另一方面来说
on the contrary 正相反	for the sake of contrast 为了对照起见

表让步

although 尽管	even though/if 即使
though 尽管	in spite of 尽管，不管
despite 不管，任凭	

表因果

because 由于	with the result that 其结果是……
now that 既然	owing to 由于
accordingly 因此；于是；相应地	result from 由……而产生
as a result 结果；所以	since 因为
result in 结果为，导致	consequently 因此
by reason of 凭……的理由	the cause of ……的原因
due to 由于	the reason for ……的理由
for this/that reason 为此	therefore 因此，所以
for some reason 由于某种原因	otherwise 否则，不然
hence 因此，所以	considering that 考虑到

表结论或概要

all in all 总的来说，总之	in other words 换句话说
as has been noted 如上所述	in plain terms 简单来说
as I have said 正如我所说的	in summary 概括地说
in a few words 一言以蔽之	on the whole 总的来看；大体上
to conclude 最后	overall 一般来说；总体上
to sum up 概括，总结	in conclusion 总之；最后
in brief/short/sum 总之，简言之	in one/a word 总而言之
to put it in another way 换句话说	to summarize 总的来说

表强调

above all 尤其是；最重要的是	for this purpose 为此目的
particularly 特别；尤其；格外	indeed 确实
primarily 首先；主要地	to repeat 重复一下
in particular 特别是	truly 真正；确实
more significantly 更有意义的是	especially 特别是
more importantly 更为重要的是	only in this way 只有这样
anyway/anyhow 无论如何；不管怎样	

表时间或顺序

in the end 终于	after an interval 一段时间后
at the same time 同时	eventually 最后，终于

（续表）

afterwards 后来，其后	finally 最终，最后
first of all 第一，首先	as soon as 一……就……
formerly 以前，从前	at present 目前
in the first place 首先	nowadays 现今，现在
in the meantime 在这期间	previously 先前地
recently 最近	currently 当前
no sooner... than... 一……就……	around the corner 即将来临
immediately 立即	no matter when 无论何时
right away 马上	at once 马上
in time 及时	in the second place 其次
until 直到，直至	subsequently 其后，接着
simultaneously 同时；一齐	later on 以后，过后
temporarily 暂时	meanwhile 在此期间，与此同时
to begin with 首先，第一	ultimately 最后，最终

表地点或空间

beside 在……旁边	in the center/middle of 在……中间
in front of 在……前面	in the distance 在远处
across from 在……对面	at the bottom of 在……底部
adjacent to 邻近的；毗连的	at the other end 在另一端
at one end 在一端	close to 接近
at the back of 在……后面	nearby 在附近
at the end of 在……末端	next to 紧靠……旁边；贴近
below 在……下面	on the top of 在……上面
beyond 在……那一边	elsewhere 在别处；到别处
opposite to 在……对面	no matter where 无论哪里
in the neighborhood of 在……附近（表空间）	

表目的

for the purpose of 为了	in order that 为了
so that 以便	in case 以备；以防

表条件

unless 除非	provided 假如；倘若
on condition that 如果	if 如果
as long as 只要	

表转折

but 但是	yet 然而
all the same 还是	while 然而
nevertheless 不过	however 然而

比如：Do you still remember the day when I failed to pass the examination? I was shedding tears in the rain. Nobody solaced me **although** they saw me. **At the moment**, you came up to me **and** comforted me with a soft velvety tone, suggesting that life is full of ups and downs. Then I continued working hard. **In the end**, I succeeded. Today, I must attribute my progress and success to your inspiration.

④ 多用代词代替已经出现过的名词。比如：

I bought a dog yesterday and **it** looks lovely.

Cultural exchange makes university students understand the world better. Moreover, **it** can let common people know the differences among nations.

English is regarded as an international language. **It** is spoken and written by more than 375 million people all over the world.

（3）内容第三

大纲明确规定，对内容的要求就是"切题"两个字。也就是说，作文内容只要别跑题，写得是惊天地泣鬼神还是平平淡淡，没有根本上的差别。这就提醒我们，得高分的关键是意思相同的句子，我们该用什么样的单词和语法来表述，这个很重要。比如：

我爱你。

I love you.（趋于通俗）

You never fail to fascinate me.（文采飞扬）

我不会嫁给你。

I will never marry you.（普通表达）

By no means will I marry you.（倒装强调）

如果有梦想，就应该会成功。

If you have a dream, you will succeed.（鼓励对方）

If there exists a dream in your heart, glory cannot fail to be achieved.（意志坚定）

4. 全国硕士研究生入学考试样文分析

（1）2000 年全国硕士研究生入学考试样文评析

Directions:

For this part, you are allowed 40 minutes to write a composition according to the pictures. Your composition should be no less than 150 words. You must base your composition on the following instructions.

A. Study the following two pictures carefully and write an essay of at least 150 words.

B. Your essay must be written neatly on ANSWER SHEET 2.

C. Your essay should meet the requirements below:

1) Describe the pictures.

2) Deduce the drawer's purpose in the pictures.

3) Suggest your counter-measures. (15 points)

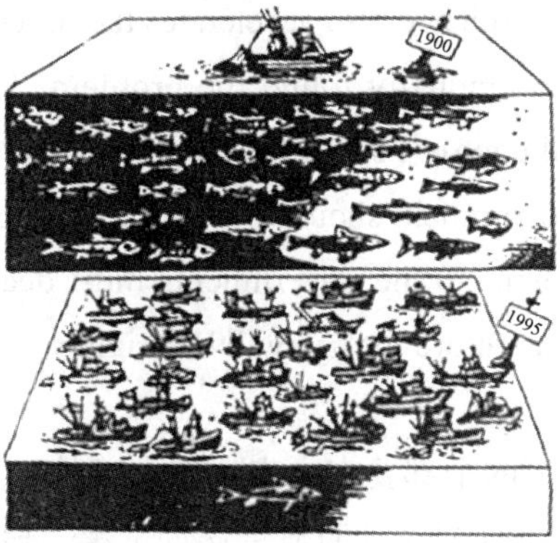

A Brief History of World Commercial Fishing

样文一

As is shown in the pictures, we can clearly that with the increase of commercial fishing, the number of fishes sharply decreased. In the first picture, there were various kinds of fish and only one fishing-boat in 1900. **On the contrary**, in 1995 there was only one fish, **but** many fishing-boats.

The purpose of the pictures is to show us that due attention has to be paid to the decrease of ocean resources. **Owing to** over-fishing, the number of fishes has obviously decreased. **If** we let this situation go as it is, we won't know where fishes are in the future. **By that time**, our environment will suffer a great destruction.

Therefore, it is imperative for us to take drastic measures. **For one thing**, we should appeal to our authorities to make strict laws to control commercial fishing. **For another**, we should enhance the awareness of people that the ocean resources are very vital to us. **Only in this way** can we protect our ocean resources. **Also**, I believe that we human beings can overcome this difficulty, and we will have a bright future.

评分：14 分

评语：其实这篇文章没有特别之处，但达到了作文大纲的基本要求：内容切题，涵盖了提纲的全部要点；文章通顺，语言流畅，句式丰富多样；用词面较宽；虽有个别不妥之处，但基本功较好；表达能力较强；篇幅符合要求。明显错误如：首段中的 we can clearly that 显然没有谓语，应修改为 we can see clearly that。注意黑体词和短语的使用，对比、转折、原因、条件、强调、顺序、递进等使文章一气呵成。

样文二

Now we can see two pictures about the history of world commercial fishing. **The first** picture shows us a fishing-boat and a water rich in fishes in 1900. **On the contrary**, we learn that, according to **the second** picture, the number of fishes decreased sharply to only one with the increase of boats in 1995.

The purpose of the pictures is to warn us that the sea resources are being ruined, and we need to protect our ocean now. As far as I am concerned, this kind of fishing **attributes to** the drive of money. To earn money, some people just want to catch fish whether it is small or big. **Secondly**, some people ignore fish has its growing time. Excessive fishing in a short time causes decrease of fish population. **In**

addition, the development of modern science **also** accelerates the process.

Nowadays, many people have gradually found the problem. They appeal to taking measures to developing the resources of fish and control fishing for commercial aim, which is also the purpose of the drawer of the pictures. **First**, the government should introduce laws to stop the operation of commercial fishing. **Second**, it is a world problem, so the governments must decide to punish people who fish too much. **To conclude**, it is clear that the future for fish will be bright with the solution of the problem.

评分：11 分

评语：内容切题，包括了提纲的全部要点；表达基本清楚，文字连贯；句式变化较多；结构与用词有少量一般性错误；篇幅符合要求。明显错误如：第二段中，this kind of fishing attributes to the drive of money 句子逻辑关系有问题，应该改为 this kind of fishing is attributed to the drive of money；第三段中，many people have gradually found the problem，found 用词不准确，应该修改为 realized；appeal to taking measures 中的 appeal to 后应该跟 sb.，表示“向某人呼吁”。再次注意黑体部分，表示时间、顺序、转折、递进等，使行文流畅。

（2）2001 年全国硕士研究生入学考试样文评析

Directions:

Among all the worthy feelings of mankind, love is probably the noblest, but everyone has his/her own understanding of it.

There has been a discussion recently on the issue in a newspaper. Write an essay to the newspaper to

1) show your understanding of the symbolic meaning of the picture below,

2) give a specific example, and

3) give your suggestion as to the best way to show love.

You should write about 200 words on ANSWER SHEET 2. (20 points)

样文一

It is generally believed that love is a hot topic which is most talked about. This is true not only in China but also in other countries. We live in different countries, speak different languages, but love is something common to us all. But how to show love may be different with different people in different countries. This is something we should give more thought to.

As shown in the picture, love is like a lamp which shines brighter in darker places. This tells us a simple truth: Love is like a lamp. It is most valuable when it is most needed. For example, once I saw a foreign lady get lost in the street. She could not speak Chinese and nobody seemed to be able to help her. Though my English is not very good and I am a shy person, I thought she needed help very much. I asked her what she wanted. She told me she lost her way, so I showed her the way to her hotel. It was a small thing, but she thanked me very much because my help was needed very much. My help was like a lamp in a dark place.

I think we all should be like a lamp in a dark place, showing our love, giving our help to others, even to strangers. In this way, we can make this world harmonious and peaceful.

评分：12 分

评语：内容切题，包括题目要求的全部要点；表达基本清楚，文字连贯；结构与用词有少量一般性错误，并且单词和句型偏简单和重复；篇幅符合要求。明显错误如：第一段第一句改为 Love is an eternal topic。第一段第四句改为 But how to show love varies from person to person。第二段第一句 As shown in the picture，应该在 As 和 shown 中间加 is。第三段第一句改为 I think we all should be like a lamp when someone is in a dark place。

样文二

I saw a picture recently in your newspaper. There is a small lamp in the picture and a flame on the lamp, which is smiling. The lamp says, “Love is a lamp, it will be brightest in the darkest place.” I think it shows us a vivid picture: Where and who need live, love is the noblest feeling. So I believe that we should give our love to those who are in need. If everyone can give his love to whom in need, then the world will be filled with love.

For example, in the countryside, there are millions of pupils, who can’t afford to attend school, Some of them never attend school. They are unfortunate, but now there are many warm-hearted people who give help to the pupils. Of course, we can also show our love in many other ways. For instance, as a friend, we should help our friends when they are in trouble. There is a saying, “A friend in need is a friend indeed.” As a young man, we should respect the old. When we walk on the street, we can help the blind or old people and children to cross the road.

In a word, there are many ways to show our love. People all over the world should love and respect each other. The best way to show our love is to help others when the are in difficulties.

评分：10 分

评语：首段中的 it will be brightest，最高级前应该加 the，并且 it 前应该加 and；Where and who need live 中，where 和 who 是不能并列的，因为词性不同，并且显然考生把 love 不小心写成了 live；If everyone can give his love to whom in need, then the world will be filled with love 中 whom 应该修改为 those，因为 whom 是疑问代词，应该放在句首或是作为关系代词引导从句。第二段 there are millions of pupils, who can’t afford to attend school, Some of them never attend school 中，定语从句不应该写成非限制性定语从句，应该去掉 who 前的逗号，并且 Some of 这句话前面应该用句号，而不是逗号；There is a saying, “A friend in need is a friend indeed.” As a young man, we should respect the old. 这两句话之间没有逻辑关系，前面说朋友，后面突然说要尊重老人，衔接有问题；When we walk on the street 中的 on the street 应该修改为 in the street。第三段 when the are in difficulties 中，the 应该修改为 they，in difficulties 应改为 in difficulty。

样文三

Among all the worthy feelings of mankind, love is probably the noblest. It is of utmost importance to human beings. Everybody not only needs love, but also should give love.

As is described in the picture, "Love is a lamp which is brighter in darker place." This is indeed true. People in darker places need more light. Maybe even a dim light can give them much hope for a better life and progress. Maybe just a thread of light will call forth their strength and courage to step out of their difficulties.

For instance, when someone is starving to death, just a little food and water from you may save his life. Or when a little girl in a poor rural area drops out of school because of poverty, just a small sum of money from you may support her to finish her schooling and change her life. The love you give is like a lamp in a dark place where light is most needed.

To sum up, we should offer our help to all that are in need. We expect to get love from others and we also give love to others so when you see someone in difficulty or in distress and in need of help, don't hesitate to give your love to him. I believe that the relationship between people will be harmonious and our society will be a better place for us to live in.

评分：14 分

评语：虽然有个别小错误，但是考生语言功底还是很深厚的；单词准确多变，语言流畅；结构清楚，内容切题。明显错误如：第二段第一句中的 in darker place 应该修改为 in darker places。最后一段第二句中的 we also 改为 we should also；so 的前面加句号，so 首字母大写。

样文四

In the picture below, in the fully dark situation, a little of spark enlightens the dark. The naive spark smiles so sweet. It seems to be saying, as the caption in the picture reads. I am a light of love, the more dark where I am, the more enlighten.

Among all the worthy feelings of mankind, love is probably the noblest. As a matter of fact, all of us survive in a love world. We offer love, more important, we need love. I am a hardworking student that is specialized in Computer Science and Application. Once a time, I lost my mind accidentally as a result I dropped down from the downstairs, and badly injured. But for my roommates' help I couldn't live up not only in physics but also in spirits. I thanked them genuinely. What I accomplished today party attribute to all of them giving me a hand to my school work. I hope I can live up to myself as well as my roommates.

As far as I am concerned, love should be showed by two means as follows. At the first place, we should keep a critical eye on others' love showed to us. Of course, most of the love is good for us, nevertheless, some does harm to us, such as helping us to cheating in exams. The last but not the least, we should show love hearts to those needing them. As we know, Hope Project is the largest love project in our country, and we should pay highly attention on it rather than neglect. In addition, we should cultivate the awareness to help others in our daily life. Let's hold our hands to build our country filled in love hearts.

评分：7 ～ 8 分

评语：这篇作文是各种错误的集合体，写作中能犯的错误，这篇作文全犯了。单词和语法水平有很大问题。优点是没有跑题，篇幅符合要求，虽然有很多错误，但是一直围绕中心展开。因为本文错误过多，所以直接在原文的基础上以黑体形式修改，如下：

In the picture **above**, in the fully dark situation, **a little** spark enlightens the **darkness**. The naive spark smiles so **sweetly**. It seems to be saying, as the caption in the picture reads, "I am a light of love. The **darker** where **a person is**, the **brighter I will be in his eyes**."

Among all the worthy feelings of mankind, love is probably the noblest. As a matter of fact, all of us **can live in a world full of love**. We offer love, **especially when others need it**. I am a hardworking student **specializing in** Computer Science and Application. Once **upon** a time, I lost my mind accidentally. **As** a result I dropped down from the **upstairs**, **and** was badly injured. But for my roommates' help I couldn't **have recovered physically or mentally**. I thanked them genuinely. What I **have** accomplished today **is partly attributed** to all of **those** giving me a hand to my school work. I hope I can live up to myself as well as my roommates.

As far as I am concerned, love should be **shown** by two means as follows. **In** the first place, we should keep a critical eye on others' love **shown** to us. Of course, most **forms of love are** good for us. **Nevertheless**, some **do** harm to us, **like** helping us to **cheat** in exams. **Last but not least**, we should show **love** to those **in need of it**. As we know, Hope Project is the largest love project in our country, and we should pay **close** attention **to** it rather than neglect **it**. In addition, we should cultivate the awareness to help others in our daily life. Let's hold our hands to **make** our country **filled with** love.

（3）2002 年全国硕士研究生入学考试样文评析

Directions:

Study the following picture carefully and write an essay entitled "Cultures—National and International". In the essay you should

1) describe the picture and interpret its meaning, and

2) give your comment on the phenomenon.

You should write about 200 words neatly on ANSWER SHEET 2. (20 points)

An American girl in traditional
Chinese costume（服装）

样文一

It is in the vivid photograph that stands a cute American girl who wears a traditional Chinese costume. Her bright smile perfectly matches the traditional Chinese clothes, hat, necklace, etc., all of which seem to belong to a Chinese minority. In such a simple way, the designer of the picture managed to reflect rapidly growing exchanges between different cultures, especially between Chinese and western cultures.

Most individuals would agree that the issue should be brought into the limelight. They believe that exchanges between these two distinguished cultures will lead to a better understanding between China and the western world, which will inevitably bring tremendous changes to our future world. There is no doubt that with better understanding, things like confrontation, conflicts and wars can be avoided and that the blend of different cultures will lead to lasting peace and prosperity of the world.

I, as a young university student, firmly believe that globalization is the tendency of today's world, and there is nothing to hold it back. The idea that western cultures would be a threat to the traditional Chinese cultures has been out of date, and it should be abandoned gradually. What we ought to think seriously about is probably not whether this kind of blend is needed or not, but what we could do in order to let this process make positive contributions to the development of Chinese cultures, and how we can make the traditional Chinese cultures known to the world and be accepted by the world. That is the very idea that the designer of this picture wants to tell us. It is probable that only in this way will the balance of exchanges be kept and both sides benefit from the process of globalization.

评分：20 分

评语：这是一篇很成功的满分作文。开头明显运用了一个强调句型，文章主题明确，论证很充分，重点突出，内容切题，合理地按照题目要求进行论述；逻辑关系很清楚，层次分明；语言通顺流畅，用词及语法正确、多样，文中多处使用了动词短语和固定搭配；这篇作文还运用了修辞手法；第三段中使用的倒装结构，体现了一定的语言功底；另外，文章篇幅符合要求。整篇文章表现出作者非常不错的英语写作水平和很强的文字表达能力。

样文二

What we can see in the picture is an American girl in Chinese traditional costume which is of characteristics of Dai people according to its style. This phenomenon reveals a form of culture communication—cultural globalization, which is an overwhelming trend, as the worldwide exchange become more and more frequent.

Confronted with this inevitable fact, we are fully aware that without communication, there will be no development. And it is just the same with the cultural communication. As it is said in a famous saying, "Things belonging to a nation belong to the whole world." There is no doubt that only by worldwide exchanges can the national cultures step into the world stage and gain new development. In this way, exchange do good to the national cultures, helping them to be known to the world.

Now is an age when China is entering the world and other countries are approaching to us. We should make good use of this opportunity and make contributions to the world civilization. We are looking forward to the day when there is only peace but no wars; there is only happiness but no pains; there is only friendship but no conflicts; there is only abundance but no poverty and there is only harmony but no misunderstandings.

评分：16 分

评语：内容切题，题目要求的内容也都有阐述；表达清楚，文字连贯，句式变换较多。美中不足的是结构与用词有少量错误，明显错误如：第一段第一句中 costume which is of characteristics of Dai people 应改为 costume which is characteristic of Dai people；而 as the worldwide exchange become more and more frequent 中 exchange 后应加 s；第二段中的第一句话意思不完整，最后一句 In this way, exchange do good to the national cultures 中的 exchange 应改为复数；第三段中，第一句话 Now is an age when China is entering the world 的主语应该是 it，所以应该在 Now 和 is 中间加 it; are approaching to us 应改为 are approaching us。文章篇幅符合要求，而且尾部的排比也显示作者具有较好的英语基本功和语言表达能力。这篇文章提醒我们高分作文的关键在于单词和语法，所以没有良好的基础，作文只靠模板是不靠谱的。

（4）2003 年全国硕士研究生入学考试样文评析

Directions:

Study the following set of drawings carefully and write an essay in which you should

1) describe the set of drawings, interpret its meaning, and

2) point out its implications in our life.

You should write about 200 words neatly on ANSWER SHEET 2. (20 points)

温室花朵经不起风雨

样文一

As depicted in the pictures, the flower in green house cannot stand for the severe storms and may be dead in the near future. What does the author really want to tell us? In my opinion, the real implication of the author is that everyone will meet difficulties in their life experiences, so we have to make adequate preparations for them.

There is no denying that a majority of young people, especially who are supported by their rich parents, take their happiness for granted. I am fully convinced that they may inevitable suffer from failures in their future lives. For the simple reason is that they are like the flowers in green house. Therefore, it is necessary for those parents to take some measures to control this trend which may lead to their children's failure. The best way to solve this problem, I think, is to give young people opportunities to do things independently. Only in this way can young people confront with difficulties and deal with them on their own.

As far as I am concerned, I am greatly in favor of the idea that encouraging young generations practice in hard environments. Because young people can benefit a lot from their own experiences in hard times and earn enough confidence to face their future challenges.

评分：16 分

评语：内容切题，句式有一定变化，表达清楚，语言错误少，但第一部分对图画几乎没有描述，没有按提纲要求写作。明显错误如：第一段第一句中 As depicted in the pictures, the flower in green house cannot stand for the severe storms...，stand for 中去掉 for；第二段第一句中的 who 前面应加上 those，第二句中的 inevitable 应改为 inevitably；第三段第一句中的 practice 改为 to practice；Because 前面的句号改为逗号，Because 首字母小写。

样文二

It goes without saying that the drawings aim at revealing a common and serious problem in China: how to educate and cultivate the young. Let's take a closer look at the drawings. In an ideal condition, the flower blooms. But when moved out of the greenhouse, it perishes under the rain and storm. It is obvious that the flower in greenhouse can't withstand wind and rain.

Nowadays the young generations in China, like the flower in the greenhouse, live under the full protection of their parents. Parents are eager to show all their love to their children. They give their children all the best things they can afford and do not ask their children to do anything at home. Self-centeredness and arbitrariness have become a trait of the young generations. Once leaving their parents, many young people cannot make a living on their own. They get lost when stepping into the complex reality and cannot face any hardships or difficulties.

Child education has become one of the most popular topics discussed not only by educational experts, but also by people in all walks of life. The failure of child education does more harm to the development of our society and our civilization than to the children themselves. Thus, it's high time that parents, educators and the government made concerted efforts to put an end to this situation.

评分：20 分

评语：内容切题，包含了题目要求的全部要点；表达清楚、连贯，符合英语表达习惯；句式多样，用词恰当。该作文之所以能获高分，主要是因为切中题目，而且语言规范、行文通畅，语句富有变化，用词准确、生动、具体。

（5）2004 年全国硕士研究生入学考试样文评析

Directions:

Study the following drawing carefully and write an essay in which you should

1) describe the drawing,

2) interpret its meaning, and

3) support your view with examples.

You should write about 200 words neatly on ANSWER SHEET 2. (20 points)

终点又是新起点

样文一

The cartoon depicts a vivid picture in which an athlete, dripping sweat, is rushing to the end. Obviously, he wins the match, but this is not the key message conveyed by the picture. The most striking feature of the drawing is that the same line is marked as both "the start" and "the end", which indicates that when the athlete came to the end, a new race is waiting for him.

The idea conveyed by the cartoon is apparent: the end is a new start. It is widely accepted that we should not be satisfied with the present achievement, for nowadays new challenges and competition never stop. The market economy and competitive society drives many people studying hard for higher academic degrees, and some of them even seek the opportunities to study abroad. We should spare no efforts improving ourselves, master high technology and professional skills. Then we can make use of them to devote ourselves to society.

Take my father as an example. He was denied higher education for historical reasons. But by self-study he became a technician in a factory. Many people thought he was content. But he never stopped studying. He took courses of law in his spare time. Later he became a lawyer. "The finishing point is just a new starting point", he said to me.

评分：16 分

评语：内容切题，单词表达正确、准确，但是结构安排不合理，例子放在了最后一段。并且文中有不少错误出现。明显错误如：第一段最后一句 when the athlete came to the end, a new race is waiting for him 中前后动词的时态应该保持一致，came 应改为 comes；第二段第二句 new challenges and competition never stop 中，stop 后应该加上 appearing；第三句 The market economy and competitive society drives many people studying hard 中，drives 应去掉 s，并且 studying 应改为 to study，因为 drive sb. to do sth. 是固定用法，倒数第二句 We should spare no efforts improving ourselves, master high technology and professional skills 中，improving 应该改为 to improve，master 后应该加 ing。

样文二

As is shown in the picture, on arriving at the finishing line of a race on the playground, the lovely young man has to continue his new journey in no time instead of stopping to take a rest. He has successfully settled the puzzle of "stopping or going on" which might have confused many others.

With the increasing pace of modern life, perhaps no change has characterized the past decade more dramatically than that of people's view on their own life. It is generally agreed that people have to adjust themselves to this new change. On the one hand, no doubt, people will gain a lot by setting new goals in their daily life. Take the famous scientist Thomas Edison for example. He had done very well in his early life, but still continue to pursue something more difficult all through his life. On the other hand, if one is satisfied with the success he has achieved, he will lose the chance to pursue new success. What is more, he may become the slave of his success. There are many cases showing that people lose their courage to better themselves after becoming successful.

To sum up, one's view on his success determines his future. In my opinion, it is necessary to carry out a nation-wide campaign publicizing people who have a burning desire for more and ever greater achievement when they are already well-known. So that people will develop a forward-looking attitude and make their life worth living and the world more beautiful as well.

评分：18 分

评语：内容切题；表达清楚、连贯，句式有变化；句子结构和用词正确，仅有个别小错误，这也说明了个别小错误是不影响得高分的。明显错误如：第二段第五句中的 continue 应改为 continued。

第二章

写作高分词汇

一、常见单词替换

认为：hold the (opinion/belief/position/standpoint/idea) that, assume, believe, deem, reckon, argue, maintain, suppose, conceive, insist, be convinced, to my knowledge, personally, from my personal perspective, as far as I am concerned, from my point of view, from my angle

举例 Quite a few individuals hold the standpoint that English will become increasingly crucial in our communication.

知道，了解：realize, comprehend, identify, distinguish, discern, notice, perceive, recognize, see, understand, figure out, be acquainted with, be familiar with

举例 To identify the issue clearly, there exist certain elements as follows.

好的：excellent, wonderful, terrific, fabulous, brilliant, favorable, fantastic, magnificent, splendid, beneficial, promising, conducive

举例 A promising future is around the corner.

坏的：awful, horrible, harmful, adverse, improper, unfavorable, dreadful

举例 If the trend continues, a dreadful tomorrow will come.

高兴的：pleased, delighted, joyful, cheerful, rosy, pleasurable

看见：notice, observe, catch sight of, perceive, discern

非常：greatly, highly, badly, extraordinarily, exceedingly, distinctly, intensely, outstandingly

举例 The problem about keeping pets becomes highly severe in our daily life.

喜欢：have a passion for, be crazy about, be addicted to, be absorbed in, be keen on, be fond of

举例 Many teenagers have a passion for worshipping superstars.

重要的：crucial, significant, vital, critical, indispensable

普遍的：common, universal

人：human being, the folk, the public, individual, citizen, all children and adults, all men and women in all walks of life

举例 It is high time for all children and adults to realize the significance of cooperation in current society.

越来越：an increasing amount of + 不可数名词，increasingly + 形容词或副词

举例 It would also require utilities to generate an increasing amount of power from renewable sources.

事情：matter, affair, business

产生，导致：lead to, result in, give rise to, bring about, render, be responsible for

举例 A sea of examples in our society could be responsible for my perspective.

许多，大量：abundant, ample, plentiful, a sea of, multitudes of, immense amounts of

能，可以：(would) be able to, have the chance/opportunity to do, get to be capable/competent

应该：be supposed to, shall, have to, must, be required to, it is necessary for sb. to

举例 Students are supposed to spend more time on their study instead of surfing on the Internet every day.

上升，增加：increase, go up, rise, raise, grow

举例 The number of private cars, from 2000 to 2005, went up by 20 percent.

下降，减少 / 小：decrease, reduce, lower, fall, go/come down, decline

查明：find out, discover, figure out

限制：limit, restrict, confine, put an end to

举例 Strict laws and regulations should be set to put an end to illegal companies.

因素：cause, factor, reason, element

合适：fit, suit, be suitable/fit/right

需要：require, need, it is necessary for, demand

不变的，稳定的：fixed, constant, stable, unchanged (unchanging)

举例 The figure in the past 5 years has stayed constant.

担心：worry about, be concerned about, care about

解决：solve/resolve, address, deal/cope with, work out, tackle, handle

举例 I did not work out what was causing this.

证实，表明：suggest, indicate, make it clear that，confirm, verify

举例 Abundant examples could indicate my point. However, the following one is most favorable here.

很大程度上：greatly, considerably, enormously, significantly, basically, dramatically

举例 The function of pets has basically been accepted by a sea of senior citizens.

提高，变好：improve, make better, enhance

采取措施：adopt/take measures/actions/steps

举例 It is high time actions should be adopted to protect the environment.

提出（政策）：propose, offer, put forward

举例 Laws and regulations could be proposed to secure wild animals.

废除：eliminate, get rid of, do away with, dispense with

任务：assignment, job, work, task, mission

有用，帮助：beneficial, helpful, useful, be a great help to, do good to, bring benefit to, be good for

举例 Cooperation proves to be definitely beneficial to the efficiency of our work.

方法：approach, strategy, method, solution

观点：idea, belief, view, opinion, viewpoint, perspective

影响：affect, influence, have/exert influence/effect/impact on

举例　Spoiling kids exerts great influence on the normal growth of them.

允许：allow, permit, be free to do

阻止：prevent, stop, keep sth./sb. from doing sth., ban, forbid, prohibit

花费：take, cost, consume

参加：join, take part in, participate in, engage in, get involved in, attend, be a part of

举例　Welcome to take part in our activity.

调整，调节：adjust, regulate, control

产生，创造：create, produce, generate, bring about, form, manufacture

确保：ensure, guarantee, assure (of), promise

举例　To ensure a glorious future, effective actions should be adopted.

最后：in the end, eventually, at last, finally, last but not least

建议：suggest, recommend, propose, have a proposal

决定：decide, choose, make up one's mind, make a determination

问题：problem, issue, question, case, trouble, difficulty, dilemma

举例　I am in a dilemma of whether to go or not to go.

会议：conference, discussion, assembly, congress, convention, gathering, session

对抗，争论：encounter, confrontation, argument, controversy

优势，优点：advantage, benefit, dominance, precedence, profit, superiority, merit, priority

缺点：disadvantage, shortcoming, weakness, inconvenience, drawback, deficiency, flaw, handicap, downside, limitation

举例　There exist more limitations than its benefits about worshipping stars blindly.

二、写作常用分类表达

1. 经济

生活节奏加快。	The tempo/pace of life has accelerated.
疲劳	fatigue, exhaust, be worn out
导致人与人之间的疏远	create alienation between people
经济利益和价值	economic interest and value
开阔眼界	expand one's vision/horizons
经济全球化	economic globalization
不正当竞争	unfair competition
打假	crack down on fake commodities
繁荣	boom, prosperity
激烈竞争	fierce competition
信用危机	credit crisis
稳定物价	stabilize prices

2. 政府

当务之急	priority, first order
把……当作当务之急	give priority to sth.
促进经济增长	promote economic growth
规范；管理；监管	regulate, monitor, oversee
政府开支	government spending/expenditure
削减预算	budget cuts
严禁	strictly prohibit, ban altogether
规章制度	rules and regulations
严格的法律	stringent laws/legislations
缩小贫富差距	close/narrow the gap between the rich and the poor
减少社会矛盾	reduce social contradictions
立法	legislate (*v.*), legislation (*n.*), make laws
社会保障	social security
减轻社会压力	release the pressure of society
福利	welfare

3. 动物

温顺的	docile
忠诚的	loyal
可爱的	cute
宠物是主人的伙伴。	Pets are their masters' companions.
陪伴	accompany, keep sb. company
给它们的主人以心理安慰	offer their masters consolation and comfort
毛皮	fur
生态系统遭到破坏。	Ecosystems have been destroyed.
灭绝	extinction/disappearance
影响	impact, implication, effect
过度捕捞	over-fishing
缺乏环保意识	lack of environmental awareness
坚持和谐相处	uphold harmonious coexistence
禁止虐待行为	the prohibition of torture
加大宣传力度	increase the publicity
增强保护意识	raise protection consciousness/awareness

4. 文化

文物古迹	cultural relics and historic sites
遗址	ruins

因为……而闻名 / 作为……而闻名	be famous for/as...
名胜古迹	places of interest
饮食	food and drink, diet
剪纸	papercutting
文化差异	cultural gap
文化冲突	cultural conflict
文化融合	cultural integration
少数民族	ethnic minorities
保护	preserve, protect
互相影响	interaction
古代文明	ancient civilization
中国传统道德规范	the classic Chinese moral ethics
美德	virtue
毅力	perseverance
合作	cooperation
忠诚	loyalty
礼貌	courtesy, politeness
道德	morality
善良	kindness
博大精深	great and profound
融合交汇	integration and interaction
碰撞	crash
有魅力的	charming
壮丽的，雄伟的	splendid, magnificent, grand
“英语热”	“English fever”

5. 环保

气候变化	climate change
温室效应	greenhouse effect
热带雨林	tropical rainforest
全球变暖	global warming
酸雨	acid rain
北极冰融	Arctic melting
垃圾	dust, waste, rubbish, garbage
白色污染	white pollution
用尽	use up, exhaust
污染	pollute, contaminate
严重的	severe, grave, grievous, serious

城市废物	municipal waste
一次性筷子	disposable chopsticks
一次性饭盒	disposable meal boxes
塑料袋	plastic sacks, plastic bags
污染源	source of contamination, pollution source
污水	sewage, effluent
摩托车	motorcycle
汽车	automobile
噪声污染	noise pollution
废物回收利用	waste reclamation, waste recycling, waste recovery
环境保护	environmental protection/conservation
环保意识	environmental awareness/consciousness
生态系统	ecosystem
可持续发展	sustainable development
生态平衡	ecological balance/equilibrium
国家立法	national legislation
增强 / 提高环保意识	enhance/raise/elevate the environmental awareness
促进经济体制和经济增长方式的转变	promote shifts in the economic system and mode of economic growth
治理环境污染	curb environmental pollution, bring the pollution under control
开发可再生资源	develop renewable resources

6. 科技

科技成果	scientific and technological achievements
科技进步	advance of science and technology
科技创新	technological innovations
信息时代	information age/era
信息爆炸	information explosion
自动化	automation
互联网的广泛使用	the proliferation of the Internet, the extensive use of the Internet, the widespread use of the Internet
对生活质量要求更高	higher demand on living standards
促进跨境贸易活动	promote trade activities across the border
无处不在的	prevalent, pervasive

网上购物	online shopping
娱乐	amusement, recreation, entertainment
方便	convenience
网上冲浪	surf the Internet
沉溺网络	net addiction
盗版产品	pirated products
电脑游戏	computer games
网红	Internet celebrity
电脑犯罪	cyber computer crime
电子商务	e-commerce
虚拟生活	virtual life

7. 就业

就业	employment
劳动力储备	labor pool
就业不足	under-employment
就业机会	job opportunities, employment opportunities
贫穷的	needy, impoverished, deprived, destitute, indigent
富裕的	affluent, wealthy, well-off
就业市场	job markets
找工作	apply/hunt/look for a job
薪水	salary, pay, wage
稳定的工作	stable jobs
职业发展	career development
接受培训和指导	receive training and counseling
充分发挥潜能	attainment of full potential
充分利用自己的能力	make the best use of one's abilities
接受新的挑战，把握机会	take on new challenges and seize opportunities
竞争激烈的	competitive
培养良好的心态	nurture a good state of mind
申请人	applicant
职位空缺	position available, vacant position
能胜任的	competent
合格的	be qualified for
熟练程度	proficiency
工作待遇和福利	job treatment and benefit
晋升	promotion

性别歧视的	gender-biased
相貌歧视的	appearance-biased

8. 大学生活 / 教育

独立思考	think independently
自学	self-study, study on one's own
适应能力	adaptability
适应	adapt to sth., adjust oneself to sth., become accustomed to sth.
全面发展	all-round development
心理健康	psychological soundness, psychological well-being
促进学生身心及情感健康的发展	promote the healthy development of students both physically and mentally, promote the students' physical, mental and emotional development
素质教育	quality-oriented education
责任感	sense of obligation/responsibility/duty
团队精神	team spirit
就业 / 市场技能	employable/marketable skills
激发学生的学习兴趣	stimulate students' interest in learning
提高学习的积极性	improve learning initiative
提高教学质量	enhance the quality of teaching
学校教育	schooling
家庭教育	family education
职业教育 / 培训	vocational education/training
应试教育	exam-oriented education
陶冶情操	cultivate one's taste and temperament
德才兼备	combine ability with integrity, equal stress on integrity and ability
青少年	youths, youngsters, adolescents
科目	subjects
学科	disciplines
培养	cultivate
深造	further one's study
培养能力	foster ability
减轻学生负担	relieve the burden on students
忙于功课	be busy/occupied with schoolwork

以……为重心	place emphasis on
全面的，广泛的	comprehensive
实际能力	practical capability
填鸭式	duck-stuffing
课外活动	extra-curricular activities
必修课	required/compulsory course
选修课	optional/elective course
学费	tuition

9. 社会现象

青少年犯罪	juvenile delinquency
开明的社会	progressive/enlightened society
两性平等	gender equality
性别歧视	gender discrimination, sexism
机会均等	equality of opportunity
老年人	elderly people, senior citizens
照顾	take care of, look after, care for
养育孩子	child rearing, raise a child
家庭暴力	domestic violence
触犯法律	break/violate/disobey the law
犯罪	commit a crime
执法机构	law enforcement agencies
刑事责任	criminal liability/responsibility
遵守法律	abide by the law
富有启发的	enlightening
引起了警惕和重视	cause alarm and attention
为……树立榜样	set a good example for
确保实施活动	ensure implementing activities
易受伤害的	vulnerable

10. 人物特征、情感描写

坚持的	persistent
意志坚强的	strong-minded
勤奋的	industrious
有前途的	promising
有活力的	energetic, dynamic
有影响力的	influential
忠实的，投入的	devoted

热心的	warm-hearted
诚信	integrity, honesty
好客的，热情的	hospitable
爱社交的，友善的	sociable
脾气好的	good-tempered
勤奋的，用功的	diligent
天真的，清白的	innocent
残忍的	cruel
精力充沛的，充满活力的	vigorous
自信的	confident
可怜的，令人同情的	pitiful
调皮的	naughty
伤心的，难过的	sorrowful
俭朴的	frugal
宽宏大量的	generous
精神饱满的，喧闹活泼的	hearty
谦逊的	humble
幽默的	humorous
有才干的，能干的	able
适应性强的	adaptable
有进取心的	aggressive
有雄心的	ambitious
和蔼可亲的	amiable
友好的	amicable, friendly
有志气的，有抱负的	aspiring
无畏的，鲁莽的	audacious
有能力的，有才能的	capable
仔细的	careful
坦率的	candid
能胜任的	competent
合作的	cooperative
富有创造力的	creative
主动的，活跃的	active
好争辩的	argumentative
有魅力的	attractive
有才气的	brilliant
仁慈的，宽厚的	charitable

愉快的	cheerful
幼稚的	childish
认真的，尽责的	conscientious
体贴的	considerate
建设性的	constructive
喜欢沉思的	contemplative
勇敢的，有胆量的	courageous
老练的，外交的	diplomatic
沮丧的	depressed
守纪律的	disciplined
尽职的；忠实的	dutiful
认真的	earnest
随和的	easy-going
有效率的	efficient
充满热情的	enthusiastic
善于表达的	expressive
守信的，忠诚的	faithful
直率的，真诚的	frank
有趣的，古怪的	funny
公正的	impartial, fair
不顾及别人的，轻率的	inconsiderate
有主见的	independent-minded, strong-minded
灵巧的，聪明的	ingenious
主动性	initiative
智力的	intellective
有智力的	intelligent
有发明才能的	inventive
好心的	kind-hearted
有见识的	knowledgeable
开明的，自由的	liberal
合逻辑的，条理分明的	logical
情绪化的，喜怒无常的	moody
顺从的，忠顺的	obedient
客观的	objective
乐观的	optimistic
有独创性的	original
外向友好的	outgoing
辛勤的，苦干的，刻苦的	painstaking

悲观的	pessimistic
受欢迎的	popular
实际的	practical
意志坚强的	purposeful, strong-willed
理性的	rational
实事求是的	realistic
讲道理的	reasonable
可信赖的	reliable
负责的	responsible
自觉的	self-conscious
自私的	selfish
无私的	selfless
敏感的	sensitive
真诚的	sincere
多疑的	skeptical
务实的	down to earth
坦率的，直截了当的	straightforward
严格的	strict
助人的	supportive
有同情心的	sympathetic
性情温和的	sweet-tempered
有才能的	talented
胆小的，羞怯的	timid
孜孜不倦的	tireless
容忍的	tolerant
容易相信人的	trustful
值得信任的	trustworthy
正直的	upright

11. 人生哲理

毅力	willpower, persistence
经得住挑战	withstand challenges
有进取心的	aggressive
进取精神	striving spirit
心胸开阔	open-mindedness
增长见识	increase one’s knowledge
创新	innovation
自信心	self-confidence

雄心壮志	ambition
爱	love
幸福	happiness
成功	success, triumph
压力	pressure, stress
困难	difficulty
满足	satisfaction
团队合作	teamwork
勤奋	diligence
积极态度	positive attitude

第三章

写作满分句型

第一节　英语句子的基本结构

一、什么是英语句子

英语句子按其结构分为简单句、并列句和复合句。简单句含有一个主谓结构。并列句是用连词连接两个或两个以上句子。复合句是由一个主句和一个或几个从句组成的句子。考研常考的从句是名词性从句、定语从句和状语从句。

二、基本句型

1. 主谓

谓语是不及物动词。

He passed away.

The sun is rising.

2. 主谓宾

谓语是及物动词。

He bought a computer.

I like dancing and singing.

3. 主谓表（同学们经常说是主系表）

谓语是系动词，系动词包括四类：

① be 动词；

② 感官动词：look, smell, taste, sound, feel;

③ 表变化：get, become, turn, go;

④ 表保持：keep, stay, remain.

4. 主谓双宾

I bought Michael a dog.

其中，a dog 是直接宾语，Michael 是间接宾语。

5. 主谓宾宾补

The dog makes him happy.

如何区别主谓双宾和主谓宾宾补？

① 从字面意思区别：

双宾，就是两个宾语，你是你，我是我，关系很疏远。

宾补则不同，补语不就是为了补充说明吗？所以宾补和前面的宾语得有关系。

② 最简单的区别方法：

在两个宾语中间，或者宾语和宾补中间加个系动词，如果读起来意思说得通就是宾补；反之，则是双宾。

三、句子的成分

1. 谓语

实义动词或系动词，一般要体现时态，并且一句话中有且只能有一个谓语；其余动词都要变成非谓语动词形式。

举例

① Loving me is supporting me.

爱我就是支持我。

② He clapped me on the shoulder, saying nothing, and left.

他拍了拍我的肩膀，一句话也没有说就离开了。

③ I am in favor of your idea.

我赞同你的观点。

④ I am in Beijing.

我在北京。

2. 主语

（1）常见的主语成分，如：名词、代词、非谓语和从句

My job is to teach English.

I am a teacher.

Helping you learn English well is my task.

That I love you is my fault.

（2）主语不能缺失

中文句子很多时候没有主语，翻译成英文的时候怎么办？

① 用 it 作主语：表示天气、温度、时间、物质、动物、植物等的句子，主语可用 it。比如：

外面很热。 It is very hot outside.

此时的重庆很冷。It is very cold in Chongqing now.

下雨了。 It is raining.

这是一本指导书。 It is an instructive book.

这是一朵漂亮的花。It is a beautiful flower.

② 用 there be 句型：一句话没有主语，并且谓语是“有”的意思，可以用 there be 句型。there

be 中的 be 通常可以换为：exist，remain，seem，stand。比如：

有很多人喜欢我。There exist a large number of individuals having affection for me.

有很多原因能够解释我的观点。There remain numerous factors which can account for my perspective.（多用于大作文第二段第一句）

总结

there be 写作句型总结：

There seems strong evidence to show that...

似乎有确凿的证据表明……

There exists a growing worldwide awareness that...

越来越多的人认为……

There remains absolutely no reason for us to believe that a brighter future for the world is an impossibility.

我们完全有理由相信一个更加美好的未来是有可能的。

There exist those who claim that...

很多人认为……

③ 变主动为被动，比如：

必须指出语法在考研中很重要。Grammar must be pointed out to be quite crucial in the examination of postgraduates.

不应该盲目追星。Superstars should never be worshipped blindly.

许多人认为孝敬父母是很重要的。Respecting parents is argued to be of great importance by a sea of individuals.

总结

被动语态的知识总结：通过以上例子，我们发现只要中文句子中是人称代词作主语，句子都可以考虑写成物作主语的被动形式。推荐在首段的尾句引出主题的时候使用。

但是需要注意以下情况没有被动：

1）不及物动词没有被动。比如：listen to music 写成被动——音乐被我听了，汉语表达不通顺。

2）系动词没有被动。“刘老师看起来很漂亮”中的“刘老师”其实是被看，但是这句话仍然翻译成 Miss Liu looks so graceful.

3）have 表示“有”的意思时，没有被动。

④ 加人称代词：I，you，we。比如：

期待收到你的回信。I am looking forward to your reply.

3. 宾语

常见的宾语成分，如：名词、代词、非谓语和从句

I love that white dog.

I love you.

I love singing songs.

I am thinking whether I need to lose weight or not.

4. 表语

常见的表语成分，如：名词、代词、非谓语、形容词、介词短语和从句

I am a teacher.

—Who is it in the picture? —It is me.

My dream is becoming a poet.

I am beautiful.

I was in the kitchen when it happened.

The key is that your dream is impossible.

5. 定语

详见第 49 页。

6. 状语

详见第 54 页。

7. 插入语

详见第 66 页。

四、时态

现在迅速数一下，已经学过多少种时态？估计很多人数也数不清。事实上，在讲时态之前，先澄清一点，在考研英语中时态能有什么考点？思考后发现写作是关键，它不太影响长难句的意思（阅读、翻译的文章以一般现在时居多）。所以，本书时态就是为写作而讲，那写作经常会涉及什么时态呢？

1. 一般过去时

定义：表示在过去的某个时间点发生了某个动作。

构成：一般在动词的后面加 -ed，但是不规则动词除外。

写作中的用处：一般在描述图表或举例的时候使用。

举例

① 2010 年，手机用户量增长到 1 500 万。

The number of subscribers using mobile phones increased to 15 million in 2010.

②有一次我生病了，没有人照顾我。

Once I got sick but nobody took care of me.

2. 一般将来时

定义：表示动作尚未发生。

构成：will + *v.*。

写作中的用处：状语从句中经常会用到。（在“状语和状语从句”中细讲）

举例

①当爱来临的时候，我要牵住他的手。

When love comes, I will hold his hands.（“主将从现”原则）

②因为他很正直，所以他注定是这场斗争的牺牲品。

Because he is pretty honest, he will be doomed to be the sacrifice in the fight.

3. 现在完成时

定义：A. 表示动作发生在过去，但是对现在造成了影响；B. 动作从过去开始发生，持续到现在，并且还可能持续下去。

构成：have + done。

写作中的用处：只要汉语中出现“已经”或“曾经”，一般都可以用该时态。

举例

①环境污染这个话题已经成了公众关注的焦点。

The subject of environmental pollution has become the public concern.

②父母花费了那么多时间和精力把我们抚养长大。

Parents have spent a lot of time and energy bringing us up.

4. 现在进行时

定义：表示一个动作正在发生。

构成：be + v-ing。

写作中的用处：多在描述图画的时候使用，语言显得生动。

举例

①守门员正在把自己想象得像蚂蚁一样小。

The goalkeeper is imaging himself as small as an ant.

②图片中一盏小油灯正在微笑。

An oil lamp is smiling in the picture.

5. 一般现在时

定义：表示动作经常发生或客观真理。

构成：使用动词原来的形式。切记，如果主语是第三人称单数，实义动词后加 -s 或 -es。

写作中的用处：考生们可能认为，这种时态应该放在第一个讲。之所以放在最后，是因为写作以一般现在时为主，也就是说，考研英语写作基本上是该时态的天下。

举例

①合作能使我们尽快地完成工作。

Cooperation enables us to finish our jobs as quickly as possible.

②孝敬父母是中华民族的传统美德。

Respecting parents is a traditional virtue of the Chinese nation.

五、简单句在写作中的使用

1. 所有不会写的单词都写成自己会的单词

举例

刘老师是一个风情万种的女人。

思路分析：会写“风情万种”吗？英文中根本就找不到一个完全对应“风情万种”的单词，

那怎么办？想过吗？阅卷老师只能看到写的单词对不对，而无法知道考生内心的想法。所以，不会写，为什么非得说刘老师“风情万种”呢？写“强壮”行吗？可以，阅卷老师也不知道她是否强壮，大不了写 beautiful，再不行还有 good 呢！所以，写作是一个主观性很强的事情，会写什么单词写什么单词，能写对什么写什么。永远记住：正确才是写作最重要的评判标准。

2. 所有写不来的长难句都用简单句来表达

举例

温室里的花朵不能经受风雨，这个事实表明孩子不应该被过分溺爱。

正确翻译：The evidence that the flower in the greenhouse fails to endure any storms indicates that kids should never be spoiled too much.

思路分析：该句两个 that 引导的分别是同位语从句和宾语从句。相信能搞懂宾语从句和同位语从句的考生不是很多吧！能写出来这种句子的考生，更是少之又少。与其写错，不如写个简单但正确的答案。

The flower in the greenhouse cannot suffer the rain.

We should not protect our children too much.

课后练兵

1. 这两天我心情不是很好。

____

2. 全球在变暖。

____

3. 重庆有很多人口。

____

4. 如果有毅力，迟早都会成功。

____

5. 有意义就是好好活，好好活就是做有意义的事情。

____

6. 笑并不意味着快乐。

____

7. 妒忌本身就是一种崇拜。

____

8. 建议政府采取措施来缓解这个问题。

____

9. 毫无疑问，溺爱孩子的问题越来越严重了。

____

10. 保护运动员是应该的。

____

11. 我弟弟每天上网，花大量的时间浏览不同的网页。

____

12. 恨一个人其实就是用别人的错误惩罚自己。

____

13. 他外表看起来很邋遢，但是内心却很高贵。

____

14. 生气会使人变得愚蠢，这个道理是显而易见的。

____

15. 最值得思考的问题是不少顾客对买不起的商品感兴趣。

____

答　案

1. I do not feel very good recently.
2. It is becoming warm throughout the world.
3. There exist a sea of citizens in Chongqing.
4. If there appears persistence in your mind, success will be achieved sooner or later.
5. Being meaningful is to live happily and living happily is to do something meaningful.
6. Smiles don't always mean happiness.
7. Jealousy itself is a kind of worship.
8. Authorities should be suggested to take measures to relieve the problem.
9. There is no doubt that the issue of spoiling children is becoming growingly severe.
10. Athletes ought to be protected.
11. My brother surfs the Internet every day, spending a lot of time browsing different websites.
12. Hating a person is penalizing yourself with other's faults.
13. He looks indecent in appearance, but he is very noble in his mind.
14. Outrage will make people foolish. This is quite obvious.
15. What's worth considering is this—many consumers are interested in those products they cannot afford.

第二节　并列句

一、什么是并列句

并列句是用连词连接两个或两个以上的句子。

比如：I love you but you spend more time on your career.

二、常见的并列连词

平行关系：and, both... and... 等。

转折关系：but, while, yet, whereas 等。

选择关系：or, whether... or not... 等。

因果关系：for, so 等。

递进关系：not only... but also... 等。

其实句子间的逻辑关系，不仅可以用连词，还可以用一些副词或介词短语来体现。

平行关系：similarly, equally, likewise, at the same time, in the meanwhile 等。

转折关系：conversely, however, nevertheless, nonetheless, unexpectedly, unfortunately, on the contrary, in/by contrast 等。

因果关系：therefore, thus, consequently, as a result 等。

递进关系：besides, additionally, subsequently, in addition 等。

选择关系：alternatively 等。

三、逻辑关系词在写作中的使用

1. 第一种用途：描述主体动作

首先我们将图画作文分类如下。

（1）一幅图：一个主体，两个动作

举例

你一条腿，我一条腿；
你我一起，走南闯北。

（2）一幅图：两个主体，两个动作

举例

（3）两幅图

举例

相携

所以在描述之前先分清图画是属于以上三种情况的哪一种。

举例

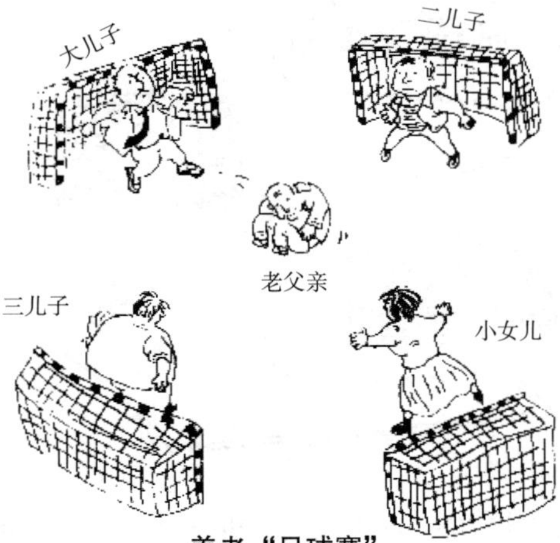

养老“足球赛”

这是一幅图，两个主体（大儿子和其他三个孩子），两个动作（大儿子的动作是踢老父亲，其他三个孩子的动作是防守）。描述如下：

In the vivid and simple cartoon, the eldest son who looks exceedingly ugly and cruel is kicking out his old father crouching in the center of the ground like a ball. **At the same time**, the other three children like their brother are keeping guard in order to stop their old father coming in their goals.（平行关系）

举例

温室花朵经不起风雨

这很明显是两幅图的作文，描述如下：

In the former caricature, the flower in the greenhouse is growing healthily when it is raining heavily outside. **By contrast**, it is withering in a heavy storm.（转折关系）

（注意：当在作文中用这些非连词替换连词时，一定要记住它们前面不能用逗号，或不用标点符号，而通常用句号，因为副词或介词短语是不能连接两个句子的。）

总结 并列结构的逻辑关系词中的平行关系和转折关系可以用在描述两幅图的作文和一幅图“两个主体，两个动作”的作文。

举例

In the vivid cartoon, the goalkeeper is imaging himself as small as an ant. **On the contrary**, the football player is visualizing his opponent as large as an elephant.（转折关系）

举例

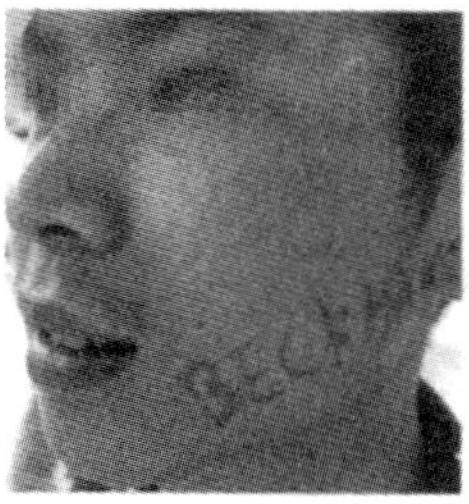

把崇拜写在脸上
注：Beckham（贝克汉姆）——英国足球明星。

花 300 元做个“小贝头”

In the former caricature, a football fan is wearing the name of Beckham on his face. **At the same time**, another one is spending 300 RMB having his hair cut into Beckham’s style.（平行关系）

图表作文也可根据相应主体的具体情况进行描述。

举例

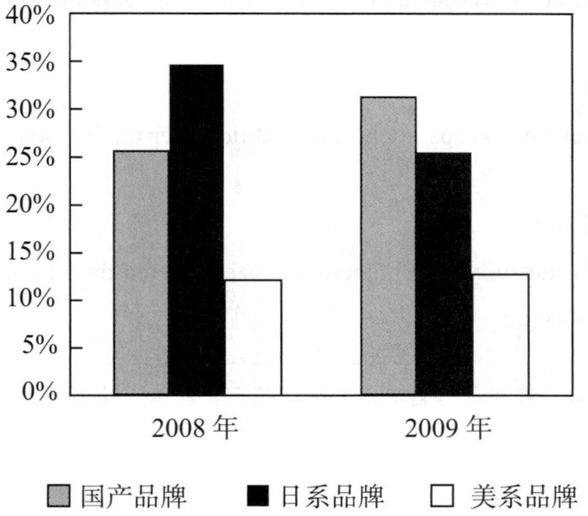

2008、2009 年国内轿车市场部分品牌市场份额示意图

In the bar chart, the proportion of Japanese brands, from the year of 2008 to 2009, dropped by nearly 10 percent in the Chinese market. **On the contrary**, the quantity of Chinese cars rocketed from about 25 percent to 33 percent.（转折关系）

举例

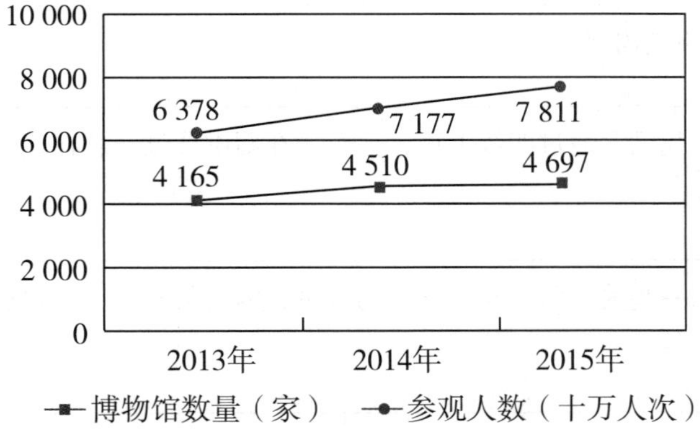

2013—2015 年我国博物馆数量和参观人数

As is shown in the graph, the number of museums, during the 3 years from 2013 to 2015, experienced a gradual rise. **At the same time**, the number of museum visitors ascended gradually from 637.8 million to 781.1 million.（平行关系）

2. 第二种用途：串联要点，以 not only... but also... 为例

举例

①养宠物的缺点是什么？

Pets may bite others especially our neighbors or strangers.

解析：如果只有这一个原因，会显得句子有点单薄。再想一个养宠物的缺点吧。

Keeping pets usually makes our living environment rather nasty.

把两个原因用 not only... but also... 连成一个长句。那就是：

Pets may **not only** bite others especially our neighbors or strangers **but also** usually make our living environment rather nasty.

②为什么要孝敬父母？

Respecting parents **not only** keeps a Chinese traditional virtue **but also** proves the duty of their offspring.

③为什么文化交流很重要？

Cultural exchange can **not only** help numerous citizens widen their horizons **but also** prompt the economic development of a nation.

总结　not only... but also... 常常在作文中用于分析原因，把两个表原因的短句连成一个长句子。

课后练兵

1. 她不但英语讲得流利，而且日语说得也很地道。

______

2. 爱情早已不在了，没想到他还停留在过去。

______

3. 如果你想成为一名志愿者，那么你必须要有足够的耐心，因为照顾孩子需要良好的心态。

______

4. 有朋自远方来，不亦乐乎？

______

5. 还记得那天吗？我没有通过四级考试，一个人在雨中哭泣。就在这时，你走过来，拍拍我的肩膀，安慰我。

______

6. 你们可以多增加一些关于历史和文学书的数量，因为很多学生喜欢这两类书目，导致很难借到。

______

7. 这部电影不但剧情惊险，而且男演员是莱昂纳多，所以推荐你看。

______

8. 孩子应该乐于助人、性格外向，因为心理健康很重要。

______

9. 我之所以决定辞职是因为这份工作不但薪水低，而且也接触不到太多的朋友。

______

10. 文化交流不但能开阔我们的视野，而且还能让我们交到更多的朋友。

______

11. 滥用手机不但影响我们的健康，而且影响人与人之间的交流。

______

答 案

1. She **not only** speaks English smoothly **but also** speaks Japanese well.
2. Love has gone. **Unexpectedly**, he still remains there.
3. If you desire to be a volunteer, you must have sufficient patience **because** taking care of kids needs a good mentality.
4. There comes a friend from afar. **Therefore**, I feel pretty delighted.
5. Do you still remember that day? I failed to pass the College English Test Band 4. **As a result**, I was shedding tears in the rain. **At the very moment**, you came up to me, touched my shoulder, and then you comforted me.
6. More historical and literary books could be increased **for** there exist **so** many students enjoying such books **that** it is hard to borrow one.
7. The movie proves thrilling and the actor in it is Leonardo. **As a result**, I desire to recommend it to you.
8. The kid should be helpful and outgoing **because** mental health is really crucial.
9. The salary keeps so low **and** I cannot get in touch with many friends, **so** I decide to quit.
10. Cultural exchange **not only** broadens our horizons **but also** enables us to make more friends.
11. Heavy use of cellphones **not only** does harm to our health **but also** exerts great influence on the communication among individuals.

第三节 复合句（名词性从句）

一、什么是名词性从句

1. 什么是从句

引导词＋句子（即引导句＋主语＋谓语）。

2. 什么是名词性从句

What I saw repeatedly is so moving and encouraging.

I admire **what his mother said**.

Gump is **who we should learn from**.

I enjoy the part **that a feather is flying in the sky**.

一个从句作主语，就是传说中的主语从句；同样，从句作宾语，就是宾语从句。

所以，名词性从句就是名词（短语）能够充当的成分，从句也能充当。它一共包括四类：主语从句、宾语从句、表语从句和同位语从句。

3. 名词性从句的引导词

名词性从句的引导词按照从句的类型来划分，一共分成三类：

① that：当从句是陈述句时。

② whether：当从句是一般疑问句时。

③ 特殊疑问词：当从句是特殊疑问句时。

比如：

That he married a rich woman is well-known in our neighborhood.

Whether he married a rich woman is still a mystery in our neighborhood.

When he married a rich woman is still a mystery in our neighborhood.

二、名词性从句在写作中的使用

1. 主语从句

读书的目的是涤荡我们的思想，这是毋庸置疑的。

That reading is to purify our minds is beyond dispute.

英语中通常把主语从句放到句末，用 it 作形式主语，结果就是：

It is beyond dispute that reading is to purify our minds.

总结

主语从句的满分表达就是 it 作形式主语：

It is common knowledge that... ……是一个常识。

It is my belief that... = I think that... 我认为……

It is self-evident that... ……是显而易见的。

It has been found that... 人们已经发现……

It is beyond dispute that... ……是毋庸置疑的。

It is universally acknowledged that... 人们普遍认为 / 众所周知……

It has been widely accepted that... 人们普遍认为 / 众所周知……

It is generally agreed that... 人们普遍认为 / 众所周知……

主语从句更高级的表达是：What... is that...

比如：

It is common knowledge that... 就可以表达为：What is common knowledge is that...

It has been found that... 就可以表达为：What has been found is that...

It is universally acknowledged that... 就可以表达为：What is universally acknowledged is that...

总结

推荐将主语从句写在第一段的开头以引出所描述图画的内容。就是：显而易见，在图画中……

举例

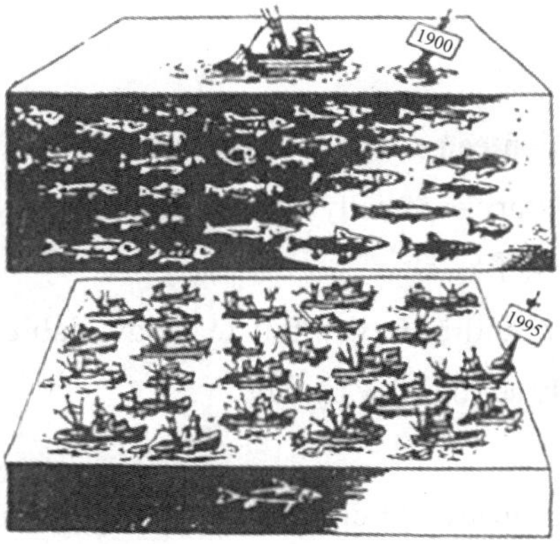

A Brief History of World Commercial Fishing

What can be seen clearly is that in the former caricature, there existed plenty of fishes with only a ship in 1900. Conversely, with the sharp increase of ships, there seemed few fishes left in 1995.

举例

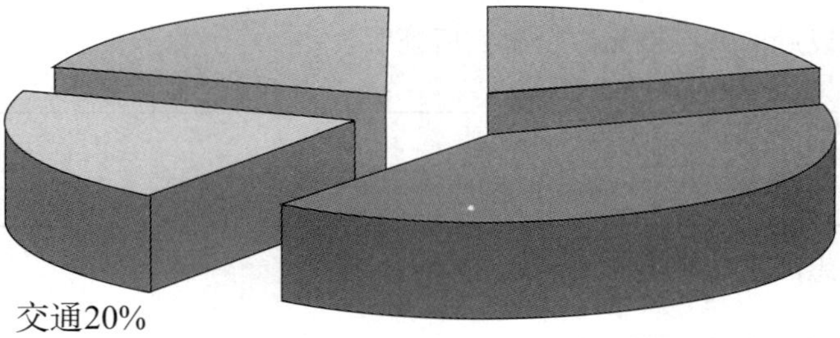

我国某市居民春节假期花销比例

What looks quite self-evident is that in the pie chart, the proportion of money, in one city of China, spent on various affairs demonstrates obvious differences during the Spring Festival. The money spent on buying gifts for others takes the lion's share, accounting for 40%. While transportation and dinner party take 20% of the whole proportion respectively.

2. 同位语从句

没有人不努力就会变得优秀，这个事实总是被很多年轻人忽略。

The truth that nobody can become brilliant without endeavors is ignored by a sea of youngsters.

没有什么能够掩盖她正在变老这个事实。

Nothing can hide the truth that she is growing old.

很多女生都穿上了漂亮的裙子，这个事实表明夏天就要来临。

The evidence that many girls have worn attractive skirts manifests that summer is coming.

总结

同位语从句的满分表达就是：

The evidence/truth that... manifests/indicates/suggests that...

翻译成汉语就是：……这个证据/事实表明……该句型可以用在大作文第二段分析原因处。

用该句型练习：

①为什么说合作很重要？

The evidence that cooperation can make colleagues finish their jobs more quickly and effectively indicates that it is definitely necessary especially when we face difficulties.

②为什么说污染越来越严重了？

The evidence that fresh air and blue sky fail to be available in cities and towns suggests that pollution has become increasingly serious day by day.

③为什么很多人养宠物？

The truth that pets can accompany old citizens when they are alone manifests that raising pets has indeed been a part of quite a few private individuals' life.

④为什么文化交流很有必要？

The evidence that one can understand the world better with cultural communication manifests that it is quite crucial in the current society.

课后练兵

1. 成功属于全力以赴的人已被无数个事实所证明。

______

2. 问题的关键是谁应该为道德的沦丧负责。

______

3. 不劳而获这种想法是非常不对的。

______

4. 显而易见，图片中两个残疾人在扔掉拐杖后，相互搀扶着往前跑。

______

5. 我的性格比较内向，不太喜欢与别人交流，这个事实表明，这个工作不适合我，所以我要辞职。

______

6. 很多市民认为，一个城市应该拆除旧的历史建筑，用现代建筑取而代之。

______

7. 你不能否认你没有努力学习这一原因。

______

8. 尽管孩子可以向父母寻求建议，但他们最终还是应该自己决定学什么方面的知识，以及将来从事什么职业。

______

9. 因此，从我所有的分析看来，我强烈反对那些认为老师应该为学生的学习负全责的看法。

______

10. 现在最紧迫的问题是父母应该提高警惕，让孩子多参加有意义的活动来融入班集体。

______

11. 我们再也看不见明亮的星星和月亮了，这个事实表明污染变得越来越严重了。

______

12. 合作能使我们更快地完成工作，这个事实表明我们都应该培养自己的团队合作精神。

____

答 案

1. It has been validated by numerous facts that triumphs belong to those who spare no efforts.
2. The core of the problem is who should be responsible for the decline of ethics.
3. The viewpoint that people can reap without sowing is never right.
4. It looks beyond dispute that in the caricature, after they threw away their walking sticks, the two disabled men are supporting each other to run forth.
5. The truth that I am relatively introverted and dislike communicating with others indicates that the job is not for me. Therefore, I decide to quit.
6. Quite a few citizens are of the opinion that a city should destroy its old historic buildings and replace them with modern ones.
7. You can't deny the reason that you didn't study hard.
8. Children should decide what kind of knowledge they will master and which profession they plan to engage in on their own even though they can consult their parents.
9. Therefore, according to my analysis, I strongly oppose the viewpoint that teachers should be fully responsible for the learning of students.
10. The most urgent problem, at present, is that parents should be on the alert, asking their kids to take an active part in more meaningful activities to become a part of the class.
11. The evidence that bright stars and the moon fail to be detected manifests that pollution is becoming increasingly grave day by day.
12. The evidence that cooperation enables us to finish the task faster indicates that team spirit should be cultivated by all of us.

第四节 复合句（定语从句）

一、什么是定语

定语就是修饰名（代）词的成分。

二、定语的成分

1. 形容词作定语

举例

① She is really a **graceful** lady.

她真是一位优雅的女士。

② An **innocent** girl is looking at you when you are having dinner.

一个天真的女孩在你用餐的时候看着你。

2. 名词作定语

举例

① He dropped the **coffee** cup and broke it.

他把咖啡杯打碎了。

② The policeman conducted us safely to the **railway** station.

警察把我们安全地护送到火车站。

3. 介词短语作定语

举例

① The nightingale **out of the window** heard the sighs of the young man.

窗外的夜莺听到了年轻人的感叹。

② I will never fall in love with the boy **in front of me**.

我绝不会爱上我前面的那个男生。

4. 分词、不定式（非谓语）作定语

举例

① In the end, the **singing** nightingale died because of love.

唱歌的夜莺最终因爱而死。

② The innocent nightingale must love the student **deceived by the girl**.

单纯的夜莺一定爱那个被女孩欺骗的学生。

5. 从句作定语

举例

① The rose **which the bird swaped her life** failed to help the man.

鸟儿用生命换来的玫瑰花并没有帮到那个人。

② The girl **who looks so innocent** is actually a cheater.

那个看起来很单纯的女孩事实上是个骗子。

三、定语的位置

前小后大——当一个单词修饰名词时，这个单词通常放在名词前面；当两个以上的单词修饰名词时，这些单词通常放在名词的后面。但是，注意过去分词作定语时，即使是一个单词也通常放在名词后。

比如：他是一个被抛弃的男人。

He is a man abandoned.

四、定语在写作中的使用

1. 每当出现名词都可以试着加定语成分，把句子拉长并且使语言生动

比如：

① 养宠物可以缓解孤独感。

Keeping pets can relieve loneliness.

加上定语的效果是：

Keeping pets **which look so cute and lovely** can relieve loneliness **of some old citizens and children who stay at home alone**.

② 盲目追星会浪费时间。

Worshipping stars blindly will waste time.

加上定语的效果是：

Worshipping stars **looking so handsome or beautiful** blindly will waste time **of youngsters who should spend more time and energy on their studies**.

③ 描述图画时给名词加定语就显得很生动了。

2006 年英语作文描述示范：

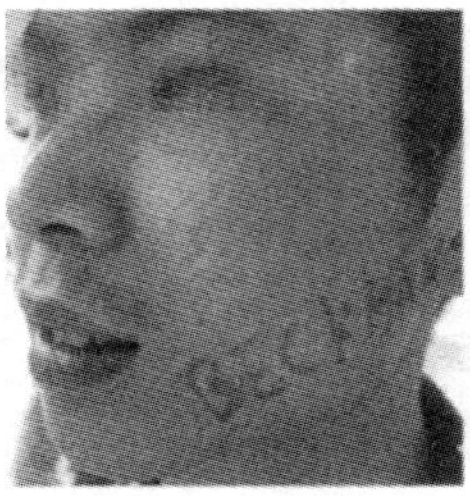

把崇拜写在脸上

注：Beckham（贝克汉姆）——英国足球明星。

花 300 元做个“小贝头”

In the former photograph, a young man **who is a crazy football fan**, wrote Beckham, **the name of a well-known superstar in the world**, on his face. **Similarly**, in the latter one, another **fashionable young man** is spending 300 RMB making his hair into Beckham's style in a barbershop.

2010 年英语（一）作文描述示范：

文化“火锅”，
既美味又营养

In the **simple and vivid** cartoon, a hot pot **which looks not only delicious but also nutrient**, cooking while it is smoking, is filled with different cultures **including Chinese and western ones such as Buddha, Beijing Opera and Shakespeare**.

2011年英语（一）作文描述示范：

旅程之“余”

In the **simple and vivid** caricature, two kids **sitting on the boat** are throwing rubbish into the river **where there have existed so many dirty items already**.

> **总结** 作文中只要写到名词就试着给它加定语，第一段描述图画时通常都要加定语，这样可以使语言生动。

2. 使用非限制性定语从句，补充说明前面的内容

① ...which has been widely accepted by the public.

② ...which leaves readers quite a deep impression.

③ ...which has provoked the public's widespread attention.

④ ...which might have brought us unexpected troubles.

⑤ ...which may give rise to even more dreadful consequences.

举例

Cultural exchanges may lead Chinese to a more brilliant future, which has been widely accepted by the public.

Parents have spent years of energy and time bringing their kids up, which leaves readers quite a deep impression.

> **总结** 建议把本句型用在第二段某个比较短的原因后面，补充前面内容，并且拉长句子。

课后练兵

1. 外表看起来非常邋遢的他其实内心很高尚。

____

2. 人生最大的精神财富是笑容、优雅、自信，拥有了它们你就拥有了一切。

____

3.《孤儿怨》是我看过的最恐怖的一部电影。

____

4. 父亲经常在假期时带她出国旅游，这让她的朋友羡慕不已。

____

5. 足球是一项培养孩子跟别人合作能力的团队活动。

____

6. 这个世界上，没有一个人可以让你一直依靠，路需要自己走。

____

7. 曾经全力以赴实现梦想的人即使最终没有成功也不会感到遗憾，这很重要。

____

8. 课堂上不集中精力、希望通过自己的课下努力通过考试的学生，常常会发现事倍功半。

____

9. 孩子能选择学习的科目越多，家长就越能发现他们感兴趣和擅长的领域。

____

10. 能澄清我观点的例子有很多，但是下面的这个是最合理的。

____

11. 追那些帅气而年轻的明星浪费了年轻人很多宝贵的时间，而这些时间本可以花在他们的学习上。

____

12. 一只肥胖又骄傲的老母鸡正在给自己刚刚下的蛋打广告。

____

答 案

1. The one who looks extremely indecent is actually noble in nature.
2. The greatest spiritual wealth in one's life is smile, elegance and self-confidence. If you possess them, you will have everything.
3. *Orphan* is the most horrible movie that I have ever seen.
4. Her father often takes her to travel abroad during the holidays, which makes her friends envy her.
5. Football is a team sport which trains children to cooperate with one another.
6. In the world, there exists no one whom you can count on all the time. So you need to walk your own way.
7. Those who spare no efforts to realize their dreams will never feel regretful even if they fail finally, which is quite significant.
8. Those who fail to concentrate in class but hope to pass the examination by their own endeavors after class often find that they just get half the result with twice the effort.
9. The more subjects kids can choose, the better chances parents will discover the field which their kids have interest in and are good at.
10. There exist abundant cases which can be used to clarify my point. Nevertheless, the following one is the soundest.
11. Worshipping stars who look rather handsome as well as young is a great waste of the precious time of youngsters which could have been spent on their study.
12. A hen being fat and proud is making an advertisement for her egg which was laid by herself just now.

第五节 复合句（状语从句）

一、什么是状语

状语就是在一个句子中修饰实义动词、形容词、副词或整个句子的成分。

二、状语的成分

1. 副词作状语

举例

① She smiles **sweetly**.

她笑得很甜。

② She cries **sadly**.

她哭得很悲伤。

2. 介词短语作状语

举例

① He runs fast **like a crazy dog**.

他跑得像疯狗一样快。

② He always sits **in front of me**.

他总是坐在我前面。

3. 分词、不定式（非谓语）作状语

举例

① He leaves, **crying**.

他哭着离开了。

② All kids went home, **accompanied by their parents**.

所有孩子都在他们父母的陪同下回家了。

③ He hurried to the station only **to find that the train had left**.

他匆忙赶到火车站，却发现火车已经发车了。

4. 从句作状语

举例

① They were singing songs **when the teacher came in**.

老师进来时，他们正在唱歌。

② They are absent from class **because they all dislike the teacher**.

他们没来上课，因为他们都不喜欢这位老师。

三、状语的位置

状语的位置极其灵活，可以随便放，但是通常放在句首或句末。如果放在句首的话，通常用逗号隔开。

比如：**In Chongqing**, I am now working.

I am now working **in Chongqing**.

四、状语从句

1. 状语从句的分类

状语从句按照引导词本身的意思一共分为九类：时间状语从句、地点状语从句、原因状语从句、目的状语从句、结果状语从句、条件状语从句、让步状语从句、方式状语从句和比较状语从句。

2. 九大状语从句及其引导词

（1）时间状语从句

常用引导词：when, as, while, as soon as, before, after, since, till, until, not... until 等。

举例

① When love comes, I will hold her hands.

当爱来临的时候，我会牵住她的手。

② I fell in love with the girl as soon as I saw her.

我一见到那个女孩就爱上她了。

（2）地点状语从句

常用引导词：where, wherever 等。

举例

① Wherever you go, and whatever you do, I am just here waiting for you.

无论你去哪里，无论你做什么，我都会在这里等你。

② The flower grows well where it is moist.

这种花在潮湿的地方生长得很好。

（3）原因状语从句

常用引导词：because, since, as, for 等。

需要注意的是一些介词短语，也翻译成“因为”，但它们后面只能跟名词，不能跟从句，如：because of, due to, owing to, thanks to, for the sake of, as a result of 等。

举例

Because he was careless, he had a car accident yesterday.

或者：Because of his carelessness, he had a car accident yesterday.

因为粗心，他昨天出了一场车祸。

需要注意的是在这些表示“因为”的介词短语中，due to 通常放句末，不放句首；而 owing to 通常放句首，不放句末。其他短语的位置则可前可后。

举例

The marriage can last long due to tolerance between the couple.

Owing to tolerance between the couple, the marriage can last long.

夫妻之间的相互包容才得以使婚姻长久。

（4）目的状语从句

常用引导词：so that, in order that 等，其后跟主谓结构。

常见的动词不定式也可以表示目的：to, in order to, so as to, 其后跟动词原形。

举例

① I am determined to take part in the examination of postgraduates so that I could have a brighter future.

或者：I am determined to take part in the examination of postgraduates in order to have a brighter future.

为了能有一个更美好的未来，我决定考研。

② Parents getting old gradually are telling a variety of lies in order that their daughters or sons will not worry about them.

或者：In order not to make their children worry about them, parents getting old gradually are telling a variety of lies.

为了不让儿女担心，慢慢老去的父母总是对他们说着各种各样的谎话。

（5）结果状语从句

常用引导词：so... that 等。

举例

① It is so hot in summer here that I decide to depart.

这里夏天太热了，以至于我决定离开。

② My mother is so nice a teacher that many students love and respect her.

我妈妈是如此好的一位老师，以至于很多学生都敬爱她。

③ I am so delighted that I cannot help singing at midnight.

我特别开心，以至于我在半夜情不自禁地唱起了歌。

④ Chinese become so self-confident at present that they dare to pursue their dreams without any fear.

中国人现在变得如此自信，以至于他们敢无所畏惧地追求自己的梦想。

总结　结果状语从句是写作满分表达。只要出现形容词或副词的地方都可以写成该句型。推荐在大作文第三段第一句总结的时候使用。

举例

① As a consequence, pollution becomes so grave that quite a few measures should be taken to relieve the current situation.

总之，污染变得很严重，以至于需要采取很多措施来缓解目前的情况。

② Filial piety is so important that it is time for us to go home to visit our elders.

孝敬长辈很重要，所以对我们来说是时候回家看看长辈了。

（6）条件状语从句

常用引导词：if, unless, so long as, on condition that 等。

举例

① I will never give up so long as there is a ghost of chance.

只要有一丝机会，我就不会放弃。

② You can borrow the album, on condition that you don’t lend it to anyone else.

你可以借这张专辑，条件是不把它借给别人。

（7）让步状语从句

常用引导词：though, although, even if, even though 等。

举例

① Liu is a beauty although she has a pair of small eyes.

虽然刘眼睛小，但她是一个美女。

② I love my boyfriend although he is a little lazy.

虽然我男朋友有点懒，但是我爱他。

> **总结**
>
> 在作文中，几乎每句话的后面都可以加一个由 although 引导的让步状语从句。推荐在第二段分析原因时，用在某个比较短的原因后面，用来拉长句子。

举例

① Worshipping stars blindly will waste a lot of time and energy although it may bring us much fun.

盲目追星会浪费我们很多时间和精力，即使它可能会给我们带来很多乐趣。

② Pets indeed bring much delight for my grandma although taking care of them needs time and energy.

虽然照顾宠物需要时间和精力，但是它们的确给我的奶奶带来了很多快乐。

（8）方式状语从句

常用引导词：as, as if, as though 等。

举例

It looks as if the weather may warm up soon.

看来天气很快就会暖和起来。

（9）比较状语从句

常用引导词：as... as..., than, the more... the more... 等。

举例

① as... as... 和……一样……

1）She looks as graceful as a red rose, who can take many people's breath away.

她像红玫瑰那样优雅，美得令人窒息。

2）Pollution is as serious as earthquakes, which has threatened our existence or even taken people's lives away.

污染跟地震一样严重，它已经威胁到我们的生存，甚至夺去了许多人的生命。

> **总结**
>
> 作文中出现形容词、副词的地方都可以考虑使用该句型。
>
> 该句型的结构是：
>
> Something（文章中心词）proves as important as air and water, which plays a key role in our daily life.
>
> 或者：Something（文章中心词）proves as grave as fatal diseases, which has threatened the existence of human beings.
>
> 推荐将该句型用在第一段的最后一句话或第三段的第一句话，来总结中心。

② the more... the more... 越……越……

举例

1）The harder one works, the luckier he will be.

越努力，越幸运。

2）The higher one climbs, the farther he will look.

爬得越高，看得越远。

3）The more quickly authorities take measures, the more effectively the issue will be resolved.

政府越快采取措施，就能越有效地解决这个问题。

总结 推荐将该句型用在第二段分析原因或第三段喊口号的地方。

举例

① The more frequently cultures are exchanged, the more rapidly the economy will develop.

文化交流越频繁，经济发展越快。

② The more intimately humans cooperate with their partners, the more effectively their work will be finished.

人们与同伴合作得越密切，他们越能高效地完成工作。

五、分词作状语

1. 如何把状语从句转化成分词作状语呢?

比如（状语从句）：

When I was a little girl, I was especially eager to grow up.

当我还是一个小女孩的时候，我特别渴望长大。

第一步：把状语从句最明显的标志——引导词 when 去掉，那现在就出现了一个语法错误——逗号连接了两个句子。

I was a little girl, I was especially eager to grow up.（错误句）

第二步：既然逗号不能连接两个句子，那就把前面的句子变成非句子就行了。怎么把句子变成非句子呢？只需要把动词变成非动词（即非谓语结构）。

I being a little girl, I was especially eager to grow up.（错误句）

第三步：看分词的主语和后面句子的主语是否一致，如果一致，分词的主语省略；如果不一致，分词的主语保留。本句话，显然主语一致，所以去掉分词的主语。

Being a little girl, I was especially eager to grow up.

2. 是不是非得出现状语从句才能使用分词作状语呢?

当然不是，你只要有意识地用逗号连接两个句子，都可以把那个次要的句子变成分词作状语。

比如：自信是一种积极的心态，它能使很多奇迹降临。

Self-confidence is a positive attitude, it enables many miracles to happen.（错误句）

Being a positive attitude, self-confidence enables many miracles to happen.

把分词作为插入语的结果就是：

Self-confidence, being an active mentality, enables many miracles to happen.

总结 该句型虽然可以改造任何两个句子，但是推荐在作文第一段描述一幅有一个主体、两个动作的图画时使用。

举例

你一条腿，我一条腿；
你我一起，走南闯北。

如果用简单句描述图画就是：The two disabled men threw away their walking sticks. They are helping each other by running shoulder by shoulder.

合成的效果就是：The two disabled men, throwing away their walking sticks, are helping each other by running shoulder by shoulder.

加上定语的效果就是：The two disabled men looking confident as well as vigorous, throwing away their walking sticks, are helping each other by running shoulder by shoulder.

举例

网络的“近”与“远”

如果用简单句描述图画就是：A sea of children and adults are surfing the Internet in narrow space. They are separated by the Internet which looks like a spider net.

合成的效果就是：Surfing the Internet in narrow space, a sea of children and adults are separated by the Internet which looks like a spider net.

六、状语在写作中的使用

任何一个句子都可以加状语成分，拉长句子并且使句子完整。尤其是第一段描述图画时，如果句子不够长，别忘了加状语。

比如：

我正在看刘晓艳写的书。

I am reading the book written by Liu Xiaoyan.

①加副词：I am reading the book written by Liu Xiaoyan diligently.

②加时间状语：I am reading the book written by Liu Xiaoyan at the moment.

③加地点状语：I am reading the book written by Liu Xiaoyan either on the sofa or on the bed.

④加原因状语从句：I am reading the book written by Liu Xiaoyan because it is so interesting and attractive.

⑤加让步状语从句：Although I don't want to take part in any examination, I am reading the book written by Liu Xiaoyan.

⑥加结果状语从句（必须出现形容词或副词）：I am reading the book written by Liu Xiaoyan so crazily that I forget to sleep at night.

⑦加目的状语从句：I am reading the book written by Liu Xiaoyan in order that I can improve my grammar as quickly as possible.

⑧写成比较结构：As diligent as a bee, I am reading the book written by Liu Xiaoyan.

举例

描述图画：

In the **simple but meaningful** caricature, as water is dropped on the ground, a man **who looks rather less impressive** is saying "all is over" **when covering his face with a hand**. By contrast, the other one, **active as well as optimistic** is saying "Luckily, there still exists a little."

总结

描述图画的万能状语是：in the vivid cartoon

论述原因的万能状语是：

with the rapid advance of science and technology

in our contemporary society

in the routine of everyday life

although quite a few adults fail to pay attention to it

举例

①为什么说追星不好？

Worshipping stars will definitely exert great influence on our normal study **although quite a few adults fail to pay attention to it**.

②为什么做人要讲诚信？

Integrity still keeps a Chinese traditional virtue **in our contemporary society**.

课后练兵

1. 你可以像猪一样生活，但是你永远不会像猪一样快乐。（使用状语从句）

____

2. 我想借这次机会向给我第一手帮助的老师表示真心的感谢。

____

3. 虽然几乎每个人从小就知道，一个诚实的人才是一个完整的人，但是社会上仍有很多不诚实的人。

____

4. 时间是如此宝贵，以至于无论如何度过都是一种浪费。

____

5. 因为我的母亲需要人照顾，而这份工作又让我很忙，所以我决定辞职。

____

6. 为了实现我的梦想，我一直在思考该不该和男朋友分手。

____

7. 在有学校的地方，司机应该缓行。

____

8. 看完北大的宣传片——《星空日记》，我明白了其实有时候梦想比苟活更重要。（使用分词作状语）

____

9. 他们在墙壁上刻字，以便后人记得他们做过的事情。

____

10. 如果你知道自己的目标是什么，知识就能帮你达到这个目标。

____

11. 虽然很多人还没有意识到，但是乐观的心态在我们的事业和学习中都很重要。

____

12. 虽然网络使我们的生活更便利，但是每天在网上购物和打游戏上花费大量时间还是不好的。

____

答　案

1. Although you can live as if you were a pig, you will never be as happy as a pig.
2. By the chance, I want to show sincere gratitude to my teacher who gave me first-hand help. 或 I want to take the chance to show sincere gratitude to my teacher who gave me first-hand help.
3. Although almost every kid knows that a man of integrity is a complete man, there still exist a sea of dishonest people in our society.
4. Time is so precious that it is a waste however we spend it.
5. I am determined to quit because my mother needs to be taken care of while the job keeps me busy all the time.
6. In order to realize my dream, I am thinking whether I should break up with my boyfriend.

7. Drivers should slow down where there are schools.
8. Having seen the advertising video about Peking University—*Journey to the Star*, I realize that dreams, to be sure, sometimes are more important than ignoble existence.
9. They carved the words on the wall in order that the future generations can remember what they had done.
10. Knowledge helps you to reach your destination provided that you know what the destination is.
11. Although quite a few people fail to realize it, positive attitude indeed plays an essential role both in our career and in our study.
12. It is unfavorable for us to spend too much time shopping online and playing video games although the Internet really makes our life more convenient.

第六节　英语句子的特殊结构

一、强调句型

1. 构成：It is... that/who...

that 可以指人，也可以指物，但是 who 只能指人。比如：

我昨天在街上遇到了我的旧情人。

I met an old flame in the street yesterday.

如果强调主语：

正是我昨天在街上遇到了我的旧情人。

It was I that met an old flame in the street yesterday.

如果强调时间：

就在昨天我在街上遇到了我的旧情人。

It was yesterday that I met an old flame in the street.

解析：当强调句型 It is... that 在句子中出现的时候，它们是不作成分的，意思是“就在；正是”，它们就像一个框架，强调哪部分内容，就把哪部分内容放在 It is... that 的中间，被强调部分不允许有任何修改。但是需要注意的是一般情况下强调句型不能强调句子的谓语。

强调句型既然只是一个框架，那么当它在意群中时，必须遵守意群的时态（就两种时态：要么是 is，要么是 was，过去时态用 was, 其他时态都用 is）。

它和主语从句的区别在于把 It is... that 去掉后，如果句子成分依然完整的话，就是强调句型；如果句子成分残缺，就是主语从句。比如：

It is obvious that one should make friends with those who can make you become aggressive and optimistic.

去掉 It is... that 后，句子变成：Obvious one should make friends with those who can make you aggressive and optimistic。该句显然不正确，如果 obvious 放在句首，应该用副词形式 obviously。所以，这个是主语从句。

2. 强调句型在写作中的使用

强调句型可以强调除谓语外的任何部分。推荐在第二、三段首句使用。比如：

The existing numerous factors account for the phenomenon.（第二段首句）

It is the existing numerous factors that account for the phenomenon.

As a consequence, measures should be adopted to relieve the current situation.（第三段首句）

As a consequence, it is to relieve the current situation that measures should be adopted.

二、倒装

1. 定义

倒装就是把一句话写成一般疑问句的语序，也就是将助动词或 be 动词放在主语前面。

Do you love me?

Is your father an official?

Have you been to Europe?

2. 倒装在写作中的使用

（1）否定词放在句首时

① The public can fail to pay attention to the issue of pollution under no circumstances.

倒装为：Under no circumstances can the public fail to pay attention to the issue of pollution.

② Respecting parents not only keeps a Chinese traditional virtue but also proves the duty of their offspring.

倒装为：Not only does respecting parents keep a Chinese traditional virtue but also proves the duty of their offspring.

③ Cultural exchange not only enables Chinese citizens to widen their horizons but also promotes the friendship between nations.

倒装为：Not only does cultural exchange enable Chinese citizens to widen their horizons but also promotes the friendship between nations.

> **总结**　该倒装可以在第二段分析原因的时候或者是第三段首句总结的时候使用。

比如：

在任何情况下，父母都不能忽略培养孩子自信的重要性。

Under no circumstances could parents neglect the importance of cultivating children's confidence.

（2）含有 so... that... 结构的句子将 so 引导的部分置于句首时

① He was so excited that he could not help laughing at midnight.

倒装为：So excited was he that he could not help laughing at midnight.

② He is giving a speech so forcefully that everyone present is convinced.

倒装为：So forcefully is he giving a speech that everyone present is convinced.

③ She looks so gorgeous that she can catch the eyes of everyone.

倒装为：So gorgeous does she look that she can catch the eyes of everyone.

总结 这个句型请参看前面状语从句部分，出现形容词和副词的地方都可以写成 so... that... 句型。也就是说，只要出现形容词或副词的地方都能出现该倒装句型。

（3）“only+ 状语”位于句首时

① You will call your mother only when you need additional pocket money.

倒装为：Only when you need additional pocket money will you call your mother.

② The problem could be resolved only by taking these actions.

倒装为：Only by taking these actions could the problem be resolved.

③ The couple can lead a happy and comfortable life only when the issue is tackled.

倒装为：Only when the issue is tackled can the couple lead a happy and comfortable life.

总结 该倒装可以在第三段尾句喊口号的时候使用。

（4）as 引导让步状语从句，从句的表语放在句首时

① As I look ugly, I am quite gentle.（错误句）

倒装为：Ugly as I look, I am quite gentle.

② As the drawing seems simple, the meaning behind it is far-reaching.（错误句）

倒装为：Simple as the drawing seems, the meaning behind it is far-reaching.

（注意：as 的倒装结构为形容词 + as + 主谓。）

三、虚拟语气

1. 定义

虚拟语气表示与事实相反或语气委婉。

2. 一般用法

if 引导的非真实条件句（用于假设不太可能发生或者与事实相反的事）

（1）if 虚拟语气假设与现在事实相反

if 从句的谓语为动词的过去式（be 动词不论人称，一律用 were），主句谓语为 would/should/could/might + 动词原形

① If I were rich, I would travel around the world.

如果我有钱，我就周游世界。（事实上我现在没钱）

② If I knew his address, I would tell you.

如果我知道他的地址，我就会告诉你。（事实上我不知道）

（2）if 虚拟语气假设与过去事实相反

if 从句的谓语为 had + 过去分词，主句谓语为 would/should/could/might + have + 过去分词

① If it hadn't rained yesterday, we would have had a party in the garden.

如果昨天没有下雨，我们就在花园开派对了。（事实上昨天下雨了，我们没有在公园开派对）

② If he had taken my advice, he would not have made such a mistake.

如果他听了我的劝告的话，就不会犯这样的错误了。（事实上他没有听我的劝告，犯了错误）

（3）if 虚拟语气假设与将来事实相反

if 从句的谓语为动词过去式 /should + 动词原形 /were to + 动词原形，主句谓语为 would/should/could/might + 动词原形

① If it were to snow tomorrow, they would not go out.

如果明天下雪，他们就不出去了。（事实上明天不太可能下雪）

② If he should come here someday, I would talk to him.

如果他哪天来这儿的话，我就跟他谈谈。（事实上他来的可能性很小）

总结　if 引导的虚拟语气可以在第二段尾句进行反面论证的时候使用。

3. 特殊用法

（1）以下情况，从句用"should + 动词原形"表示虚拟，并且 should 可以省略

以防：in case that, for fear that, lest 等

命：order, direct, command 等

建（贱）：suggest, advise, propose 等

要求：ask, request, require, demand 等

用虚拟：

是必要的 / 重要的 / 紧急的：It is necessary/important/urgent that...

竖着看这些汉字："以防命'贱'，要求用虚拟是必要的"（你的"命"不好，写作文的时候多用以上这些虚拟语气，"命"就好了）。

举例

①我的朋友要求我尽快减肥。

My friend asked me that I should lose my weight as quickly as possible.

②大学密切关注大学生心理健康问题是非常必要的。

It is quite necessary that universities should pay close attention to the issue of mental health of university students.

③父母应该鼓励孩子多参加一些活动并与同学和老师交流，这是非常必要的。

It is urgent that kids should be inspired to take part in some activities and communicate with classmates and teachers.

总结　该句型可以在第三段提出解决问题的具体措施的时候使用。

（2）以下情况，从句用过去时态表示虚拟

常见的有两个：would rather 和 It is high time that...

举例

①我宁愿你比我幸福。

I would rather you were happier than me.

②是我们关注这个问题并且采取必要行动的时候了。

It is high time that we paid attention to the issue and took necessary measures.

③是我们采取措施关注儿童教育这个问题的时候了。

It is high time that action was taken to attach great importance to the issue of children's education.

总结 该句型可以在第三段喊口号的时候使用。

四、插入语

1. 定义

插入语是指插在句子中的词语或句子，其位置比较灵活，通常被逗号或破折号隔开，与句子的其他部分之间没有语法上的关系。其作用是对一句话进行解释、说明或总结；有时表示说话人的态度和看法；有时起强调作用；有时是为了引起对方的注意；还可以起转移话题或说明原因的作用；也可以承上启下，使语句间的衔接更紧密。写作使用插入语，行文会更流畅。

2. 插入语在写作中的使用

（1）副词作插入语，常见的有

undoubtedly, indeed, surely, obviously, briefly, actually, similarly, exactly 等。

比如：Respecting parents, undoubtedly, is a Chinese traditional virtue.

再如：Cooperation, actually, is a necessity to success.

（2）介词短语作插入语，常见的有

for my part, from my perspective, in short, on the contrary, in other words, in a/some sense, in general, in one's opinion, in conclusion, in reality, as a matter of fact, in addition, in return, as a consequence/result 等。

比如：The story about the hen, for my part, seeks to draw our attention to the issue of honesty.

再如：The public, in conclusion, should do something to relieve the pressure.

（3）不定式短语作插入语，常见的有

to be frank, to tell the truth, to be honest, to be sure, to make the matter worse 等。

比如：Those charming actors, to be frank, are hard-working when they perform on the stage.

（4）简短句子作插入语，常见的有

I believe, I suppose, I'm afraid, what's more, you know, that is (to say), as far as I know, as far as I'm concerned, believe it or not 等。

比如：Overfishing, believe it or not, has become a widespread problem around the world.

（5）现在分词短语作插入语，常见的有

honestly speaking, generally speaking, strictly speaking 等。

比如：The number of fish, strictly speaking, has decreased sharply in ten years.

总结 插入语可以插在任何一句话的主谓之间，使语言显得很正式。但是推荐写在第一段尾句或第二段、第三段首句的主谓之间。

五、修辞

1. 比喻

...is to humans as the foundation is to high skyscrapers.

……对人类来说就像地基对高楼大厦一样重要。

...is to humans as water is to fish.

……对人类来说就像水对鱼一样重要。

...is to the common as incurable diseases are to poor patients.

……对民众来说就像无法治愈的病对可怜的病人一样严重。

Men fear..., as children fear to walk in the dark.

人类害怕……，就像孩子害怕在黑暗中行走一样。

As every coin has two sides, ...is no exception.

事物都有两面性，……也不例外。

As no garden has no weeds, ...has its own shortcomings.

就像没有花园无杂草一样，……也有它自己的缺点。

As every magic book has its weak points, ...has its own weaknesses.

就像每一本魔法书都有它的缺点一样，……也有它自己的缺点。

总结 比喻可以在第一段尾句或第三段首句总结文章中心的时候使用。

2. 排比

（1）名词排比

History, philosophy, fundamental mathematics, and other abstract subjects have to be learned from books, or primarily from books.

历史、哲学、基础数学或其他抽象学科的知识必须从书本或者主要从书本中获得。

Three passions, simple but overwhelmingly strong, have governed my life: the longing for love, the search for knowledge, and unbearable pity for the suffering of mankind.

我的一生被三种简单却又无比强烈的激情控制着：对爱的渴望、对知识的寻求和对人类苦难的难以忍受的同情。

With God's help, the future of mankind will be assured in a world of justice, harmony, and peace.

在上帝的庇佑下，人类的未来将在一个公正、和谐、和平的世界里得到保障。

（2）形容词或副词排比

a small and peaceful town

一个小而安静的城镇

a stupid and incorrect decision

一个愚蠢而错误的决定

a direct and simple yet magically effective method

一个直接而简单但是有着神奇效果的方法

A conscientious professor always prepares his lecture carefully, intelligently and prudentially.

一个尽职尽责的教授总会认真、明智、谨慎地准备他的讲课。

We are creating a nation once again vibrant, robust and alive. But there are many mountains yet to climb. (Ronald Reagan, American president)

我们正再次创建一个繁荣、强大和生机勃勃的国家，但是仍然有很多的困难要克服。（美国总统，罗纳德·里根）

We were in the midst of shock—but we acted. We acted quickly, boldly, decisively. (Franklin D. Roosevelt, American president)

我们正处在危机之中，但是我们行动了。我们快速、大胆、果断地采取了行动。（美国总统，富兰克林·德拉诺·罗斯福）

（3）比较级排比

The impact that technology has had on our modern life and society, in general, is undeniable. The computer will become even greater as it gets faster, smaller, smarter, and so inexpensive is it that virtually everyone will be able to own one.

技术对我们现代生活和社会的影响通常是不可否认的。在电脑变得更快、更小、更智能的同时，其功能会变得更强大，而且价格低得几乎每个人都可以拥有它。

（4）非谓语动词排比

As one of modern college students, I get online everyday to acquire the information I need, to download the music and movies I like, and to chat with the friends I miss.

作为一名当代大学生，我每天上网获取需要的信息，下载喜欢的音乐和电影，和想念的朋友聊天。

This great nation will endure as it has endured, will revive and will prosper. (Franklin D. Roosevelt, American president)

这个伟大的民族将会忍受它曾忍受的一切，将会复苏，将会繁荣昌盛。（美国总统，富兰克林·德拉诺·罗斯福）

（5）从句的排比

If there is anyone out there who still doubts that America is a place where all things are possible, who still wonders if the dream of our founders is alive in our time, who still questions the power of our democracy, tonight is your answer.

如果有谁在怀疑美国是否是一个万事皆可能发生的国度，有谁在怀疑我们祖先的梦想在我们这个年代是否依然存在，有谁还在怀疑我们国家民主的力量，今晚就是给你们答案的时候。

Let us take as our goal: where peace is unknown, make it welcome; where peace is fragile, make it strong; where peace is temporary, make it permanent. (Richard Nixon, American president)

让这些成为我们的目标：让世界上不知道和平的地方有和平；在和平脆弱的地方使其强大；在和平短暂的地方使其长久。（美国总统，理查德·尼克松）

课后练兵

1. 文化交流不但能促进我们国家经济的发展，而且还能开阔个人的眼界。（使用倒装）

______

2. 在任何情况下，父母都不能忽略培养孩子自信的重要性。（使用倒装）

______

3. 我累得浑身都没有劲儿了。（使用倒装）

______

4. 就是在我的女儿出生以后，我才意识到母亲的伟大。

______

5. 你至今仍然没有意识到就是因为你交友不慎，你才没有考上心目中理想的大学。

______

6. 如果你要远行，我会掩上所有的窗户；世界上的风景为了所有的眼睛而生，而我只为你。（使用虚拟语气）

______

7. 当外面下雨的时候，只有在自己的家里，我才感到安全和放松。

______

8. 对于普通市民来说，保护小区环境、不随便丢垃圾是非常必要的。

______

9. 随着科学和技术的快速发展，各国人民交流日益频繁。（插入语）

______

10. 只有通过节食和多运动你才能成功减肥。（倒装）

______

11. 只有通过以上方式，过度捕捞这种现象才能得到缓解。

______

12. 如果孩子能常陪老人聊聊天，老人们会觉得生活更有意义和快乐。

______

答　案

1. Not only can cultural exchanges promote economic development in our country but also widen the horizons of individuals.

2. Under no circumstances could parents neglect the importance of building children's confidence.
3. So exhausted am I that I have no energy all over.
4. It is after my daughter was born that I knew the greatness of a mother.
5. Till now, you fail to be aware that it is because of bad companions that you did not go to your ideal university.
6. If you were to go on a long journey, I would close all my windows. Although sceneries of the world are for all the eyes, I am the one just for you.
7. When it rains outside, only at my own home will I feel safe and relaxed.
8. It is very necessary that common citizens should protect their community environment and not dump rubbish at random.
9. There, with the rapid development of science and technology, is more communication among people from different nations.
10. Only by eating less and exercising more could you lose weight successfully.
11. Only in these manners above could the phenomenon of overfishing be relieved.
12. If children spend more time accompanying the elderly, chatting with them, the elderly will find life more meaningful and happier.

第四章
段落写作

一、段落写作原则

段落是构成文章的整体单位，考研英语写作分为三段，几乎每段的写作都有统一的形式。段落通常分为四个部分：起、承、转、合——先有一个该段的中心句（topic sentence），然后有若干个对一个主要观点展开论述的相关联的句子。但段落并非句子的随意堆砌，句子之间应该具有连贯性和逻辑性。段落表达的内容应该是单一的，一个段落只能表达一个中心，而不能把意思上互不关联的句子堆砌在一起，造成段落内容的庞杂与错乱；段落表达的内容应该是完整的，一个中心应当尽量集中在一个段落里论述，最好不要把一个中心分割成两段或几段，这样会导致段落内容支离破碎。

在句子写作已经阐述清楚后，很有必要进行段落写作训练，它是考研英语写作的重要环节。首先，应该学习怎样写好一个段落，掌握段落的写作方法和技巧，然后再学习怎样组合和扩展段落，从而写成文章。学会了段落的写法，书写文章也就水到渠成了。

段落通常由三个主要部分组成：主题句、辅助句（正面论述和反面论述）、总结句（如果段落字数已经够了，可以考虑省略）。

请读下面的段落范例并注意分析其结构。

这是关于快乐和金钱关系的一段文字。

Opponents, however, hold the view that happiness does not depend on economic success but completely on other factors. First of all, numerous studies show that happy individuals are successful across multiple life domains, including marriage, income, work performance and health. The happiness exists not only because economic success makes people happy, but also because positive effect engenders happiness. What’s more, it is indisputable that there are millions of people who still have a miserable life and have to face the dangers of starvation and cold, but some of them still lead a happy life because they keep the happy spirit. Last but not least, money cannot buy everything, such as friendship, love or health. You can buy corporeal things, but you can never use money to buy more time. Therefore, if one only enjoys economic success, he will never grasp the truth of life.

【参考译文】然而，反对者认为幸福并不取决于经济上的成功，而完全取决于其他因素。首先，大量研究表明，快乐的人在多个生活领域都是成功的，包括婚姻、收入、工作业绩和健康。幸福的存在不仅是因为经济上的成功使人幸福，而且是因为积极的影响产生幸福。更重要的且无可争辩的是，现在有数百万人仍过着挨饿受冻的艰苦生活，但其中一些人仍感到生活幸福，因为他们保持着幸福的精神。最后但同样重要的是，金钱不能买到一切，如友谊、真爱和健康。你可以买有形的东西，但你永远不能用钱换来更多的时间。因此，如果一个人只享受经济上的成功，他永远不会领悟生活的真相。

主题句（起）：在段落中用于总领段落主旨大意的句子。一个好的主题句能够准确地表达作者的观点和态度。关于主题的观点和态度被称为主题思想（controlling idea）。主题句限定在一个单独的段落中，是被充分讨论的内容。上例中的主题句是首句。

辅助句（承）：在段落中对主题句进行具体阐述的句子。辅助句用来解释、说明或扩展主题句所表述的主题思想。请看上例中对主题句加以阐述的几个辅助句，即 2~6 句。

总结句（合）：在段落中重述或强调主题思想的句子。上例的总结句是最后一句。

总之，段落的结构图示如下：

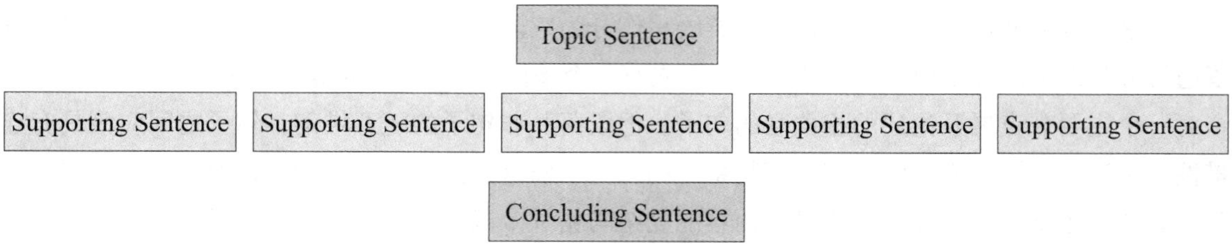

再如例文：In the contemporary society, there exist almost no areas on the earth that have not been spoiled by industrial development and pollution. The air that we breathe is **more often than not** polluted by the smoke from factory chimneys and the exhaust fumes of motor vehicles, while chemical waste poisons our rivers, lakes and seas. And by covering more and more of the earth's surface with buildings and roads, we are erecting huge barriers of concrete between ourselves and nature. It would appear that we are purposely cutting ourselves off from nature and destroying wildlife as we do so.

【参考译文】当今社会中，地球上几乎没有地方不受工业发展和污染的破坏。我们呼吸的空气多半被从工厂烟囱里冒出来的气体和汽车排放的尾气污染。同时，化学垃圾污染着我们的河流、湖水和海洋。大量的建筑和公路覆盖越来越多的地面，我们正在人类和自然之间竖立起巨型混凝土屏障。好像我们这样做是故意切断我们自己和自然界的关系并且伤害野生动物。

词组：more often than not 通常；多半

这段例文中，所有的句子都是围绕着“我们的生存环境被污染，生态环境被破坏”这一主题论述的，具有较好的统一性。

下面这篇作文中，作者列举并解释了养狗的三点意义：维护主人的健康，培养孩子的责任心，增强家庭关系的和睦和感情的稳定。作者强调最后一点是狗的主人所得到的最有意义的收获。

Keeping Pets

Keeping dogs as pets has more benefits than most people recognize.

Firstly, they contribute to the good health of their owners. Often their demands for walks and play improve their owners' exercise routine. In fact, statistics show that dog owners get more regular exercise than those without a dog. Also, they enhance their owner's health simply by being around to be petted. Secondly, they provide a means for parents to teach their children responsibility. When parents give children a dog, they provide them the opportunity to fulfill the responsibility of walking, feeding, and caring for its other needs. Finally and the most importantly, dogs enhance the well-being and emotional stability of families. Older people who live alone especially rely on dogs to give them joy and companionship. Children also find a great deal of comfort in their dogs. For example, a family dog helps a little boy adapt when his mother leaves him with a sitter and goes to work.

In brief, although dogs cause their owners trouble and extra expense, these animals may at the same time have unrealized value.

【参考译文】

养宠物

把狗作为宠物来养的好处比大多数人认识到的要多。

首先，它们对主人的健康有好处。因为狗需要散步和玩乐，所以这会加强它们主人的日常锻炼。事实上，数据表明，养狗的人比不养狗的人有着更规律的锻炼。并且，狗可以通过陪伴和爱抚来增进主人的健康。其次，它们也为父母提供了教育孩子责任感的方法。当父母送给孩子一条狗时，他们就给孩子提供了去履行他们责任的机会，比如遛狗、喂狗和满足狗的其他需要。最后也是最重要的一点是，狗可以增强家庭的幸福感和情感的稳定性。独居的老人对狗更充满依赖，它们可以给老人带来快乐和陪伴。孩子们在狗身上也可以找到很多慰藉，比如说，当母亲把孩子留给一个临时看管的人出去工作时，家犬能帮助孩子适应这种生活。

总之，虽然狗狗会给主人带来一些问题，也会产生额外的费用，但是这些动物同时也有一些未被察觉的价值。

二、写作论述方式

其实到现在为止，如果单词、句子能做到正确、准确、多变，再加上我们讲解的段落写作原则，同学们已经可以自己写出一篇高分作文了。但遗憾的是，很多时候由于思维的局限性，即使被要求写出一篇中文作文，同学们也感觉很痛苦，因为无话可说。这时候怎么办呢？这就是本模块要讲解的内容，让你的作文旁征博引，内容丰富。

1. 例证

举出实例来论证主题，可以让文章看起来“高大上”，这是写作中最常见的扩展段落的方法，也是用于说明段落主旨、阐述细节最简单有效的方法。但必须要注意的是，例子绝对要和中心相关，并且单词、语法不要出现大的错误。

比如关于谦虚的例子：

Newton, one of the most influential scientists throughout the history of mankind, could be the best case of how modesty works in the course of making further progress and achieving greater success. Just imagine, having discovered the Newton’s First Law of Motion, how could he have succeeded in establishing the Three Laws of Motion if he had simply taken pride in his past achievements?

【参考译文】牛顿是人类历史上最具影响力的科学家之一，他可能是在取得重大进步和收获更大成功的过程中，具有谦虚品德的最佳典范。想象一下，在牛顿发现运动第一定律之后，如果他对自己过去的成就感到骄傲自满，他怎么可能成功地建立起三大运动定律呢？

下面是关于勤奋的例子：

Kobe Bryant can be the most favorable example of how diligence functions in our career. When asked by one of his friends what was the secret of his success, he replied with humor and implication that, "Do you know how Los Angeles looks like at 4 o'clock a.m.? I know." Obviously, how could he, one of the greatest basketball players throughout the history of mankind, who was once deemed not appropriate for playing basketball, have achieved considerable success in NBA without diligence?

【参考译文】科比·布莱恩特是证明勤奋如何在我们职业生涯中发挥作用的最好例子。当朋友问他成功的秘诀时，他幽默地暗示道：“你知道凌晨4点时洛杉矶的样子吗？我知道。”显然，他作为人类历史上最了不起的篮球运动员之一，曾经被人们认为不是打篮球的料，如果没有勤奋，他怎么可能在NBA取得巨大的成功呢？

下面是关于勤奋和宽容的例子：

There are so many cases that could account for my perspective in which Abraham Lincoln's is pretty impressive. As he was born in a poor family, he was exceedingly diligent. As a consequence, he became President of the United States.

Apart from many fine qualities that Lincoln possessed, I appreciate him in that he dared to do what he thought was right at a time when his beliefs were very unpopular with many people. He also had infinite patience and tolerance for those who disagreed with him, and bore their discourtesy toward him with admirable restraint. He also had the manliness to forgive his opponents. When the Civil War ended, he treated his erstwhile enemies with great generosity. So the case vividly clarifies a truth that ______ has played a crucial role in our success.（横线处可填某种品质。）

【参考译文】尽管如此多的案例可以解释我的观点，但亚伯拉罕·林肯的例子令人印象尤为深刻。他出生在贫寒的家庭，所以他非常勤奋。结果，他当上了美国总统。

除了林肯所具有的许多优秀品质，我欣赏他敢于做他认为正确的事情，当时他的信仰在很多人当中非常不受欢迎。他对那些不赞同他的人也有无限的耐心和宽容，并以令人钦佩的克制忍受着他们对他的无礼。他也很有风度地原谅了他的对手。内战结束后，他对昔日的敌人非常慷慨。这个例子生动地阐明了一个事实，那就是______在我们的成功中起着重要作用。

总结

举例的时候需要注意：

- 一定要使用自己拿得准的单词和句型，正确最重要；
- 注意句子间的逻辑关系，多用逻辑关系词；
- 如果举的例子是过去的事情，一定要用过去时态。

下面按照这个思路举一个普通人的例子：

To clarify the truth that love is like a lamp, which appears brighter in scaring darkness, I would like to present a vivid case as follows. The other day, I got sick. Nobody stayed with me for all students in my dormitory went shopping. At that moment, my teacher, Mr. Liu, came in to supply me with certain medicines. Soon, I recovered and could attend class normally. It might be, in the eye of the teacher, one small thing. However, I was really grateful for his assistance. If there had been no help from my dearest teacher, I would have become worse on that day.

【参考译文】为了说明爱心就像一盏灯，它在可怕的黑暗中显得越明亮这个事实，我想举如下这个生动的例子。前几天，我生病了。没有人陪我，因为同宿舍的所有同学都去购物了。就在那时，我的老师——刘老师，进来给我送了一些药。很快，我就康复了，可以正常上课了。在老师看来，这可能是件小事。然而，我真的很感谢他的帮助。如果没有我最亲爱的老师的帮助，我那天就会病得更严重。

举例常用的表达有：

① Examples to prove the view are abundant. The most persuasive one is the case of sb. who...
证明这一观点的例子很多。最有说服力的例子是关于某人……

② This can be illustrated by the example of sb. who...
这可以用某人……的例子来说明。

③ Such stimulating/less impressive cases/stories are not rare in our daily life.
在我们的日常生活中，这样给人印象深刻 / 不那么令人印象深刻的案例 / 故事并不罕见。

④ To illustrate this, let's return to the example of sb./sth.
为了说明这一点，让我们回到某人 / 某物的例子。

⑤ There exist too plentiful cases like this in the routine of our life to list. However, the most impressive one is about myself.
在我们的日常生活中，这样的例子不胜枚举。但最令人印象深刻的例子是关于我自己的。

⑥ Although so abundant cases can support my simple view, the following one is the most favorable.
虽然有这么多的例子可以支持我的简单观点，但下面这个例子是最合适的。

⑦ So the case vividly clarifies a truth that... has played a crucial role in our success/life.
因此，这个例子生动地阐明了一个事实：……在我们的成功 / 生活中起了至关重要的作用。

⑧ If there were no..., sb./sth. would do...
如果没有……，某人或某物将会……

当然图表作文如果无话可说，举例也是最佳方式，比如 2012 年英语（二）写作 Part B：

某公司员工工作满意度调查

满意度 / 年龄组	满意	不清楚	不满意
≤ 40 岁	16.7%	50.0%	33.3%
41~50 岁	0.0%	36.0%	64.0%
＞ 50 岁	40.0%	50.0%	10.0%

该篇文章，我们需要论述为什么年龄大的人对工作满意度很高，举例是最佳的论证方式。

It's not hard to think of some reasons why older people are more satisfied with their jobs. First and foremost, older employees have lower expectations than younger employees, and they can adjust themselves better. Secondly, older employees have higher job satisfaction because they have gone through the process of getting better jobs or more satisfying positions in their careers. Finally, the older they are, the higher their income is and the more likely they are to be satisfied, and the lower their "career expectations" are, the less likely they are to be disappointed.

【参考译文】关于为什么年龄大的人对工作满意度高不难想出以下几点理由。首先，年长员工的期望值要比年轻员工的低，他们能更好地调节自己的状况。其次，年长员工具有较高的工作满意度是因为他们在自己的事业中经历了获得更好的工作或更满意的职位的过程。最后，年龄越大，收入就越高，带来满足感的可能性也就越高，他们的"职业期望度"越低，带来失落感的可能性也就越低。

2. 数据列举

我们在阅读中经常见到这种论证方式。通常都是先说一个论点，然后用数据支撑，这是很真实有用的论述方式。在段落扩展中，引用统计数据是论证作者观点的最有效的方法之一。比如你的观点是：污染很严重。用数据列举就铁证如山，很有说服力！百分之多少的人因空气质量问题得什么病，百分之多少的污水都被排放到江河。很多同学会说，我不知道百分比是多少啊，那你觉得批卷老师知道这个百分比吗？那些阅读中的数据一定是真实准确的吗？我们无从考证。

比如以下统计数字的表达方式：

Surveys have shown that almost half of all male high school seniors—and nearly 20 percent of all ninth-grade boys—can be called "problem drinkers" ... Over 5,000 teenagers are killed yearly in auto accidents due to drunken driving.

【参考译文】调查显示，几乎一半的高三男学生（几乎 20% 的九年级男孩）都有酗酒习惯……每年有超过 5 000 名青少年因为酒驾死于交通事故。

A national survey by the Institute for Social Research of the University of Michigan, in which 17,000 of the nation's 2.7 million high school seniors were questioned about their use of drugs, revealed a continuing downward trend.

【参考译文】一个由密歇根大学社会研究机构组织的国民调查表明，在 270 万的高三学生中，有 1.7 万被怀疑有吸毒行为，这个趋势呈现持续下降的势头。

According to a recent investigation by Chinese Academy of Social Sciences, the majority of university students are of the opinion that cooperation is quite essential in both our life and our career.（这个没有使用精确数字）

【参考译文】根据中国社会科学院最近的一项调查，大部分大学生都认为无论在我们的生活还是工作中，合作都是重要的。

数据列举常用的表达有：

① In light of the latest survey by the Chinese Academy of Social Sciences, an increasing number of people harbor the idea that...

根据中国社会科学院的最新调查，越来越多的人认为……

② A recent study revealed the shocking/surprising/delightful fact that...

最近的一项研究揭示了一个令人震惊 / 惊讶 / 高兴的事实……

③ On the basis of the proximate statistics by the Department of Social Sciences in a university, 78~85 percent of adults especially youngsters argue that...

根据一所大学社会科学系的最新统计，78%～85% 的成年人（尤其是年轻人）认为……

④ Official figures released by the Ministry of Transportation/Education show that...
交通运输部 / 教育部发布的官方数据显示……

⑤ The ratio of smokers to non-smokers is 3∶2.
吸烟者和非吸烟者的比例是 3∶2。

⑥ The number of computer companies has increased sevenfold.
计算机公司的数目增加了七倍。

⑦ The statistics showed that there was a 30% increase in the sales over the previous year.
统计数据表明，销售额比去年增加了 30%。

在列举数据的时候，如果能用到下面的专业表达，其真实性就进一步增加了。

（1）数字增加主要有以下几种表达方式（注意翻译的意思）

①表示两倍，一般用 twice 或 double

twice

twice as much/many as...　　是……的两倍（比……大一倍）

twice as large as...　　（意思同上）

twice larger than...　　（意思同上）

double

be the double of...　　（意思同上）

举例

The statistics showed that the number of postgraduates who could persist reading at least 10 books per year is twice as large as that of those who fail to enjoy reading books.

统计数据表明，每年坚持读至少十本书的研究生是那些不喜欢读书的同学的两倍。

②表示三倍或三倍以上一般用数词加 times 或 -fold

times

increase by 5 times　　增加了 5 倍（增加到 6 倍）

increase to 6 times　　增加到 6 倍（增加了 5 倍）

6 times larger/greater than...　　增加到 6 倍（增加了 5 倍）

fold

increase fivefold（意思同上）

（2）数字减少主要有以下几种表达方式（注意翻译的意思）

reduce to 30%　　下降到 30%

reduce by 30%　　下降了 30%

reduce to 1/3　　减少到 1/3（减少了 2/3）

reduce by 2/3　　减少了 2/3（减少到 1/3）

1/3 as large as...　　为……的 1/3

2/3 smaller than...　　为……的 1/3

3. 引用名人名言

考研英语写作中，恰当地引用名言来证明自己文章中的观点要比用自己的话更有说服力，也可以使问题和观点的阐述更为深刻有力，有时会达到画龙点睛的效果。如果出现了名人的名字，引文一定要准确无误，并且引用内容要与文章内容紧密相关。不能断章取义，牵强附会，并要正确地使用标点符号。如果用引语来证明自己的观点，就要知道怎样使用不同的短语和从句把引语自然流畅地插入到段落中。当然了，我们事先准备好的名言不一定能写到作文中去，下面我会帮助同学们列出一些万能名言以备考试时使用。

写作中常用到的名人名言（可以选择每组背一个句子）。

理 想 篇

Do not, for one repulse, give up the purpose that you resolved to effect. (William Shakespeare, British dramatist)

不要只因一次失败，就放弃你原来决心要达到的目的。（英国剧作家，威廉·莎士比亚）

Don't part with your illusions. When they are gone you may still exist, but you have ceased to live. (Mark Twain, American writer)

不要放弃你的幻想。当幻想没有了，你还可以存活，但是你虽生犹死。（美国作家，马克·吐温）

I want to bring out the secrets of nature and apply them for the happiness of man. I don't know of any better service to offer for the short time we are in the world. (Thomas Edison, American inventor)

我想揭示大自然的秘密，用来造福人类。我认为，在我们短暂的一生中，最好的贡献莫过于此。（美国发明家，托马斯·爱迪生）

Ideal is the beacon. Without ideal, there is no secure direction; without direction, there is no life. (Leo Tolstoy, Russian writer)

理想是指路明灯。没有理想，就没有坚定的方向；没有方向，就没有生活。（俄国作家，列夫·托尔斯泰）

If winter comes, can spring be far behind? (P. B. Shelley, British poet)

冬天来了，春天还会远吗？（英国诗人，P·B·雪莱）

If you doubt yourself, then indeed you stand on shaky ground. (Ibsen, Norwegian dramatist)

如果你怀疑自己，那么你的立足点确实就不稳固了。（挪威剧作家，易卜生）

If you would go up high, then use your own legs! Do not let yourselves carried aloft; do not seat yourselves on other people's backs and heads. (F. W. Nietzsche, German philosopher)

如果你们想走到高处，就要使用自己的两条腿！不要让别人抬到高处；也不要坐在别人的背上和头上。（德国哲学家，F·W·尼采）

It is at our mother's knee that we acquire our noblest and truest and highest, but there is seldom any money in them. (Mark Twain, American writer)

就是在我们母亲的膝上，我们获得了最高尚、最真诚和最远大的理想，但是理想中很少有金钱。（美国作家，马克·吐温）

Living without an aim is like sailing without a compass. (Alexander Dumas, French writer)

生活没有目标就像航海没有指南针。（法国作家，大仲马）

The ideals which have lighted my way, and time after time have given me new courage to face life cheerfully—have been kindness, beauty and truth. (Albert Einstein, American scientist)

有些理想曾为我指引过道路，并不断给我新的勇气以欣然面对人生，那些理想就是——真、善、美。（美国科学家，阿尔伯特·爱因斯坦）

The important thing in life is to have a great aim, and the determination to attain it. (Johan Wolfgang von Goethe, German poet and dramatist)

人生重要的事情就是确定一个伟大的目标，并决心实现它。（德国诗人、剧作家，约翰·沃尔夫冈·冯·歌德）

The man with a new idea is a crank until the idea succeeds. (Mark Twain, American writer)

具有新想法的人在其想法实现之前是个怪人。（美国作家，马克·吐温）

The only limit to our realization of tomorrow will be our doubts of today. (Franklin D. Roosevelt, American president)

实现明天理想的唯一障碍是今天的疑虑。（美国总统，富兰克林·D·罗斯福）

When an end is lawful and obligatory, the indispensable means to it are also lawful and obligatory. (Abraham Lincoln, American president)

如果一个目的是合法且必须做的，则达到这个目的的必要手段也是合法且必须采取的。（美国总统，亚伯拉罕·林肯）

奋斗篇

Genius only means hard-working all one's life. (Mendeleyev, Russian chemist)

天才只意味着终身不懈的努力。（俄国化学家，门捷列夫）

I have nothing to offer but blood, toil, tears and sweat. (Winston Churchill, British politician)

我所能奉献的没有其他，只有热血、辛劳、眼泪与汗水。（英国政治家，温斯顿·丘吉尔）

Man errors so long as he strives. (Johan Wolfgang von Goethe, German poet and dramatist)

人只要奋斗就会犯错误。（德国诗人、剧作家，约翰·沃尔夫冈·冯·歌德）

My fellow Americans: ask not what your country can do for you—ask what you can do for your country. My fellow citizens of the world: ask not what America will do for you, but what together we can do for the freedom of man. (John F. Kennedy, American president)

美国同胞们，不要问国家能为你们做些什么，而要问你们能为国家做些什么。全世界的公民们，不要问美国将为你们做些什么，而要问我们能共同为人类的自由做些什么。（美国总统，约翰·F·肯尼迪）

Our destiny offers not the cup of despair, but the chalice of opportunity. (Richard Nixon, American president)

命运给予我们的不是失望之酒，而是机会之杯。（美国总统，理查德·尼克松）

Patience is bitter, but its fruit is sweet. (Jean-Jacques Rousseau, French thinker)

忍耐是痛苦的，但它的果实是甜蜜的。（法国思想家，让－雅克·卢梭）

Progress is the activity of today and the assurance of tomorrow. (Emerson, American thinker)

进步是今天的活动、明天的保证。（美国思想家，爱默生）

The world can be changed by man's endeavor, and that this endeavor can lead to something new and better. No man can sever the bonds that unite him to his society simply by averting his eyes. He must ever be receptive and sensitive to the new; and have sufficient courage and skill to novel facts and to deal with them. (Franklin D. Roosevelt, American president)

人经过努力可以改变世界，这种努力可以使人类达到新的、更美好的境界。没有人仅凭闭目、不看社会现实就能割断自己与社会的联系。他必须敏感，随时准备接受新事物；并有足够的勇气和技能去面对新的事实，解决新问题。（美国总统，富兰克林·D·罗斯福）

There is no royal road to science, and only those who do not dread the fatiguing climb of its steep paths have a chance of gaining its numinous summits... (Karl Marx, German revolutionary)

在科学上没有平坦的大道，只有不畏劳苦沿着其崎岖之路攀登的人，才有希望到达它光辉的顶点……（德国革命家，卡尔·马克思）

The man who has made up his mind to win will never say "impossible". (Napoléon Bonaparte, French emperor)

凡是决心取得胜利的人是从来不说“不可能”的。（法国皇帝，拿破仑·波拿巴）

To do whatever needs to be done to preserve this last and greatest bastion of freedom. (Ronald Reagan, American president)

为了保住这最后的、最伟大的自由堡垒，我们必须尽我们所能。（美国总统，罗纳德·里根）

We cannot always build the future for our youth, but we can build our youth for the future. (Franklin D. Roosevelt, American president)

我们不能总是为我们的青年创造美好未来，但我们能够为未来造就我们的青年一代。（美国总统，富兰克林·德拉诺·罗斯福）

Where there is a will, there is a way. (Thomas Edison, American inventor)

有志者，事竟成。（美国发明家，托马斯·爱迪生）

成功篇

Achievement provides the only real pleasure in life. (Thomas Edison, American inventor)

有所成就是人生唯一的真正乐趣。（美国发明家，托马斯·爱迪生）

But has the last word been said? Is all hope to be lost? Is the defeat final? No! (Charles de Gaulle, French president)

但是难道败局已定，胜利已经无望？不，不能这样说！（法国总统，夏尔·戴高乐）

I succeeded because I willed it; I never hesitated. (Napoléon Bonaparte, French emperor)

我成功是因为我有决心；从未踌躇。（法国皇帝，拿破仑·波拿巴）

If you wish to succeed, you should use persistence as your good friend, experience as your reference, prudence as your brother and hope as your sentry. (Thomas Edison, American inventor)

如果你希望成功，当以恒心为良友、以经验为参谋、以谨慎为兄弟、以希望为哨兵。（美国发明家，托马斯·爱迪生）

Only those who have the patience to do simple things perfectly ever acquire the skill to do difficult things easily. (Friedrich von Schiller, German dramatist and poet)

只有有耐心圆满完成简单工作的人，才能够轻而易举地完成困难的事。（德国剧作家、诗人，弗里德里希·冯·席勒）

Power invariably means both responsibility and danger. (Theodore Roosevelt, American president)

权力永远意味着责任和危险。（美国总统，西奥多·罗斯福）

Success covers a multitude of blunders. (George Bernard Shaw, British dramatist)

成功由大量的失望铸就。（英国剧作家，乔治·萧伯纳）

The people who get on in this world are the people who get up and look for circumstances they want, and if they cannot find them, make them. (George Bernard Shaw, British dramatist)

在这个世界上，取得成就的人是那些努力寻找他们想要的机会的人，如果找不到机会，他们就去创造机会。（英国剧作家，乔治·萧伯纳）

You have to believe in yourself. That's the secret of success. (Charlie Chaplin, British actor)

你必须相信自己，这是成功的秘诀。（英国演员，查理·卓别林）

幸福篇

Happy is the man who is living by his hobby. (George Bernard Shaw, British dramatist)

醉心于某种爱好的人是幸福的。（英国剧作家，乔治·萧伯纳）

Happiness lies not in the mere possession of money; it lies in the joy of achievement, in the thrill of creative effort. (Franklin D. Roosevelt, American president)

幸福不在于仅仅拥有金钱，而在于获得成就时的喜悦以及产生创造力的激情。（美国总统，富兰克林·D·罗斯福）

Human felicity is produced not so much by great pieces of good fortune that seldom happen, as by little advantages that occur every day. (Benjamin Franklin, American politician)

与其说人类的幸福来自偶尔发生的红运，不如说来自每天都有的小实惠。（美国政治家，本杰明·富兰克林）

Most folks are about as happy as they make up their minds to be. (Abraham Lincoln, American president)

对于大多数人来说，他们认定自己有多幸福，就有多幸福。（美国总统，亚伯拉罕·林肯）

The secret of being miserable is to have leisure to bother about whether you are happy or not. (George Bernard Shaw, British dramatist)

痛苦的秘密在于有闲工夫担心自己是否幸福。（英国剧作家，乔治·萧伯纳）

The supreme happiness of life is the conviction that we are loved. (Victor Hugo, French novelist)

生活中最大的幸福是坚信有人爱我们。（法国小说家，维克多·雨果）

There is no paradise on earth equal to the union of love and innocence. (Jean-Jacques Rousseau, French thinker)

人间最大的幸福莫过于爱情与纯洁相融合。（法国思想家，让－雅克·卢梭）

To really understand a man we must judge him in misfortune. (Napoléon Bonaparte, French emperor)

要真正了解一个人，需在不幸中考察他。（法国皇帝，拿破仑·波拿巴）

We have no more right to consume happiness without producing it than to consume wealth without producing it. (George Bernard Shaw, British dramatist)

正像我们无权只享受财富而不创造财富一样，我们也无权只享受幸福而不创造幸福。（英国剧作家，乔治·萧伯纳）

时间篇

At twenty years of age, the will reigns; at thirty, the wit; and at forty, the judgment. (Benjamin Franklin, American politician)

二十岁时起支配作用的是意志，三十岁时是才智，四十岁时是判断。（美国政治家，本杰明·富兰克林）

Do you love life? Then do not squander time; for that's the stuff life is made of. (Benjamin Franklin, American politician)

你热爱生命吗？那么，别浪费时间，因为生命是由时间组成的。（美国政治家，本杰明·富兰克林）

Each moment in history is a fleeting time, precious and unique. (Richard Nixon, American president)

历史巨轮飞转，分分秒秒的时间都十分宝贵，也独具意义。（美国总统，理查德·尼克松）

Fish and visitors smell three days. (Benjamin Franklin, American politician)

鱼放三天发臭，客住三天讨嫌。（美国政治家，本杰明·富兰克林）

I am a slow walker, but I never walk backwards. (Abraham Lincoln, American president)

我走得很慢，但是我从来不会后退。（美国总统，亚伯拉罕·林肯）

If you want to understand today, you have to search yesterday. (Pearl S. Buck, American female writer)

想要懂得今天，就必须研究昨天。（美国女作家，赛珍珠）

In delay there lies no plenty. Then come kiss me, sweet and twenty. Youth's a stuff that will not endure. (William Shakespeare, British dramatist)

迁延蹉跎，来日无多，二十丽姝，请来吻我，衰草枯杨，青春易过。（英国剧作家，威廉·莎士比亚）

Never leave that until tomorrow, which you can do today. (Benjamin Franklin, American politician)

今天的事不要拖到明天做。（美国政治家，本杰明·富兰克林）

Ordinary people merely think how they shall spend their time; a man of talent tries to use it. (Arthur Schopenhauer, German philosopher)

普通人只考虑如何度过时间，有才能的人设法利用时间。（德国哲学家，亚瑟·叔本华）

The golden age is before us, not behind us. (Mark Twain, American writer)

黄金时代在我们面前，而不是在我们背后。（美国作家，马克·吐温）

The time of life is short; to spend that shortness basely, it would be too long. (William Shakespeare, British dramatist)

人生苦短，若虚度年华，则短暂的人生就太长了。（英国剧作家，威廉·莎士比亚）

Time is money. (Benjamin Franklin, American politician)

时间就是金钱。（美国政治家，本杰明·富兰克林）

To choose time is to save time. (Francis Bacon, British philosopher)

合理安排时间就是节约时间。（英国哲学家，弗朗西斯·培根）

We always have time enough, if we will but use it aright. (Johan Wolfgang von Goethe, German poet and dramatist)

只要我们能善用时间，就永远不愁时间不够用。（德国诗人、剧作家，约翰·沃尔夫冈·冯·歌德）

Weep no more, no sigh, nor groan. Sorrow calls no time that's gone. (John Fletcher, British dramatist)

别哭泣，别叹息，别呻吟。悲伤唤不回流逝的时光。（英国剧作家，约翰·弗莱切）

知识篇

Activity is the only road to knowledge. (George Bernard Shaw, British dramatist)

行动是通往知识的唯一道路。（英国剧作家，乔治·萧伯纳）

A free man obtains knowledge from many sources besides books. (Thomas Jefferson, American president)

自由人可以从除了书本以外许多别的来源获得知识。（美国总统，托马斯·杰斐逊）

A great part to the information I have was acquired by looking up something and finding something else on the way. (Adams Franklin, American humorist)

我的大部分知识都是这样获得的：在寻找某个资料时意外地发现了其他资料。（美国幽默作家，亚当斯·富兰克林）

If a man empties his purse into his head, no man can take it away from him. An investment in knowledge always pays the best interest. (Benjamin Franklin, American politician)

倾己所有追求知识，没有人能夺走它；投资知识，收益最佳。（美国政治家，本杰明·富兰克林）

Imagination is more important than knowledge. (Albert Einstein, American scientist)

想象力比知识更重要。（美国科学家，阿尔伯特·爱因斯坦）

Knowledge is power. (Francis Bacon, British philosopher)

知识就是力量。（英国哲学家，弗朗西斯·培根）

The empty vessels make the greatest sound. (William Shakespeare, British dramatist)

满瓶不响，半瓶咣当。（英国剧作家，威廉·莎士比亚）

教育篇

And gladly would he learn, and gladly teach. (Chaucer, British poet)

勤于学习的人才能乐意施教。（英国诗人，乔叟）

Better be unborn than untaught, for ignorance is the root of misfortune. (Plato, Ancient Greek philosopher)

与其不受教，不如不出生，因为无知是不幸的根源。（古希腊哲学家，柏拉图）

Genius without education is like silver in the mine. (Benjamin Franklin, American politician)

未受教育的天才，犹如矿中之银。（美国政治家，本杰明·富兰克林）

The roots of education are bitter, but the fruit is sweet. (Aristotle, Ancient Greek philosopher)

教育之根是苦，但果实香甜。（古希腊哲学家，亚里士多德）

文 化 篇

A great poem is a fountain forever overflowing with the waters of wisdom and delight. (P. B. Shelley, British poet)

伟大的诗篇就是永远喷出智慧和欢欣之水的喷泉。（英国诗人，P·B·雪莱）

A novel is a mirror walking along a main road. (Stendhal, French writer)

一部小说犹如一面在大街上走的镜子。（法国作家，司汤达）

Art is a lie that tells the truth. (Picasso, Spanish painter)

艺术是揭示真理的谎言。（西班牙画家，毕加索）

Humor has been well defined as thinking in fun while feeling in earnest. (Mark Twain, American writer)

幽默被人正确地解释为“以诚挚表达感受，寓深思于嬉笑”。（美国作家，马克·吐温）

The decline of literature indicates the decline of a nation; the two keep in their downward tendency. (Johan Wolfgang von Goethe, German poet and dramatist)

文学的衰落表明一个民族的衰落。这两者在齐头并进地走下坡路。（德国诗人、剧作家，约翰·沃尔夫冈·冯·歌德）

When one loves one's art no service seems too hard. (O. Henry, American novelist)

一个人一旦热爱艺术，什么奉献也不难。（美国小说家，欧·亨利）

万能名人名言

Once, there was a celebrity having gained great reputation all around the world who stated that ______ proves to human beings as blue sky is to little larks.（sth. 很重要）

Once, there was a celebrity having gained great reputation all around the world who stated that ______ proves to human beings as fatal disasters are to pitiful patients.（sth. 很严重）

4. 定义和解释

给一个事情或概念下定义，就是运用简明扼要的语言，对某事物的本质特征或一个概念的内涵和外延做确切的说明，从而把这一事物和其他相似或同类的事物区别开来。这需要一个最基本的语言思维过程，定义对于说服读者或论证观点是一种有效的策略。

因为我们主要针对的是考研英语写作的定义和解释，所以不需要像学术写作的定义那样清晰完整。

下面我们举几个比较学术的例子：

Social economics may be defined as the branch of economics which is concerned with the measurement, causes and consequences of social problems.

社会经济学可以被定义为经济学的一个分支，它关注社会问题的度量、原因和后果。

再如：

As an introduction of SIS, let us review what a computer is and what computerization means. A computer is a machine—a complex, sophisticated machine but a machine nonetheless. It is not magical, and it cannot think. Its value lies in the fact that it can handle and organize large amounts of detailed information very quickly. Using a computer, you will find that you can do your job more efficiently and have time to do other necessary jobs that you have not had time for before. (Neufeld, 1987)

作为 SIS 的介绍，让我们回顾一下什么是计算机以及计算机化意味着什么。计算机是一台机器——一台复杂、精密的机器，但它仍然是一台机器。它没有魔法，也不会思考。它的价值在于能够非常快速地处理和组织大量的详细信息。使用电脑，你会发现你可以更有效地做你的工作，有时间去做你以前没有时间做的其他必要的工作。（诺伊费尔德，1987）

这种学术性的论述听起来很抽象，所以在考研英语作文中，还是应使用简单、直白的语言。此处所说的下定义并不是要写得很抽象，而是你自己对这个概念的理解。比如：什么是水？你不需要说两个氢原子和一个氧原子。生活中的水是什么？就是一种液体，或者说是可以喝的东西。

如果是非学术的例子，就非常容易表达了，比如：

① 解释下什么是美女。

美女就是有一双大眼睛，有迷人身材和迷人脸蛋的女士。

② 解释下什么是污染。

污染是一个严重的全球性问题，这意味着随着环境问题变得越来越糟糕，我们不能呼吸到新鲜的空气，不能喝到干净的水，不能看到纯净的天空。

③ 解释下什么是孝敬父母。

孝敬父母是中国的传统美德，这意味着当他们慢慢变老的时候，我们买礼物给他们，我们为他们洗衣服，我们为他们做美味的食物。

④ 解释下什么是乐观。

乐观是一种心态，它意味着当一个人在生活和事业中遇到困难时，他不害怕挫折，敢于面对任何困难，并且坚持做他想做的事情。

总结

定义和解释的模式是：sth.（文章中心）is a Chinese conventional virtue/a pervasive social trend/an active/negative mentality/a hot social topic + which means that + 三个并列的排比句 + 状语从句。

需要注意的是这种论证方式，如果确定用在作文中，那就放在第二段的首句，因为它的作用是引出下面的原因分析。

在实际写作中，我们在论述内容和分析原因时，有时候需要几种论证方式同时采用，而不是单一地采取某种论证方式，这样能使结构和形式丰富多彩，论述更加充分。

比如 2019 年英语（一）写作 Part B，主题是“坚持很重要”，那第二段我们就可以用多种论述方式，说明坚持的重要性。

比如：

My argument is as follows. To begin with, persistence requires us to keep a positive mentality which means that you fear no difficulties, believe your faith and dare to challenge yourself whenever confronted with frustrations in your study and career.（定义和解释）A case in point is Ma Yun, a well-noted entrepreneur throughout the world. He had endured immense number of failures before he achieved great success. He, in public places, expressed the significance of persistence for many times—"It is not easy to see the sun the day after tomorrow."（举例论证）As a matter of fact, if one gives up on the road to success, he or she will achieve nothing in his or her life.（反面论证）

课后练兵

1. 什么是追星?
2. 什么是上网?
3. 什么是文化交流?

答　案

1. 追 星：Worshipping stars means that teenagers worship their idols through buying their photos, going to their concerts and imitating their hairstyles.
2. 上网：Surfing the Internet means that citizens go shopping online, see their favorite movies online and have their entertainments through Internet technology which has advanced rapidly.
3. 文化交流：Cultural exchanges mean that Chinese can travel abroad, understand different cultures and make more foreign friends.

第五章

由段成篇

第一节　应用文写作

考研英语写作 A 节部分是应用文写作，要求写 100 个单词左右。主要内容包括私人和公务信函、备忘录、报告等。

一、书信的结构

1. 书信形式

（1）齐头式

信函各行，包括信头、信内地址、称呼、主标题、正文和结束语，都要从左边缘栏线开始。日期写在右上方（也可不写日期）。

Dear my friend,

I am delighted to know that you have a strong desire to learn Chinese recently. Therefore, the letter, to be honest, is written to recommend a city for you.

When the idea occurs to me, the first city flashing in my mind is Beijing, the capital of China. The primary reason is that almost every person you will meet can speak relatively standard Chinese, which plays a key role in the process of language learning. As a result, as a modern city, it provides an excellent language environment for language learners. Besides, in Beijing, one of the most advanced cities, people are open-minded, hospitable, and inclusive. You will soon find that you can make friends with them and feel easy in such an environment.

Finally, I hope that you could take my suggestions into serious consideration, and I am looking forward to your reply at your earliest convenience.

Yours sincerely,

Li Ming

（2）缩进式

这种格式要求每段首行都要留出四个字母的空白。这也是我们考试中最常用的格式。

Dear my friend,

I am delighted to know that you have a strong desire to learn Chinese recently. Therefore, the letter, to be honest, is written to recommend a city for you.

When the idea occurs to me, the first city flashing in my mind is Beijing, the capital of China. The primary reason is that almost every person you will meet can speak relatively standard Chinese, which plays a key role in the process of language learning. As a result, as a modern city, it provides an excellent language environment for language learners. Besides, in Beijing, one of the most advanced cities, people are open-minded, hospitable, and inclusive. You will soon find that you can make friends with them and feel easy in such an environment.

Finally, I hope that you could take my suggestions into serious consideration, and I am looking forward to your reply at your earliest convenience.

Yours sincerely,

Li Ming

2. 日期

书信作文没有要求写日期，如果自己想要写，应该写在书信作文的右上角。常见英式写法：日、月、年，如 4 July, 1998。美式写法：月、日、年，如 July 4, 1998。其中月份和日期之间不用标点，但在年份前要用逗号隔开；若日期省略，月与年之间不用逗号，如 August 2005。日期可用基数词，也可用序数词，但最好用基数词，简单明了。

注意年份和月份均应写全，不能随意简略或以阿拉伯数字来代替，如不能用 26/03/99，应该是 March 26, 1999。正式信函中的月份一般不缩写，非正式信函中的月份可使用缩写形式：Jan.（January），Feb.（February），Mar.（March），Apr.（April），May，Jun.（June），Jul.（July），Aug.（August），Sept.（September），Oct.（October），Nov.（November），Dec.（December）。

3. 称呼语

称呼语是书信的开头对收信人的敬称。写称呼时无论齐头式还是缩进式都是顶格写，都自成一行并带有标点（一般用逗号）。

称呼因人而异，对不是很熟悉的男性收信人一般称 Dear Mr. ×，Dear Sir，My dear Sir 等。对女性收信人，一般用 Dear Mrs. ×，Dear Madam，Dear Lady 或 Dear Miss ×，不过现在人们比较常用 Dear Ms. ×。如果书信要求是写给一个机构，没有说男女，那就称呼：Dear Sir or Madam。还可根据收信人的身份冠以学位、职称，如 Dear Mr. Manager，Dear Mr. President，Dear Mr. Editor 等。当然如果是私人书信，就直接称呼 Dear× 或 Dear my friend。

4. 正文

正文是书信的主体部分，是写信人主要叙述的部分。正文要求简明扼要、条理清楚，篇幅不宜太长。正文内容应完全按照题目中的要求来写，因为字数有限，所以建议正文直接切入主题，达到写此信的目的。后面将细致讲解公务信函和私人信函的正文如何展开。

5. 落款签名

信尾分两行，第一行为结束语，第二行为写信人的姓名。结束语单独成行，一般低于正文两行。开头第一个字母要大写，末尾加逗号。结束语应与收信人的称谓相配，常用的写法是：

写给机关、团体、学校或商业机构的信件，一般可用 Yours (very) truly，Yours (very) faithfully，Faithfully yours，Yours sincerely 等。

写给上级或长者的信件，一般可用 Yours respectfully，(Very) Respectfully yours 等。

写给朋友、熟人或同事的社交书信，一般可用 Yours (very) sincerely 等。

最后的签名，题目中一般会给出，英语（一）一般都是 Li Ming，英语（二）一般是 Li Ming 或 Zhang Wei。

二、书信的种类和特点

书信是人际、外事交往的一种重要媒介，是传递信息、交流思想的一种有效的交际方式。一般来说，信函（书信）可分为两种类型，即公务信函和私人信函。

1. 公务信函

公务信函主要用于国家、单位之间的正式信函往来，亦称为正式信函（formal letters）。这种信函用于各种业务联系，如商业信函、正式邀请函、推荐信等。信的结构和格式如前文所述。信中语言要求准确、简洁，态度应客气、礼貌，措辞应委婉、得体。不能使用口语、俚语或缩略语。

正式信函中的称呼语和结束语也比较固定。常用的称呼语均用简略形式：Dear Mr. ×，Dear Miss ×，Dear Mrs. × 或 Dear Ms. ×。一般来说，应尽量使用收信人的准确姓名和头衔，以表示尊重，比如：Dear Professor and Chairwoman，Dear Professor Xu Dehua；或只在姓前加头衔，比如：Dear Professor Lee，Dear Dr. Bliss 等。称呼语后要加逗号。

当收信人的姓名或性别不详或不明确时可用：Dear Sir/Madam（尊敬的先生 / 女士）或 To whom it may concern（敬启者），不过这两种称呼语比较泛，不太会引起别人的注意和关心。

结束语有约定俗成的客套语。常用的有 Sincerely，Sincerely yours，Yours sincerely，Truly yours，Yours truly，Respectfully，Respectfully yours 等，注意，在上述结束语后面一定要加逗号。

举例

Directions:

You want to invite Mr. Williams to give a lecture on “American literature” in your college. Suppose you are the assistant of the English Department, write a letter and say

1) the purpose of the invitation, and

2) the time of the lecture.

You should write about 100 words neatly on the ANSWER SHEET.

Do not sign your own name at the end of the letter. Use “Li Ming” instead.

Do not write the address.

参考范文

Dear Mr. Williams,

As the assistant of the English Department, I am writing on behalf of the English Department to invite you to give a lecture in our college.

As English majors, we would like to know more about American literature. We will be exceedingly grateful if you can give a lecture on "Contemporary American Literature" to the students in our department on Saturday, June 4. If you are not interested in this subject, any other similar topics will be welcome as well.

We have already had several very interesting talks with some distinguished visitors from various countries. We are looking forward to the opportunity to benefit from your experience and wisdom.

Yours truly,

Li Ming

【参考译文】

亲爱的威廉姆斯先生：

作为英语系的助理，我谨代表英语系写信邀请您来我院讲一堂课。

作为英语系的学生，我们想多了解美国文学的知识。如果您能给我们英语系的学生做一场关于“当代美国文学”的讲座，我们将会十分感激。讲座时间是在 6 月 4 日，星期六。如果您对这个话题不感兴趣，其他类似的话题也是可以的。

我们已经与来自不同国家的一些知名访客进行了多次非常有趣的会谈。我们期待有机会能从您的经验和智慧中获益。

您真诚的，

李明

举例

Directions:

Suppose you have found something wrong with the electronic dictionary that you bought from an online store the other day. Write an email to the customer service center to

1) make a complaint, and

2) demand a prompt solution.

You should write about 100 words on the ANSWER SHEET.

Do not sign your own name at the end of the letter. Use "Zhang Wei" instead.

Do not write the address.

参考范文

Dear Sir or Madam,

I am your regular customer. The other day I bought an electronic dictionary from your online store. I am writing the letter to express my dissatisfaction with the dictionary.

When I got the dictionary, I felt quite delighted. However, quickly I found the battery couldn't be charged. Several days later, some of the keys on the keyboard did not work as usual, which has brought me much trouble and I believe it has been used before.

It is to resolve the problem that I require that the dictionary should be exchanged with a new one as quickly as possible, or I will make complaints about your company. In the end, I wish you could reply at your convenience.

Yours truly,

Zhang Wei

【参考译文】

亲爱的先生或女士：

我是前几天在贵公司网店买了一本电子词典的老客户。我写这封信是为了表达我对这本电子词典的不满。

当我拿到这个电子词典的时候，我感到非常高兴。但是很快我就发现电池不能充电。几天后键盘上的一些按键也不能正常工作，这给我带来了很多麻烦，我认为它之前已经被用过。

为了解决这个问题，我要求尽快给我换一本新的电子词典，否则我就会投诉贵公司。最后，希望您在方便的时候给我回复。

您真诚的，

张伟

公务信函常用表达

• Thank you in advance for your anticipated favor.

对于您将给予的帮助，我们提前表示感谢。

• We assure you of our best service at all times.

我们保证随时提供最佳服务。

• We hope you will provide us with a continuance of your support.

我们希望您能继续给我们友好的支持。

• As the matter is urgent, an early reply would be obliged.

由于事情紧急，请早日回复。

• I apologize for the delay in replying to your letter.

迟复为歉。

• We would appreciate an early reply.

如能早日回信，我们将十分感谢。

• I appreciate your interest and good will.

非常感谢你对此的兴趣和善意。

2. 私人信函

私人信函是为了交换信息、报告近况、询问某事、表达谢意或讨论感兴趣的话题。主要用于同学、同事、朋友、亲戚或家人之间，亦称作非正式信函（informal letters）。其格式与正式信函有些不同之处：

① 称呼语、结束语以及正文开头语与正式信函不同。

② 语气亲切、表达灵活自如，缩略语和非书面用语不限。

称呼语：Dear father and mother, My dear son (daughter, niece, nephew, etc.), Dear Mary, Dear Mrs. Hu, Dear Dr. Howard, etc.

结束语：Yours, Your loving daughter (son, sister, mother, etc.), Yours ever, Yours lovingly, Yours kindly, Yours affectionately, With love from, All my love, Love, etc.

举例

Directions:

Write a letter to a friend of yours to

1) recommend one of your favorite movies, and

2) give reasons for your recommendation.

Your should write about 100 words on the ANSWER SHEET.

Do not sign your own name at the end of the letter. Use "Li Ming" instead.

Do not write the address.

参考范文

Dear my friend,

How are you getting along with your life these days? Today, I'd like to recommend you to see *Inception*, a 2010 American science fiction film written, produced and directed by Christopher Nolan, who has engaged in screenplay for a decade.

It is a movie about dreams, reality and heartbreak. The fact that *Inception* is much fun, emotional and thrilling, though not quite perfect, makes it a true marvel. As a heist film set within a brand-new universe in which dreams can be shared, it explores how two people can meet in a dream and in reality but with different results.

You will enjoy the movie. In the end, wish you happiness and good health.

With Love,

Li Ming

【参考译文】

亲爱的朋友：

你这些日子过得怎么样？我今天想推荐你去看《盗梦空间》。这是一部在2010年上映的美国科幻电影，由克里斯托弗·诺兰编剧、制作和导演，他从事剧本编写工作已经有十年了。

这是一部关于梦想、现实和心碎的电影。事实上，《盗梦空间》这部电影非常有趣，很感人，也很刺激。虽然不太完美，但是这些足以使它成为一个真正的奇迹。作为一部发生在一个可以分享梦境的全新宇宙中的盗窃电影，它探索了两个人如何在梦中相遇，在现实中却有着不同的结果。

你会喜欢上这部电影的。最后祝你生活幸福，身体健康！

爱你的，

李明

举例

Directions:

Write a reply to your friend Professor Zhang in China. You should

1) tell him how you have been recently, and

2) give your regards to him/her and his/her family.

You should write about 100 words on the ANSWER SHEET.

Do not sign your own name at the end of the letter. Use "Bob" instead.

Do not write the address.

参考范文

Dear Prof. Zhang,

How wonderful to hear from you! I am happy to learn that your family is fine and well. How is your work going?

My studies continue, and yes, I still work in the Computer Lab. I expect I will continue this job as long as I am here. My supervisor said that she thought I might take her place if she left next summer, and I would be the "boss" adviser. However, I would only be interested in doing that if they increased my pay substantially. That position is a full-time job, really, and I believe my schoolwork would suffer if I did many hours of that work.

My wife and I miss you very much. I don't know if we will be able to travel to China, but if we do I promise we will visit you. Best wishes and good fortune to you and your family!

Yours sincerely,

Bob

【参考译文】

亲爱的张教授：

收到你的来信很高兴。了解到你阖家欢乐，我很高兴。你最近的工作怎么样？

我的学业还没结束，而且我仍然在计算机实验室实习。只要我在这里，我希望我会一直做这份工作。我的导师说如果她明年夏天离开的话，她认为我可以坐上她的位置，我就会是"老板"顾问了。然而，如果他们为我大幅涨薪我才会对那个职位感兴趣。那个位置事实上是一份全职工作，如果我花好几个小时做那份工作的话，我认为我的学业会受到影响。

我和我的妻子非常想念你。我不知道我们是否会去中国旅行，但是如果我们去中国了，我们一定会去拜访你。祝你和你的家人身体健康，万事如意！

你真诚的，

鲍勃

私人信函常用表达

• It is great to hear from you again.

十分高兴再次收到你的来信。

• How are you getting along with your life?

你生活得怎么样？

• I hope that things are going well with you.

希望你一切顺利。

• Nothing could give me greater pleasure than getting news of you.

没有什么比收到你的消息更能使我高兴的了。

• You have no idea how happy I was to receive your letter.

你想象不到收到你的来信时我有多高兴！

• Thank you for the expression of joy at my recent promotion.

感谢你为我最近的晋升而高兴。

• I look forward to hearing from you at your earliest convenience.

期待着你早日回信。

• Please bring my best wishes to your family.

谨向你家人致以最好的祝愿！

• With my best wishes/regards.

谨致以最好的祝愿！

• Give my regards to your parents.

请代我向你父母致以问候。

• I wish every success for your career in the future.

祝你未来事业有成。

• I wish you good health and lots of happiness.

祝你健康幸福。

• Good luck to you!

祝你好运！

• I shall appreciate hearing from you again.

非常感谢您能再次回信。

三、考研英语写作常考书信类型

1. 邀请信（Invitation）

邀请信是人们在社会交际、外事活动和日常生活当中常用的一种信函，是为了邀请对方参加某次活动而写的信件。信的主要内容是说明邀请原因、活动时间和地点以及来访安排等。其特点是简短热情。邀请信可分为正式和非正式两种，主要取决于活动的性质和与被邀请人之间的熟悉程度。

邀请某人参加某种仪式、会议等的应用文，其写作要点如下。

① 开头首先表明写作意图，向某人发出邀请，指明地点、时间等要素。

② 表达你渴望见到对方。如果是商务性质的，除了时间、地点、发信主题、组织者、出席者等，还要留下联系人的姓名、地址和电话号码。

③ 表达你对受邀者能应邀的愉快心情，并希望尽快得到回复。

举例

Directions:

Write a letter to your former roommate in your university and invite him/her to visit your city during the summer vacation.

You should write about 100 words on the ANSWER SHEET.

Do not sign your own name at the end of the letter. Use “Li Ming” instead.

Do not write the address.

参考范文

Dear my friend,

How are you getting on recently? I am wondering if you have made a definite plan for the coming summer vacation. If not, I wish you could come here and visit my city. My family will be glad to receive you.

My hometown is a very beautiful seashore city. There are many places of interest worthy of sightseeing. Besides, the local style food here is also well-known. You did tell me in the letter that you had been dreaming of the sea many times. The place where I live is located near the sea. Everyday you can walk on the seashore, pick up seashells or enjoy swimming in the sea.

Hope to see you in my hometown as soon as possible.

Yours,

Li Ming

【参考译文】

亲爱的朋友：

你最近怎么样？我想知道你是否对即将到来的暑假有明确的计划，如果没有，我希望你能来参观我的城市。我的家人会很高兴地接待你。

我的家乡是一座非常漂亮的海滨城市。这里有很多值得参观的名胜古迹。此外，这里的特色美食也是非常著名的。你之前在信中提到你好多次梦到大海。我住的地方离海非常近。你每天都可以去海边散步、捡贝壳或者在海里尽情地游泳。

希望能尽快在我的家乡见到你。

你真诚的，

李明

举例

Directions:

Write an email of about 100 words to a foreign professor, Jim Smith, inviting him to visit Peking University.

You should include the details you think necessary.

You should write neatly on the ANSWER SHEET.

Do not sign your own name at the end of the letter. Use "Zhang Wei" instead.

Do not write the address.

参考范文

Dear Professor Smith,

I am the Head and Professor from the Department of English in Peking University. It is our great pleasure to invite you to visit our university for a month from June 1 to June 30, 2017.

We would appreciate your doing workshops with our English teachers and presenting lectures for our students during your visit. We will certainly cover your travel expenses between Beijing and your hometown and your accommodations here.

If you are pleased to accept our invitation, then you may proceed immediately with your application for visa. If you have any questions, please feel free to contact us. We are looking forward to meeting you in June 2017.

Sincerely yours,

Zhang Wei

【参考译文】

尊敬的史密斯教授：

我是北京大学英语系主任和教授。非常高兴能邀请你来我们学校访问一个月，从 2017 年 6 月 1 日到 6 月 30 日。

我们将非常感激你在访问期间给我们的英语教师们做讲座，给我们的学生做演讲。当然，我们会支付你往返于北京和家乡之间的费用，以及你在这边的住宿费。

如果你愿意接受我们的邀请，你就可以着手准备签证了。如果你有任何的问题，请随时联系我们。我们期待在 2017 年 6 月见到你。

你真诚的，

张伟

邀请信常用表达

• I am writing to invite you to...

我写信是想邀请你……

• I wonder if you can come...

我想知道你是否能来……

• I think it would be great if you could participate in...

我想如果你能参加……就太好了。

• Would you please drop me a line to let me know if you can come to...?

你可以打电话通知我你是否能来……吗？

• Be sure to let me know if you can come. My whole family is very eager for your arrival.

如果你能来请一定通知我，我们全家都非常盼望你的到来。

• We would be looking forward to your coming with great pleasure.

我们非常高兴地期待着你的到来。

• I am looking forward to seeing you.

我非常期待见到你。

• My family and I will feel much honored if you can come.

如果您能来，我和我的家人都将感到不胜荣幸。

• Please accept my invitation and let me know at your convenience as soon as possible.

请接受我的邀请并尽早通知我。

• We do hope you can join us.

真心希望你能加入我们。

• Would you be so kind as to come to our college at your convenience?

您能在方便的时候莅临我院吗？

• On behalf of... I would like to invite you to visit our university for a week.

我谨代表……邀请您来我校进行一周的访问。

• It is our great pleasure to invite you to visit our department.

我们很高兴能邀请您来我们系访问。

2. 祝贺信（Congratulation）

祝贺信是人们在社交活动中一种礼仪性的书面交流形式。正式信函用于公务方面，小到单位，大到国家之间；非正式信函则用于私人之间的祝贺，以分享幸福和喜悦。祝贺信主要就某事向对方表示祝贺，所以言辞要热情、真挚。通过祝贺信函可以交流感情、增进友谊。

举例

Directions:

Suppose your colleague Mr. Smith has been promoted, and write a congratulation letter to him.

You should write about 100 words on the ANSWER SHEET.

Do not sign your own name at the end of the letter. Use "Li Ming" instead.

Do not write the address.

参考范文

Dear Mr. Smith,

It is a pleasure to congratulate you on your recent promotion to Deputy Managing Director of ABC Trading Company.

Knowing the news that you are promoted, I feel it is the reward for your diligence. Because of our close association over the past ten years, I know how well you are qualified for this important post. You earned the promotion through years of hard work and I am delighted to see your true ability win recognition.

Again, congratulations and best wishes for your future success. In the end, please bring my best wishes to your families.

Sincerely yours,

Li Ming

【参考译文】

亲爱的史密斯先生：

很高兴祝贺你最近被提升为 ABC 贸易公司副总经理。

听到你晋升的消息，我觉得这是天道酬勤。因为过去十年我们保持着密切的联系，我知道你完全能胜任这个重要的岗位。通过几年的努力你获得了进升，得知你的能力被认可，我感到非常高兴。

再次祝贺并祝你未来取得成功！最后请把我最好的祝愿带给你的家人。

你真诚的，

李明

举例

Directions:

Suppose your uncle Jim will have his fiftieth birthday, and write a congratulation letter to him.

You should write about 100 words on the ANSWER SHEET.

Do not sign your own name at the end of the letter. Use “John” instead.

Do not write the address.

参考范文

Dear uncle,

It’s time to celebrate your special day again. Congratulations on your fiftieth birthday and best wishes for the whole year.

We want you to know our thoughts are with you every day, especially on this special day. We wish you good luck in everything.

If you are in the mood for celebrating, we would like to take you to a concert. Just let us know when you would be available and we will make all the arrangements. May this birthday be a particularly happy one.

Cordially,

John

【参考译文】

亲爱的叔叔：

又到了庆祝您生日的这天。祝贺您 50 岁生日快乐，并致以一整年最好的祝福。

我们想让您知道我们每一天都想着您，尤其是在这特别的日子里，我们祝您生活万事如意。

如果您有心情来庆祝一下，我们想带您去听音乐会。请告诉我们您什么时候有空，我们会安排好一切的。愿您这次的生日特别快乐！

真挚的，

约翰

祝贺信常用表达

• Congratulations and all the best wishes!

恭贺你并致以最好的祝愿！

• Accept my heartfelt congratulations on your success.

请接受我对你的成功的衷心祝贺。

• I congratulate you on winning a scholarship...

祝贺你获得……奖学金。

• All the luck in the world to you.

祝你幸运无比。

• Many happy returns of the day!

年年有今日，岁岁有今朝！

• Let me offer my most sincere congratulations upon your success.

我谨对你的成功表示最诚挚的祝贺！

• Best wishes from all of us for...

我们大家向……致以最美好的祝愿！

• I would like to take this opportunity to offer you my congratulations on your success.

谨借此机会向你的成功表示祝贺！

• I am very pleased to learn about your success.

我很高兴获悉你成功的喜讯。

• It is a great pleasure to hear of your success.

非常高兴听到你成功的喜讯。

3. 投诉信（Complaint）

投诉信是针对某件不满意的事情向责任人提出投诉、抱怨的信件，其写作要点如下：

① 首段开门见山指明所投诉的具体事件。

② 接着将问题清晰、简洁、公正地描述出来，指出事件给你带来的不便。

③ 感谢对方关注你的投诉，清楚地表明你想让对方如何解决，并期待对方尽早解决问题。

举例

Directions:

Suppose you have been cheated by an advertisement in a magazine. Write a letter of about 100 words to the government officers complaining about the bad effect the ad brought you.

参考范文

Dear Sir or Madam,

Enclosed is an ad which appeared in a magazine for a device which supports people with back problems.

Four months ago I mailed the money of ordering and soon received the device with instructions for its use. My mother followed these instructions. Not only did her back pain persist, but soon it began to worsen. After a month she stopped using the device and made an appointment with her doctor. "This device is worthless," he said. I told the company of my experience and asked for a refund. However, they didn't even respond.

I write to you and tell you of my mother's great suffering. I hope that you could do something to put a stop to this deceptive ad and the continuing exploitation other backache sufferers have been receiving.

Sincerely yours,

Frank Smith

【参考译文】

亲爱的先生：

随信附上的是一个在杂志上出现的能解决人们背部问题的仪器的广告。

四个月前，我把订购的钱汇出去，很快就收到了仪器和使用说明。我母亲按照说明使用了。她的背痛不仅持续存在，而且很快开始恶化。一个月以后她不再使用这种仪器，并且去看了医生。医生说："这个仪器没用。"我把我的经历告诉这家公司，且要求退款。然而，他们连回应都没有。

我写信给你，告诉你我母亲的巨大痛苦。我希望你能做些什么来制止这个有欺骗性的广告，防止其他背痛患者继续受到欺诈。

你真诚的，

富兰克·史密斯

举例

Directions:

Suppose you met a rude salesperson in a supermarket. Write to the sales manager of the supermarket to show your complaints.

参考范文

Dear Sales Manager,

This letter is a complaint concerning the action of your salesperson. On May 2, 2016, around 3 p.m., I went to your store to look for an outfit. When I asked an available salesperson, Ms. Maria Johnson, for help in finding my size, she informed me that she was busy and that I would have to find it by myself. I explained that the reason why I came to her was that I couldn't find it. She then said in a rude tone that, in that case, I needed to look somewhere else.

I felt that Ms. Johnson was rude and unnecessarily curt. I hope that you will talk with Ms. Johnson about her behavior. I buy things frequently at your store and I look forward to a more pleasurable shopping experience next time.

Sincerely yours,

Julia Taylor

【参考译文】

亲爱的销售经理：

我写这封信是要投诉贵方销售人员的行为。2016 年 5 月 2 日大约下午三点钟，我去贵店，想找一个套装。当我问一个空闲的销售人员玛利亚·约翰逊女士，让她帮我找我需要的尺寸时，她告诉我她现在忙，我得自己找。我解释说我找她就是因为我自己找不到。然后她用粗鲁的语气跟我说，这样的话，我应该到别处去找找。

我感觉约翰逊女士非常粗鲁，没必要对我这么无礼。我希望你能就约翰逊女士的行为与她当面谈谈。我经常在贵店买东西，希望下次能有更愉快的购物体验。

你真诚的，

朱丽亚·泰勒

投诉信常用表达

• I'm writing to you because I need to complain to you about...

我写这封信是需要向你投诉……

• I'm sorry to point out the defect in the...

很抱歉我得指出……的毛病。

• We wish to make the following complaint to you and hope you can do something about it.

我们想向你们投诉以下问题，希望你们能予以解决。

• I was shocked to find... purchased on... at... by us didn't function well.

我惊讶地发现，我们于……时在……购买的……不好用。

• I would appreciate it very much if you could give me the refund.

如能退款，不胜感激。

• I strongly insist that you exchange... as soon as possible.

我强烈要求尽快更换……

• I am very reluctant to complain, but...

我非常不愿意投诉，但……

• One annoying aspect of your service is...

你们的服务项目中一个令人不满的地方是……

• I have been pleased with your services for years, but now I feel very disappointed.

多年来我一直对你们的服务很满意，但现在我非常失望。

• I would like to draw your attention to the problem/fault...

我希望你注意到这个问题 / 错误……

• I am writing to inform you that I find... unsatisfactory.

我写信是为了告诉你，我发现……令人非常不满意。

• I wish to express my dissatisfaction/disappointment with...

我想表达我对……的不满 / 失望。

• It would be highly appreciated if you could...

如果你能……，我将万分感谢。

• I trust you will take my complaints seriously and...

我相信你会认真对待我的投诉，并且……

• I hope you will give due attention to this matter.

希望你能对此事给予足够的重视。

• I would like to get this matter settled by the end of this month.

我希望能在月底之前解决这件事。

• I could not be more satisfied if you can kindly...

如果能请你……，我将会非常满意。

• I would appreciate it very much if you could...

如果你能……，我将非常感谢。

4. 咨询信（Inquiry）

咨询信的主要目的是寻求所需的信息或帮助，其写作要点如下。

① 首先表明写作意图，说明写这封信是为了获得什么样的信息或帮助。

② 接着提出所咨询的具体问题，强调获得这个信息或帮助对自己的重要性。

③ 向对方表示真诚的感激，表达获取信息的强烈愿望，并提供联系方式。

举例

Directions:

Suppose you are a store holder and want to purchase goods for Christmas sales. Write to a wholesaler to ask for the detailed information of the available goods.

You should write about 100 words on the ANSWER SHEET.

Do not sign your own name at the end of the letter. Use “Li Ming” instead.

Do not write the address.

参考范文

Dear Sir/Madam,

Your advertisement in the latest edition of *Buy Now* caught my attention. I am particularly interested in your new line of gift merchandise. Since the Christmas season is nearing, we need to stock our inventory with items that will make appropriate gifts.

Please send me your current holiday catalog of gift ideas. We are usually asked to stock items that are worth $ 50 and under.

We will also need to know your terms of payment, quantity, prices, discount options and any special offers. We are also interested in how items will be shipped and the speed with which they can be delivered.

Thank you for your assistance.

Sincerely yours,

Li Ming

【参考译文】

亲爱的先生 / 女士：

贵方刊登在最新版《现在就买》上面的广告吸引了我的注意。我对贵方新的礼品系列特别感兴趣。由于圣诞节快到了，我们需要一些适合作为礼物的物品来充实我们的存货。

请寄给我贵方目前的假日礼品目录，我们通常要求库存的物品价值在 50 美元及以下。

我们还需要知道贵方的付款方式、数量、价格、折扣和一些特别优惠。我们也对货物如何运送，以及运送的速度感兴趣。

感谢您的帮助。

您真诚的，

李明

咨询信常用表达

- I'm writing to you because I need to inquire you about...

写这封信是因为我需要向你咨询……

- I'm sorry to bother you to inquire about...

抱歉打扰你，我想询问……

- Your advertisement in... caught my attention.

贵方刊登在……上的广告吸引了我的注意。

- I am particularly interested in...

我对……十分感兴趣。

- I would be highly appreciated if you could...

如果你能……，我将万分感谢。

5. 感谢信（Thanks）

感谢信是一种提供礼仪性感谢的书信形式。在社会生活和交际中，人与人之间或单位与单位之间常常需要相互帮助。受助者向提供帮助者或赞助者写信表示感谢，说明对方帮助的重要作用，并致以真诚的谢意。信函中言辞应真挚热情，但要注意不能过于谦卑。

举例

Directions:

You have just come back from the U. S. as a member of Cultural Exchange Program. Write a letter to your American colleague to

1) express your thanks for his/her warm reception, and

2) welcome him/her to visit China in due course.

You should write about 100 words on the ANSWER SHEET.

Do not sign your own name at the end of the letter. Use “Zhang Wei” instead.

Do not write your address.

参考范文

Dear Jimmy,

It is exceedingly great to recall the past week when I studied in America as a member of Cultural Exchange Program. Today, I am writing to extend my thanks and invite you to visit China.

I am much grateful for your warmhearted reception. It was your kind help that enabled me to enjoy a comfortable and fruitful study. This experience has brought me a new vision, aroused my enthusiasm for cultural communication, and helped me know America better. However, compared with America, China possesses a long and glorious history and more distinctive cultures. Thus, it is advisable for you to visit China in due course. Meanwhile, I can repay your reception.

Please accept my sincere thanks and invitation, and I am looking forward to your coming.

Yours truly,

Zhang Wei

【参考译文】

亲爱的吉米：

回忆过去一周，我作为文化交流项目的一员在美国学习，这让我非常高兴。今天我写信是为了表达我的感谢以及邀请你来参观中国。

我非常感激你热情的接待，是你善良的帮助让我享受到舒适而富有成效的学习。这次学习经历拓宽了我的视野，唤起了我对文化交流的热情，也帮助我更好地了解了美国。然而，和美国比起来，中国拥有漫长而光辉的历史和更多独特的文化。因此，非常建议你在适当的时候来参观中国。同时，我可以答谢你的款待。

请接受我真诚的感谢和邀请。我期待你的到来。

你真诚的，

张伟

举例

Directions:

The other day, you had an accident, and your English teacher spent a lot of time taking care of you. Write a special letter to express your thanks.

参考范文

Dear Ms. Liu,

I am writing to express my heartfelt gratitude. I am referring to that unfortunate accident the other day when I was hit by a taxi while riding my bike.

If there had not been your timely assistance in giving me first aid, I fear that the consequences might have been much more serious. Everyone agrees that it was your quick-witted response in that emergency that led to a less serious consequence.

In the end, I would like to show my sincere appreciation for your assistance again. If there are more people like you, this world will be a much nicer place.

Yours sincerely,

Li Ming

【参考译文】

亲爱的刘老师：

我写信是为了表达我真诚的感谢。我指的是前几天我骑车时被出租车撞到的不幸事故。

如果没有您的及时帮助，给我做急救的话，恐怕后果会更严重。大家都认同正是因为您在紧急情况下的迅速反应才没有出现太严重的后果。

最后，我想再次对您的帮助表达真诚的感谢。如果有更多像您一样的人，这个世界会变得更好。

您真诚的，

李明

感谢信常用表达

• I am sincerely grateful for your timely help.

对于你的及时帮助，我感激不尽。

• May I take this opportunity to express my hearty thanks to you.

请允许我借此机会向你们表示衷心的谢意。

• At the outset, we want to thank you for your consideration and compliments.

首先，我们要感谢您的关怀和问候。

• It is generous of you to take so much interest in my work.

承蒙您对我的工作如此费心。

• Thank you so much for your generous hospitality.

非常感谢您的盛情款待。

• I greatly appreciate your generous spirit of cooperation.

我非常感谢您慷慨的合作精神。

• I deeply appreciate your showing so much consideration for me.

您对我如此关怀，我深表感谢。

• Please accept our thanks for your attention.

承蒙重视，谨致谢意。

• We were delighted to receive your letter.

我们很高兴收到你的来信。

6. 道歉信（Apology）

由于疏忽或者客观原因造成某种损失，或由于某种原因而未能赴约或者出席会议时，应向对方道歉。如不便或者不能当面道歉，应写信致歉。

道歉信的写作策略：表示道歉→说明具体原因、提出补救办法→再次致歉，希望得到理解。

道歉信的语言要诚挚，解释的理由要真实，不要显出丝毫的虚情假意。好的道歉信不仅会获得对方的谅解，还会增进彼此的感情。在写作过程中，尽可能提供比较合理的理由。如果违反生活常识将导致扣分。在解释完原因后，尽量提供一个合适的补救办法，使文章更加完整。

举例

Directions:

You have just come back from Canada and found a music CD in your luggage that you forgot to return to Bob, your landlord there. Write him a letter to

1) make an apology, and

2) suggest a solution.

You should write about 100 words on the ANSWER SHEET.

Do not sign your own name at the end of the letter. Use "Li Ming" instead.

Do not write the address.

参考范文

Dear Bob,

I am writing to make an apology to you for I was in such a great hurry that I forgot to return the music CD which I had borrowed from you last week. Yesterday I came back home and I found it in my luggage. I am so sorry that you cannot listen to it at present.

The CD which I borrowed from you is made in Canada, so I believe you can find another one in your local store. How about you buy another CD by yourself and I pay for it? If you cannot find a similar one, I will send it back to you by post. And if there are any other solutions you like, please let me know.

I am sorry again for my carelessness. Looking forward to your reply.

Yours sincerely,

Li Ming

【参考译文】

亲爱的鲍勃：

我写信是为了向你道歉，我太匆忙了，忘了归还上一周你借给我的音乐 CD。昨天我回到家，发现 CD 在我的行李里。非常抱歉你现在没法听这张 CD。

你借给我的 CD 产自加拿大，所以我相信你能在当地的商店再买一张。你自己买一张 CD，然后由我付钱怎么样呢？如果你不能找到相同的 CD，我会把这个给你邮寄回去。如果你喜欢其他的解决方式，请告诉我。

我再次为我的粗心大意表示抱歉。期待收到你的回信。

你真诚的，
李明

举例

Directions:

Your friend Xiaoyan invites you to attend her wedding ceremony, but you cannot be there that day. Write her a letter to

1) make an apology, and

2) include the details why you couldn't attend the ceremony.

Do not sign your own name at the end of the letter. Use "Robert" instead.

Do not write the address.

参考范文

Dear Xiaoyan,

Thank you so much for inviting me to attend your wedding ceremony. I would like to apologize to you, because I cannot be there.

The primary reason why I will be absent is that my daughter has felt ill unexpectedly. We had to rush her to the hospital for an instant intravenous injection. The doctor told her to rest on bed for ten days so I have to take care of her in case that any emergency should happen.

Please accept my heartfelt congratulations on the special occasion of your marriage. Best wishes!

Affectionately,
Robert

【参考译文】

亲爱的晓艳：

非常感谢你能邀请我参加你的结婚典礼。但我要向你说声抱歉，因为我不能参加了。

我不能到场的主要原因是我的女儿突然生病了。我们不得不赶紧把她送到医院立即进行静脉注射。医生让她卧床休息十天，所以我需要照顾她，以防发生任何意外。

在你们结婚的这个特殊时刻，请接受我衷心的祝贺。祝你幸福！

挚爱的，
罗伯特

道歉信常用表达

- I am writing to apologize for... /I am writing to say sorry for...

我写这封信是为了向你致歉，因为……

- I would like to give you my apology for...

对于……我向你道歉。

- We hope you will pardon us for troubling you.

给你们添麻烦了，望见谅。

- We apologize for the inconvenience this error may have caused you.

对于这个错误可能给您造成的不便，我们深表歉意。

• It gives us deep sorrow to have to inform you that...

我们非常遗憾地通知您……

• Excuse me for my absence.

请原谅我的缺席。

• I must apologize for my delay in answering your letter.

十分抱歉，我未能及时回信。

• I hope you will accept my sincere apologies.

我希望您能接受我诚恳的道歉。

• We regret the trouble we caused you.

我们对给您造成的麻烦表示歉意。

• I wish to offer my sincere apologies for...

谨对……表示我诚挚的歉意。

• We are sorry to have to draw your attention to...

我们很抱歉得提醒您注意……

• Please accept my sincere apology for...

关于……，请接受我真诚的道歉。

• I am indeed very sorry for what I said/did, but please believe I had no intention to...

对于我说的话 / 做的事，我确实感到很抱歉。但请相信，我不是故意……

• Please forgive me for a stupid choice of words.

请原谅我说话欠妥。

• I feel awfully sorry about it and want you to know what happened.

为此我感到非常内疚，所以想告诉你实情。

• Please accept my apologies for my oversight.

请原谅我的疏忽。

• Please allow me to say sorry again.

请允许我再次表示歉意。

• I sincerely hope you can understand my situation/think in my position and accept my apologies.

我真心希望你能理解我的处境 / 设身处地地为我考虑，并接受我的道歉。

• Once again, I'm sorry for the inconvenience caused to you.

对于给您造成的不便，我再次表示歉意。

7. 推荐信（Recommendation）

推荐信可以推荐人也可以推荐事物。推荐人的信是资历较深的人以其特定的身份，如专家、教授、导师、校长、经理等，向招生 / 招聘的学校、部门或单位介绍和推荐申请人。这种推荐信与求职信的最终目标是一样的，都是要得到某个职位或某份工作。这两类信的写法也很相似，求职信是直接说明自己能够胜任某份工作，推荐信是说明他人能够胜任某份工作，因此在主体段落的写法上基本是相同的，事实上只要把求职信的第一人称换成第三人称就可以了，但是推荐信在开头和结尾与求职信略有不同，开头要说明写信人与被推荐人的关系，结尾要借推荐人之口说

“雇用他将会是一个明智的选择”，并表示“如需要更多的信息，可与我联系”。

推荐信的写作策略：表明写作意图→说明推荐原因→感谢和期待。

举例

Directions:

Write a letter to a friend of yours to

1) recommend one of your favorite movies, and

2) give reasons for your recommendation.

You should write about 100 words on the ANSWER SHEET.

Do not sign your own name at the end of the letter. Use “Li Ming” instead.

Do not write the address.

参考范文

Dear my friend,

I am writing to you to recommend one of my favorite movies, *2012*. I have sufficient reasons to introduce this movie to you and I dare to say that this is the best disaster movie ever.

This movie is about love and life from the perspective of a thrilling story of the doomsday. The fast-paced, exciting story line keeps me fidget in my seat all the way through. What's more, the scenes look so attractive that I almost think they are real. Finally, this movie successfully reminds us of our attitudes towards the world and the people around us.

I bet you will love this fantastic movie and wish you enjoy it.

Yours sincerely,

Li Ming

【参考译文】

亲爱的朋友：

我写这封信是为了向你推荐一部我最喜欢的电影——《2012》。我给你推荐这部电影有很多原因，并且我敢说这是有史以来最好的灾难片。

这部电影从一个惊心动魄的世界末日的角度讲述了爱情和生活。快节奏、令人激动的故事情节一直让我坐立不安。更重要的是，这些场景看起来如此吸引人，以至于我几乎认为它们是真的。最后，这部电影成功提醒我们要注意自己对世界和周围的人的态度。

我打赌你会喜欢这部精彩的电影，并希望你能好好享受它。

你真诚的，

李明

举例

Directions:

Write a letter to Dr. Smith who is the director of Department of Biochemistry. You should

1) recommend one of your students to join in his program, and

2) give reasons for your recommendation.

You should write about 100 words on the ANSWER SHEET.

Do not sign your own name at the end of the letter. Use "Li Ming" instead.

Do not write the address.

参考范文

Dear Dr. Smith,

I am a professor of internal medicine in Eastern University of Medical Sciences. It is my great pleasure to write this letter to support Mr. Li Dongfeng's application for a postgraduate degree in your school.

Mr. Li was my medical student from 2012 to 2017. He was awarded a bachelor's degree in medicine in 2017. Besides, he ranked third in the class of 2012 among 560 students. During his five years of study at our medical school, his grades were excellent in every subject.

Based on his excellent academic performance, I highly recommend Mr. Li to your program without any reservation. If you have any further questions, please contact me.

Yours sincerely,

Li Ming

【参考译文】

尊敬的斯密斯博士：

我是东方医科大学内科教授，我很高兴写这封信来支持李东锋先生申请贵校研究生学位。

从 2012 年到 2017 年，李先生是我的医科学生。他于 2017 年获得医学学士学位。此外，他在 2012 届 560 名学生中排名第三。在我们医学院学习的五年间，他各科成绩优异。

基于他优秀的学术表现，我毫无保留地向你的项目推荐李先生。如果你还有什么问题，请与我联系。

你真诚的，

李明

推荐信常用表达

• I strongly/highly recommend her to study in your school and get a scholarship.

我强烈推荐她进入贵校学习并获得奖学金。

• I do not hesitate to recommend Mr. × to be admitted into your program.

我毫不犹豫地推荐 × 先生加入你们的项目之中。

• It gives me great pleasure in recommending Mr. × to you for admission as a transfer student at your institution.

我非常高兴地向您推荐 × 先生作为一名转学生进入贵学院。

• I take great pleasure in recommending... to you.

我十分高兴地向您推荐……

• I recommend Mr. × to you, who wishes to obtain a position at your office.

我谨向您推荐 × 先生在贵处获得一个职位。

• It is with great pleasure to recommend Mr. × to you, and I am confident that...

非常高兴向您推荐 × 先生，我相信……

• He is a man of good education, and I am confident that he will prove his value by his industry and faithfulness.

他受过良好教育，我深信他将以勤奋和忠诚证明他的价值。

• I am confident that he will do his best in wherever he may be placed, and I cordially recommend him to you.

我诚挚地将他推荐给您，我深信无论承担什么工作，他都会尽职尽责。

• Being calm and thoughtful, he has a mature character.

他性格成熟，遇事冷静，善于思考。

• I shall greatly appreciate it if you kindly give him your assistance during his visit in your university.

如果您能在他访问贵校期间给予帮助，我将不胜感激。

• conscientious and hardworking

有责任心，工作努力

• impressive academic records

成绩优秀

• He shows diligence and ingenuity in the studies.

他在研究中表现出勤奋和独创性。

• rich practical experience

实践经验丰富

• creative imagination

富有创造性的想象力

• a reliable team player and helpful colleague

值得信赖、乐于助人的同事

• He is easy to get along with.

他很好相处。

• a stable personality and strong sense of responsibility

性格稳重并具有高度的责任感

8. 建议信（Suggestion）

举例

Directions:

Some international students are coming to your university. Write them an email in the name of the Students' Union to

1) extend your welcome, and

2) provide some suggestions for their campus life here.

You should write about 100 words on the ANSWER SHEET.

Do not sign your own name at the end of the letter. Use "Li Ming" instead.

Do not write the address.

参考范文

Dear friends,

On behalf of the Students' Union of Beijing Foreign Studies University, I would like to extend our heartfelt welcome to all of the overseas students to study in our university.

It is my great pleasure to offer you several practical suggestions. In the first place, life in this prestigious university perhaps is not as easy as you have expected. You may be tightly bound by continual classes, abundant homework and exams. Then, be prepared for the hectic life here. In the second place, in spite of all those burdens, various extracurricular activities such as sports meets, speech contests, social gatherings will still provide ample opportunities to make friends. So enjoy your life in this famous institute!

All in all, although there is a lot of pressure, the time you spend in our campus will be worthwhile. Hope you like it here!

Yours sincerely,

Li Ming

【参考译文】

亲爱的朋友：

我谨代表北京外国语大学学生会向所有从世界各地来的将在我校学习的学生表示热烈的欢迎。

非常高兴能给你们提供一些实用的建议。首先，在这所有名望的大学里生活也许不像你们想象的那样容易。你们可能会被连续不断的课程、大量的作业和考试紧紧束缚。请为这里忙碌的生活做好准备。第二，尽管有这些负担，各种各样的课外活动，比如运动会、演讲比赛、社交活动等，仍然会提供许多交朋友的机会。所以，在这所有名的大学里享受生活吧！

最后，尽管有很多压力，你们在我们大学里度过的时光将是值得的。希望你们喜欢这里！

你真诚的，

李明

举例

Directions:

Write a letter to the president of your university, giving some suggestions to improve students' physical fitness.

参考范文

Dear Mr. President,

This letter comes to you from a student named Li Ming. I am writing to you to present my suggestions in relation to the ways to improve students' physical fitness.

Nothing is more important than health because without good health we would have nothing including happiness. In my humble opinion, it will be wise of you to take the following suggestions. For one thing, we should spend one to two hours a day on regular exercise and try to walk instead of riding. For another, we should eat some healthy food such as vegetables, fruits and so on. They are able to help us maintain a healthy body.

I hope you will find these suggestions useful, and I would be ready to discuss this matter with you in further details.

Yours sincerely,

Li Ming

【参考译文】

亲爱的校长先生：

我叫李明，是一名学生。我写信是为了就如何提高学生的身体素质提供我的建议。

没有什么事情比健康更重要，因为没有健康，我们什么也没有，包括快乐。在我看来，您接受如下建议是明智之举。一方面，我们应该每天花一到两个小时进行常规锻炼，并且尝试用步行来代替骑车。另一方面，我们应该吃像蔬菜、水果等这样健康的食物。它们能帮助我们保持身体健康。

我希望您觉得这些建议是有用的，我愿意与您进一步讨论此事的详情。

您真诚的，

李明

建议信常用表达

• It is high time that we put an end to the trend.

该是我们停止这一趋势的时候了。

• It is time to take the advice of... and to put special emphasis on the improvement of...

该是采纳……的建议，并对……的进展给予特殊重视的时候了。

• It must be realized that...

必须意识到……

• I wish my suggestions could be considered carefully.

我希望我的建议能被仔细考虑。

• I hope that my suggestions are helpful. Thank you for your attention!

希望我的建议会有所帮助。谢谢关注！

• I am writing to express my views concerning...

我写信是为了表达我对于……的观点。

• I would like to suggest that...

我建议……

• I am writing to offer suggestions about...

我写信是为了提出我对……的建议。

• May I suggest that...

我建议……

• I hope you will find these suggestions/proposals/recommendations are helpful/practical/useful/beneficial.

我希望这些建议 / 提议对你们来说是有帮助的 / 实用的 / 有用的 / 有好处的。

四、其他类型应用文

1. 告示类（Notice）

告示类应用文的写法各不相同，但大致上也有统一的格式和要求。比如，首先要写标题，说明告示的种类，如寻子启事（Child Lost）、寻物启事（Lost）、招领启事（Found）、迁移启事（Removal）、征稿启事（Contributions Wanted）、鸣谢（Acknowledgements）、招标启事（Invitation for Bids）、更正启事（Corrections）、通知（Notices）、海报（Poster）、公约（Pact）、守则或规则（Rules）、书刊介绍（Preface）等。然后注明日期，接着便是公告的内容，最后是公告单位或个人的署名。告示类应用文的时态一般用现在时或将来时，也可以用现在进行时表示近期即将发生的事情。

这种文体字数更少，因为不需要自我介绍，所以这种文体写两段就够了。

举例

Directions:

Write a letter to welcome students to join in a club. In your essay, you should

1) introduce the main activities of your club,

2) analyze the advantages if students join in your club, and

3) describe how to join.

参考范文

Welcome to English Club

Do you want to improve yourself by developing your English ability? Then come and join us now. Our English club was organized 10 years ago and has more than 3,000 members. On Sunday evenings, you will see a classic English movie. Most importantly, someone will be invited to express his/her ideas about the movie, and then we will have a hot discussion on it. Besides, a foreign friend will be introduced to you if you like, which is really helpful to your oral English.

So don't hesitate to join us. If you are interested in our club, please email us at Englishclub@163.com.

English Club

【参考译文】

欢迎来到英语俱乐部

你想通过提高自己的英语水平，来提升自己的能力吗？那现在就来加入我们吧。英语俱乐部在十年前组建，有 3 000 多名成员。在星期天晚上，你可以观看一部经典的英语电影。最重要的是，我们会邀请成员就这部电影发表自己的观点，然后我们会对其进行热烈的讨论。此外，如果你愿意，我们可以给你介绍一位外国朋友，这对你的英语口语很有帮助。

所以不要犹豫，加入我们吧。如果你对我们俱乐部感兴趣，请发邮件至 Englishclub@163.com。

英语俱乐部

举例

Directions:

You are supposed to write for the Students' Union of the Department of English a notice to organize a school-wide English speaking contest. The notice should include the basic information about the contest and other information which you think is relevant.

You should write about 100 words on the ANSWER SHEET.

Do not sign your own name at the end of the notice. Use "Students' Union of the English Department " instead.

参考范文

English Speaking Contest

In order to improve students' ability to speak English and enrich after-class activities, the Students' Union of the English Department is going to hold a school-wide English speaking contest on next Saturday (September 8) at the Students' Recreational Center. Those who are interested in taking part in it may sign up at the monitor of each class before this Thursday. Six overseas teachers will be invited to be the judges. The first six winners will be given awards.

Everybody is welcome to be present at the contest. If you have any problems, please contact us.

Students' Union of the English Department

【参考译文】

英语演讲比赛

为了提高学生们说英语的能力以及丰富课外活动，英语系学生会决定于下周六（9 月 8 日）在学生活动中心举办全校范围的英语演讲赛。有兴趣参加的学生于本周四之前在各班班长处报名。六位外教老师将会被邀请来当评委。前六名会获得奖励。

欢迎所有同学出席这次比赛。如果你有任何问题，请联系我们。

英语系学生会

举例

Directions:

You are supposed to write for the Postgraduates' Association a notice to recruit volunteers for an international conference on globalization. The notice should include the basic qualifications for applicants and other information which you think is relevant.

You should write about 100 words on the ANSWER SHEET.

Do not sign your own name at the end of the notice. Use "Postgraduates' Association" instead.

参考范文

Volunteers Needed

Do you want to have a good opportunity of practice? Come and join us. We are recruiting volunteers for an international conference on globalization. To begin with, applicants should have Chinese nationality, a strong professional spirit, cheerful personality and be aged under 35. In addition, candidates must have outstanding skills in English listening comprehension and the ability to speak Chinese and English fluently. Finally, students with relevant professional experience are preferred.

Those postgraduates who are interested in taking part in it may sign up at the monitors of their classes before May 1, 2020. Everybody is welcome to join in it.

Postgraduates' Association

【参考译文】

招募志愿者

你想有一个好机会来锻炼自己吗？来加入我们吧。我们正在为一场全球化国际会议招募志愿者。首先，申请人应具有中国国籍、优秀的专业素养和开朗的个性，年龄应在35岁以下。另外，申请人一定要有优秀的英语听力理解能力以及熟练的英语和汉语表达能力。最后，有相关专业经验的学生优先。

有兴趣参加的研究生应在2020年5月1日之前在各班班长处报名。欢迎大家参加。

研究生协会

告示类应用文（如通知、启事、便条等）常用表达

• So and so is/are requested to note that...

受命通知……

• So and so takes/take pleasure in announcing that...

很高兴宣布……

• So and so has/have the honor to announce...

很荣幸宣布……

• It is hereby proclaimed/announced/made public that...

我们要公布的事情是……

• This is to notify/inform/announce that...

这篇告示是为了……

• Welcome to join us.

欢迎加入我们。

• We are waiting for your coming sincerely.

我们真诚地等待着你的到来。

• If you are interested in our club, you can call us.

如果你对我们的俱乐部感兴趣，请给我们打电话。

2. 备忘录（Memorandum）

该文体虽然大纲中有规定，但其并非考研英语写作的重点。备忘录属于广义信函中的一种，它是公司或者部门内部的通讯形式，主要用于员工之间传递信息，比如会议安排、情况通报、问题处理等。其内容要求简明准确，句式要求完整。备忘录的内容一般包括以下几个部分：

①标题：Memo位于第一行正中间。

②信头：包括TO, FROM, DATE和SUBJECT等内容。TO后面接收文人姓名、职务等，FROM后面接发文人的姓名、职务等，DATE后写日期，SUBJECT后是备忘录主要内容的概括性小标题。具体模板如下。

TO: 收文人，如All the Faculty

FROM: 发文人，如Li Ming

DATE: 日期，如January 28, 2017

SUBJECT: 主题，如Donating for the Poor

③正文段落：主题下面空两行写正文，不用写称呼和结尾礼词。

④收文人姓名首字母：写在正文末行空一行的地方。如果没有的话，也可以不写。

举例

Directions:

Write a memo of about 100 words on behalf of the Students' Union to call on students to join in the volunteer activities in Xinhua Community.

参考范文

TO: All students of Shanghai University

FROM: Students' Union

DATE: Sept. 17, 2017

SUBJECT: Volunteer activities in Xinhua Community

At the beginning of the new term, we plan to organize a series of volunteer activities in Xinhua Community, which is about 200 meters from our university.

The activities are scheduled on September 17 (this Sunday). We may do housework for the disabled or old people who live by themselves, teach children English, and publicize knowledge about healthy diet and preventing common diseases.

We believe it is a good opportunity to show our love and know more about the society. One hundred volunteers are needed. If you are willing and have time to take part in the activities, please email us at SUSU@163.com.

【参考译文】

收文人：上海大学全体学生

发文人：学生会

日期：2017年9月17日

主题：新华社区志愿者活动

在新学期的初始，我们打算在距我们大学两百米远的新华社区举办一系列志愿者活动。

这些活动定在9月17日（本周日）。我们可以给独自生活的残疾人和老人做家务，教孩子们英语，以及宣传关于健康饮食和避免常见疾病的知识。

我们相信这是一次表达我们的爱，更多地了解社会的绝佳机会。我们需要100名志愿者。如果你愿意并且有时间参加这些活动，请发邮件至SUSU@163.com。

举例

Directions:

You are the manager's assistant, and your company is going to donate some medicine to the patients in poor areas. Please write a memo to inform the staff to have a meeting next week to discuss about the donation.

参考范文

TO : All the staff

FROM: Li Ming, the manager's assistant

DATE: Dec. 25, 2017

SUBJECT: Donation of medicine to patients in poor areas

All staff are required to attend the meeting, which will be held next Friday in the meeting hall.

The meeting is to discuss the medicine donation to the patients in poor areas. As you see, people there are so poor that they could do nothing when faced with even a minor illness. Thus, it is quite necessary to help the disadvantaged. But before the discussion, every department should put forward a detailed plan.

The meeting will begin at 2 o'clock and everyone must be present on time.

【参考译文】

收文人：全体员工

发文人：李明，经理助理

日期：2017 年 12 月 25 日

主题：给贫困地区的病人捐献药品

全体员工须参加下周五在会议厅举行的会议。

这次会议的主要目的是讨论给贫困地区的病人捐献药品。正如你们所知，那里的人们非常穷，以至于即使面对很小的病也无能为力。因此，帮助弱势群体非常有必要。但在讨论之前，每个部门应该提出一个详细的计划。

会议将在两点开始，每个人必须按时到场。

五、小作文（应用文）写作总结

1. 公务书信

（1）称呼

文中已给出：按照文中要求写。

文中未给出：按下面形式写。

Dear Sir or Madam,

Dear Mr. President/Professor/Editor,

（2）正文

第一段：自我介绍 + 写作目的

自我介绍

文中已给出：按照要求写。

文中未给出：自己假定一个身份，可能是员工，可能是学生。比如：

I am a staff in a × company.

I am a senior from the × department of a/the university.

写作目的

I am writing the letter in order to...

（注意：in order to 后面的内容在提纲中一定已经有所体现，基础好的同学就把文中给出的内容稍微改写一下，基础差的同学直接抄写文中给出的内容。）

第二段

第二段写什么内容，文中一定做出了要求，按要求来写就行。需要注意的是，因为小作文字数要求比较少，就不用有“起、承、转、合”的结构了，直接论述就行。比如：to begin with, in addition, last but not least。

第三段（两句）

文中已做出要求：第一句话写文中要求的内容，不要展开论述，因为字数有限；第二句话，根据要求表示感谢或期待回信。

文中未做出要求：表示感谢 + 期待回信。

表示感谢

My thanks for your generous assistance are beyond words.

Words fail me when I desire to express my sincere gratitude to you for your kind consideration for my requirement/application/complaint.

I would like to take the opportunity to show my heartfelt appreciation for the generous assistance you rendered me.

期待回信

I am looking forward to your reply.

I look forward to a favorable reply at your earliest convenience.

Your prompt attention to my... would be highly appreciated.

当然也可以按照我们前面所讲的应用文不同书信类型的常用表达来写第三段，这样更具有针对性。比如邀请信的第三段就可以写 We would be looking forward to your coming with great pleasure.（我们非常高兴地期待着你的到来。）再写期待回信：We are waiting for your reply.（我们等你的回复。）

（3）落款

在右下角写 Yours truly 和人名（如：Li Ming）。Yours truly 后面加逗号。

举例

Directions:

You have bought an air-conditioner from the department store, but soon it does not work very well. Now write to the department store to

1) tell them what is wrong with the machine,

2) complain about the inconvenience it has brought about, and

3) express your wish that it should be repaired as soon as possible.

参考范文

Dear Sir or Madam,（公务书信的称呼）

I am a consumer who bought an air-conditioner from your store last Sunday.（自我介绍）Now, I regret to tell you that the machine is really far from satisfying.（写作目的）

At first, it made a little bit of noise, and I thought I could bear it. However, the noise became louder and louder. At the same time, its pipe began to leak, which made our whole family feel horrible and we could not fall asleep in such a hot summer.（全是简单句，本段好在连词用得好，小作文不拼长句

子，拼的是流畅度和结构）

In the end, I hope the problem could be solved as quickly as possible.（期待解决）We are looking forward to your reply.（期待回复）

Yours truly,

Li Ming

【参考译文】

亲爱的先生或女士：

我上周日在贵店买了空调。现在，我不得不遗憾地告诉你，我对这个空调非常不满意。

一开始它有一些噪音，我认为我可以忍受。然而，噪音变得越来越大。同时，它的管道开始漏水，这让我的家人感觉很讨厌，我们在如此炎热的夏天无法入睡。

最后，我希望问题能尽快得到解决，我们期待着你的回复。

你真诚的，

李明

举例

Directions:

The library in your university intends to improve its services and facilities. As a regular library user, please write a letter to the library, offering your suggestions.

Your letter should be no less than 100 words.

Do not sign your own name at the end of the letter. Use "Li Ming" instead.

Do not write the address.

参考范文

Dear Sir or Madam,

I am a sophomore from the Department of Social Sciences in our school. The letter is to offer my proposals for improving your services.（自我介绍＋写作目的）

Our library, for my part, should do its best to purchase the latest publications and make sure that it has a full set of classical and reference works in that libraries play a vital role in the education and entertainment. I also suggest that computers should be connected to the Internet. Only in this way will the library expand its services to a larger number of readers.（按照提纲要求写原因分析，因为第一个原因比较长，所以只写了两个原因）

In the end, I wish my suggestions could be considered thoroughly.（表示期待）

Yours sincerely,

Li Ming

【参考译文】

亲爱的先生或女士：

我是本校社会科学系的一名大二学生。此信是为你们改善服务提出我的建议。

在我看来，我们的图书馆应该努力购买最新的出版物，并且确保有全套的经典书目和参考文献，因为图书馆在教育和娱乐方面扮演着重要的角色。另外，我建议电脑联网。只有这样，图书馆才能为更多的读者服务。

最后，我希望你能充分考虑我的建议。

你真诚的，
李明

2. 私人书信

（1）称呼

Dear Bob/my friend,

（2）正文

第一段：问候语 + 写作目的

问候语

• How are you getting on with your life recently?

你最近生活过得怎么样？

• It is great to hear from you again.

十分高兴再次收到你的来信。

• How are you getting along with your life?

你生活过得怎么样？

• Nothing could have given me greater pleasure than getting news of you!

没有什么事比听到你的消息更使我高兴了。

• You have no idea how happy I was to receive your letter.

你想象不到我收到你的信有多么高兴。

• Thank you for the expression of joy at my recent promotion.

感谢你为我最近的晋升而高兴。

写作目的

I am writing the letter in order to...

（同公务书信，in order to 后面的内容在文中一定已经做出要求，按要求写即可。）

第二段

同公务书信，第二段写什么内容，文中一定做出了要求，按要求来写就行。需要注意的是因为小作文字数要求比较少，就无须用“起、承、转、合”的结构了，直接论述就行。比如：to begin with, in addition, last but not least。

第三段

文中已做出要求

第一句话：写文中要求的内容，不要展开论述，因为字数有限。

第二句话：祝福语。

文中未做出要求

第一句话：祝福语。

第二句话：期待回信。

祝福语常用表达

• All the best of luck to you!

祝你幸运无比。

• Please bring my best wishes to your family.

谨向你家人致以最好的祝愿！

• With my best wishes/regards.

谨致以最好的祝愿。

• I hope that things are going well with you.

祝你一切顺利。

• Give my regards to your parents.

请代我向你父母致以问候。

• I wish every success for your career in the future.

祝你未来事业有成。

• Wish you good health and lots of happiness.

祝你健康幸福。

• Good luck to you!

祝你好运！

• Best wishes from all of us for...

我们大家向……致以最美好的祝愿。

举例

Directions:

A classmate wants to go to graduate school. Give him some suggestions about choosing the major and tell him the reasons.

参考范文

Dear my friend,

I'm so delighted to hear that you decide to go to graduate school. Now, I want to give you some suggestions about choosing the major.（问候语 + 写作目的）

As far as I am concerned, English may be your best option. First, you love English and interest is the best teacher. Then, if you learn English as your major, after graduation you may become an English teacher who can help so many Chinese students to realize their dreams at last. Possibly, you can go abroad to teach foreigners how to study Chinese, which is a fantastic idea.（第二段虽然没有什么闪光点，但语言正确，逻辑关系清楚，7 分左右还是可以拿下的。）

So please consider my suggestions carefully and make a prudential decision to have a bright future. Good luck to you!（总结 + 祝福语）

Yours truly,

Li Ming

【参考译文】

亲爱的朋友：

获悉你要攻读硕士学位我感到非常高兴。现在我想给你一些关于选专业的建议。

在我看来，英语是你最好的选择。首先，你喜欢英语，而兴趣是最好的老师。第二，如果你把英语当作自己的专业来学习，毕业后你可能会成为一名英语老师，帮助很多中国学生最终实现他们的梦想。你也可能出国教外国人如何学习汉语，这是一个好主意。

所以请仔细考虑我的建议，为了有一个美好的未来，请做出一个谨慎的决定。祝你好运！

你真诚的，

李明

举例

Directions:

Write a letter of thanks to Mr. Liu who once helped you. Tell him the reasons, and then tell him what to do to repay him.

参考范文

Dear Mr. Liu,

Thank you for the expression of joy at my recent success in my career. The letter is to show my great appreciation to you for your kind help when I was a student.（问候语 + 写作目的）

Maybe you've forgotten that rainy day when I felt so bad because I failed in the College English Test Band 4. So many people passed me but nobody turned back to solace me. At that moment, you came with an umbrella. I remember clearly that you just put your hand on my shoulder, and then you told me with a slow tone: "Failure makes one wiser; Pain makes one stronger." I was stricken by your words. Quickly, by working hard, I passed the exam with a high grade.（第二段要写感谢理由，文中没有写三个理由，只是讲了一个感谢原因，一个故事，类似举例，主要注意语法正确，逻辑关系清楚）

At last, I will be a teacher just like you to help more students. Wish you happiness and good health.（文中做出了要求，所以第一句写文中要求的内容，第二句话是祝福语）

Yours truly,

Li Ming

【参考译文】

尊敬的刘老师：

感谢您对我最近事业上的成功感到高兴。此信是为了感谢您在我学生时代对我的帮助。

也许您已经忘了那个下雨天，当时我感到很糟糕，因为我没有通过四级考试。很多人从我身旁经过，但是没有人回头安慰我。这时，您带着伞来了。我清楚地记得您只是把您的手放在我的肩膀上，然后缓慢地告诉我“失败使人明智；痛苦使人强大”。您的话使我深受感动。通过努力，我很快就以高分通过了考试。

最后，我将成为一名像您一样的老师，帮助更多的学生。祝您生活幸福，身体健康。

您真诚的，

李明

3. 告示类

（1）标题

NOTICE

（2）正文

第一段：写作目的 + 具体论述（文中一定做出了要求）

Our notice is to... First..., second..., third...

写作目的常用表达

• So and so is/are requested to note that...

受命通知……

• So and so takes/take pleasure in announcing that...

很高兴宣布……

• So and so has/have the honor to announce...

很荣幸宣布……

• It is hereby proclaimed/announced/made public that...

我们要通知的事情是……

• This is to notify/inform/announce that...

这篇告示是为了……

第二段：欢迎加入＋联系方式

Welcome to join us./We are waiting for your coming.

If you intend to join us, please call us at 136××× or email us at ×××@×××.com.

（3）落款：单位名字

举例

Directions:

Write a letter to welcome students to join in a club. In your essay, you should

1) introduce the main activities of your club,

2) analyze the advantages if students join in your club, and

3) describe how to join.

参考范文

NOTICE

Do you want to improve yourself and develop your English ability? Then come and join us now.（欢迎加入＋写作目的）

Our English Club was organized 10 years ago and has more than 3,000 members. On Sunday evenings, you will see a classic English movie. Most importantly, someone will be invited to express his/her ideas about the movie, and then we will have a hot discussion on it. Besides, a foreign friend will be introduced to you if you like, which is really helpful to your oral English.（第二段就是根据题目要求来写，其实语言很简单，需要注意逻辑关系词的综合运用。）

So don't hesitate to join us. If you are interested in our club, you can call us at 136××× or email us at Englishclub@163.com.（再次欢迎加入＋联系方式）

English Club

【参考译文】

告示

你想要提升自己的能力，提高自己的英语水平吗？那现在就来加入我们吧。

英语俱乐部在十年前组建，有 3 000 多名成员。在星期天晚上，你可以观看一部经典的英语电影。最重要的是，我们会邀请成员就这部电影发表自己的观点，然后我们会对其进行热烈的讨论。此外，如果你愿意，我们可以给你介绍一位外国朋友，这对你的英语口语很有帮助。

所以不要犹豫，加入我们吧。如果你对我们俱乐部感兴趣，可以打电话至136×××或发邮件至Englishclub @163.com。

英语俱乐部

举例

Directions:

You are supposed to write for the Postgraduates' Association a notice to recruit volunteers for an international conference on globalization. The notice should include the basic qualifications for applicants and the other information which you think is relevant.

You should write about 100 words on the ANSWER SHEET.

Do not sign your own name at the end of the notice. Use "Postgraduates' Association" instead.

参考范文

NOTICE

This is to notify that volunteers are needed for an international conference on globalization. On the one hand, you should be good at English which, as is known to us all, has become the international language. If you excel at it, you can communicate with foreign experts and professors smoothly. On the other hand, you should be outgoing, sociable as well as eloquent because there may exist many possibilities that you will cooperate with certain partners. These features are quite crucial to finishing your job well.

Do not hesitate to join us. If you are interested in the activity, you can call us at 136 ××× or email us at ×××@yahoo.com.（欢迎加入＋联系方式）

Postgraduates' Association

【参考译文】

告示

现为一个关于全球化的国际会议招募志愿者。首先，你应该擅长英语，众所周知，英语是国际语言。如果你擅长英语，你就可以和国外的专家、教授流利地交流。另一方面，你应该开朗，善于交际，并且能言善辩，因为你有可能会和特定的伙伴合作。这些特征对很好地完成你的工作非常重要。

不要犹豫，加入我们吧。如果你对这项活动感兴趣，可以打电话至136×××或发邮件至×××@yahoo.com。

研究生协会

第二节　图画作文

下面列举了三篇典型的图画作文，根据提纲要求分析它们的相同点和不同点，并从中总结出图画作文的写作思路。

2007 年写作 Part B

Directions:

Write an essay of 160-200 words based on the following drawing. In your essay, you should

1) describe the drawing briefly,

2) explain its intended meaning, and then

3) support your view with an example/examples.

You should write neatly on ANSWER SHEET 2. (20 points)

2015 年英语（一）写作 Part B

Directions:

Write an essay of 160-200 words based on the following picture. In your essay, you should

1) describe the picture briefly,

2) interpret its intended meaning, and

3) give your comments.

You should write neatly on the ANSWER SHEET. (20 points)

手机时代的聚会

2016 年英语（一）写作 Part B

Directions:

Write an essay of 160-200 words based on the following pictures. In your essay, you should

1) describe the pictures briefly,

2) interpret the meaning, and

3) give your comments.

You should write neatly on the ANSWER SHEET. (20 points)

与其只提要求，不如做个榜样

这三篇作文代表了所有的图画作文：第一篇图中有两个主体，两个动作；第二篇有一个主体，两个动作；第三篇则是由两幅图画构成。图画描述就分为这三种情况，考题要求第一段都是描述图画，并引出中心。

其次看写作具体要求，第一篇作文要求举例，第二、三篇只要求给出评论，这就意味着作文第二段有所不同。如果提纲要求举例，则必须根据提纲给出例子；如果提纲没有要求举例，则可以举例也可以不举例。

第三段则是相同的，都是总结，提出建议。

1. 第一段写法

第一段为固定模式，即描述图画并且写出图画的寓意。该段的模板性不强，这里只推荐一些描述图画和表达寓意的句型。

（1）第一、二句话：用主语从句引出对图画的描述

What seems self-evident is that... 显而易见……

What has been found is that... 显而易见 / 众所周知……

What proves beyond dispute is that... 毋庸置疑 / 显而易见……

What seems universally acknowledged is that... 人们普遍认为 / 众所周知……

What has been widely accepted is that... 人们普遍认为 / 众所周知……

What is generally agreed proves that... 人们普遍认为 / 众所周知……

对图画的描述分为三种情况如下。

① 一幅图一个主体，两个动作。

In the easy and simple cartoon, sb.（定语 / 同位语）, doing sth.（次要动作）（定语 / 状语）, is doing sth.（主要动作）（定语 / 状语）

② 一幅图两个主体，两个动作。

In the easy and simple cartoon, sb. 1（定语 / 同位语）is doing sth. 1（定语 / 状语）, and/but sb. 2（定语 / 同位语）is doing sth. 2（定语 / 状语）

③ 两幅图。

In the former picture, sb. 1（定语 / 同位语）is doing sth. 1（定语 / 状语），and/but in the latter one, sb. 2（定语 / 同位语）is doing sth. 2（定语 / 状语）

（2）第三句话：引出寓意的过渡语

Personally, what the picture conveys is far beyond a new fashion trend and carries cultural implication.

The fact/story that... indicates that...

The symbolic meaning of the cartoon is quite self-evident.

The message conveyed in the picture seems to be that...

The picture has revealed, as is known to us all, a current social phenomenon that...

The picture does reflect a thought-provoking social phenomenon that...

It is apparent that the author of the drawing is trying to reveal to us...

The picture conveys a deep concern for sth.（不好的现象）+ 定语（which has exerted an adverse influence in our society）.

The purpose of the picture is to show us that due attention has to be paid to the phenomenon of sth.

Its symbolic meaning, which is quite obvious, should be taken into account more seriously.

It seems to me that the cartoonist is sending a message about the importance/seriousness of sth., which...

We can deduce from this picture that the drawer is trying to attract our attention to sth., which...

（3）第四句话：表达寓意

We should do sth.

We should never do sth.

Sth. is very important.

Sth. is very serious.

虽然第四句话需要表达这个意思，但是不能用这么简单的句型。

推荐使用如下句式。

① 被动

② as... as... 比较结构

③ so... that...

④ 比喻

无论选择这四个句型中的哪一个，都要求在主谓中间加插入语。

举例 2007 年写作 Part B 第一段（一幅图两个主体，两个动作）

What proves beyond dispute is that（主语从句开头）in the easy and simple cartoon, the goal-keeper who feels so timid is imagining himself as small as an ant. Conversely, the football player preparing to shoot is visualizing his rival as big as an elephant.（套用“一幅图两个主体，两个动作”的模板句型）The message conveyed in the picture seems to be that（引出文章中心的过渡语）confidence, as a matter of fact, should be of great significance in our contemporary society.（文章中心句，选用被动，并且用了插入语）

举例 2015 年英语（一）写作 Part B 第一段（一幅图一个主体，两个动作）

What can be seen clearly is that in the easy and simple caricature, four youngsters who may be intimate friends, sitting in front of the table served with dishes, are concentrating on their cellphones without any communication with each other. The message conveyed in the picture seems to be that nowadays, so serious is the heavy use of cellphones that it, to be frank, seems to be high time to pay attention to it.

举例 2016 年英语（一）写作 Part B 第一段（两幅图）

What has been found is that in the former cartoon while the father is playing games himself, he asks his son who gives a reluctant expression to study. Conversely, in the latter one, when the father is writing carefully, the kid is reading actively and earnestly. The message conveyed in the pictures seems to be that the action of parents, as a matter of fact, speaks louder than their words.

2. 第二段写法

第二段一般都是分析问题，所以该段以分析原因或讨论一个问题的好处或坏处为主。比如：如果是孝敬父母的话题，第二段就论述孝敬父母的原因；如果是污染的话题，第二段就写污染的危害；如果是合作的话题，第二段就论述合作的好处。当然，有时候提纲中明确规定要举例，此时的原因分析就以举例的方式展开。第二段写法分为两种：

① 举例与否均可的原因分析。

② 一定要举例的原因分析。

下面分别论述这两种情况。

（1）纯原因分析段（没有例子）的写法

首句：引出原因分析

The majority of people would agree that the issue has its deep roots as follows.

Personally some reasons could account for such a phenomenon.

If proceeding unchecked, it will undoubtedly cause many problems.

On the surface of it, this may seem to be ridiculous, but if thinking again, we will be able to point out some reasons.

It is superficially plausible, but when subjected to analysis, it really has its fundamental reasons.

If we let this situation continue as it is, we do not know what will happen about people's relationships in the future.

You may criticize for/blame for...（不好的现象，比如说不诚实）, but the causes/roots of the problem/phenomenon go far deeper.

It is not an easy task to find the reasons for the complicated phenomenon.

There stand at least two reasons, I think, for the phenomenon of...

Recognizing a problem, on the other hand, is the first step in finding a solution.

第二句：具体论述

推荐句型如下。

not only... but also...（最好写成倒装）

The evidence that... manifests that...

although 引导的让步状语从句

which 引导的非限制性定语从句

the more... the more...

if 引导的虚拟语气（反面论证）

举例 2015 年英语（一）写作 Part B（为什么滥用手机不好？）

Analyzing the issue proves the first step in finding a solution. The primary element I would like to point out here is that（相当于 firstly）heavy use of cellphones not only exerts great influence on our good health but also wastes too much precious time of teenagers and youngsters. Another factor here is that（相当于 secondly）the more frequently kids surf the Internet on cellphones, the worse their performance will become, which leaves readers quite a deep impression.（因为这个原因不够长，所以外加了一个非限制性定语从句来进行补充）In the end, if the tendency continues as it is, the grave consequence will be easy to be predicted. The users of cellphones might look like mummies, and consequently, economy will stop growing. How horrible it sounds!

举例 2014 年英语（一）写作 Part B（孝敬父母）

It keeps my belief that quite a few reasons, from my perspective, could account for the current situation. To begin with, it is a Chinese tradition to respect the elderly and take care of the young, which has been widely accepted by the public.（由于句子不够长，所以加了个 which 引导的非限制性定语从句）In addition, the evidence that senior citizens have struggled to create better living and working conditions for posterity manifests that they should be supported by their offspring when they retire. The last factor that I have to point out here is that without diligence and endeavor of the past generations, we could by no means enjoy the current prosperity and happiness.

（2）举例段的写法

首句：表示举例的总起句

Examples to prove the view are abundant. The most persuasive one is the case of sb. who...

This can be illustrated by the example of sb. who...

Such stimulating/less impressive cases/stories are not rare in our daily life.

To examine it, let's return to the example of sb./sth.

There exist too plentiful cases like this in the routine of our life to list. However, the most impressive one is about myself.

Although so abundant cases can support my simple view, the following one is the most favorable.

中间句：具体例子

尾句：总结句

So the case vividly clarifies a truth that... has played a crucial role in our success/life.

If there were no..., sb./sth. would do sth.

举例 2001 年写作（爱心是一盏灯）

Such stimulating stories as to the power of love are not rare in our society. As a matter of fact, we still remember how the Chinese people of all nationalities responded to the call to help the victims of the earthquake in Wenchuan in 2008. Although the income of common Chinese citizens was still not high enough, people all over the country did not hesitate to donate whatever they could to help their needy fellow citizens. The local in the disaster felt grateful for their assistance. As a consequence, if there had been no help from the whole nation, they would have suffered more sacrifices in the earthquake.

举例 2007 年写作 Part B（自信很重要）

To be undaunted and self-confident is of great significance. Once we believe ourselves, sparks of possibility may turn into flames of triumph. There are numerous of people who show confidence all the way and have gained remarkable achievements. Jack Welch, former CEO of General Electric, is a good example. When he was young, he has serious stammer which made him a laughingstock. However, his mother encouraged him: "Your brain is so clever that no one could catch up with it." This inspires Jack's firm self-assurance, which serves as a valuable contributor to make him blossom into a legend in the field of business.

3. 第三段写法

需要注意的是，第三段具体措施写得越准确，分值就越高。因为现在模板化很严重，所以基础好的学生最好自己写措施，以防内容太空洞导致分值不高；而基础差的学生，自己几乎写不出来，所以推荐以下内容，以供参考和使用。

首句：总结句

So crucial/grave is... that it proves it is time to attach great importance to it.

Therefore, it is high time that effective measures should be taken to solve the problem.

Therefore, it is imperative to take drastic measures to reverse this disturbing trend.

To promote..., quite a few actions could be adopted.

Accordingly, it is vital for us to derive positive implications from these thought-provoking drawings.

If we do not desire the trend to become a reality one day in the future, positive steps must be taken to put an end to... right now.

In order to promote the idea of..., tremendous tasks have to be accomplished.

To put an end to the negative situation, my suggestions are the following steps.

There is, as a matter of fact, little doubt that immediate action is required to be adopted...

We can say this and we can say that, but the most important thing is not to say, but to do.

Having recognized the problem, it follows that we must develop a plan of action.

中间句：具体方案或总结（一般一至两句话，太长会显得文章结构不够完美）

采取具体方案的主体一般为：政府、集体（企业或家庭）、个人。

需要注意：三个主体最好只选择一到两个主体采取措施，并且采取的措施要尽量具体化，可操作性越强，写作效果就越好。比如：怎么让年轻人自信?

如果你写 It is quite necessary that teenagers and youngsters should have confidence. 也可以，但是这个措施就很空洞，没有操作性。英语表达越具体准确，分值就越高。

如果你写 It is quite necessary that teenagers and youngsters should take part in more activities to show themselves in front of strangers. 就很具体，有操作性了。

再如：怎么保护环境?

如果你写 We should cultivate the awareness that environmental protection is of great importance to us. 就不够具体，没有操作性。

如果你写 We should cultivate the awareness that rubbish must be classified not only at home but also in public places. 就很具体、准确了。

这就是自己写作和使用模板的区别。但是中文表达就有问题的同学，可以使用下面推荐的表达：

（1）政府

推荐句型如下。

People's awareness must be heightened through education and publicity.

We should appeal to the authorities to make strict laws to control...

Authorities, in coordination with the press, are obliged to...

（2）企业、学校或家庭

推荐句型如下。

It is quite necessary that responsible companies should restrain themselves from doing sth.

Elders cannot have failed to educate their kids to do sth.

It is quite urgent that elders should inspire their children to do sth.

（3）个人

推荐句型如下。

Chinese citizens are expected to enhance their awareness that sth. is an indispensable part for the construction of a harmonious society.

We should cultivate the awareness that sth. is of great significance to us.

I can use my major to call on the masses to do sth.

尾句：一般是用来总结或倡议

（1）总结法

As every coin has two sides, ...is no exception. What we should pay attention to is to confine its defects and carry forward its strong points.

事物都有两面性，……也不例外。我们能做的就是限制它的缺点，并发扬它的优点。

The sooner effective measures are taken, the more glorious future we will have.

越早采取有效措施，我们的前途就会越光明。

I believe that a happy and bright future is awaiting us if we make every effort to promote/ban...

我相信如果我们全力提倡 / 禁止……，一个幸福而光明的未来就会等待着我们。

We do have a long way to go to reach our final goal, but achieving... is within the realm of possibility.

为了实现最终的目标，我们的确有很长的路要走，但是实现……还是有可能的。

（2）反问法

Isn't... indispensable for the mental/physical health of children and adults?

难道……对于孩子与成人的精神 / 身体健康不是必不可少的吗？

Shouldn't humans pay attention to the issue of...?

难道人类不应该把注意力放在……这个问题上吗？

What does the future hold if mankind persists in...?

如果人类继续……，人类的未来将是什么样子？

(3) 引语法

Just as an esteemed writer has put it that...

就像一位著名作家曾经说过的……

We have always kept in mind the world's leading writer's words that...

我们一直铭记着这位世界上一流的作家曾经说过……

(4) 建议法

It is essential that effective measures should be taken to carry forward the spirit of...

非常重要的是，我们应该采取有效措施来发扬……的精神。

It is urgent that effective actions should be taken to terminate the worse situation.

非常紧急的是，我们应该采取有效措施来终结这一恶化的形势了。

It is high time that we urged an immediate end to this phenomenon.

是我们终结这种现象的时候了。

It is high time that we fought for the end of the undesirable phenomenon of...

是我们为结束这种……的负面现象而奋斗的时候了。

举例 2014 年英语（一）写作 Part B（孝敬父母）

As a consequence, so crucial is respecting parents that it, from my perspective, proves time to attach great importance to it. The essential action, obviously, is to raise kids to honor the elderly. Apart from this, youngsters should go back to see their parents frequently in spite of busy jobs. In the end, just as an old saying has put it, "Filial piety comes ahead of any other morality."

举例 2007 年写作 Part B（自信）

What could be done, consequently, to promote self-confidence? For one thing, self-abased kids should participate in more activities in which there are many strangers to communicate with. For another, they should practice speaking loudly or walking with the head held high. Finally, as a brave lark, I just desire to say, refuse self-abasement from now on.

第三节 图表作文

图表也是信息的基本载体，即用表格、图像等形式清晰、简明地显示相关信息，常用在科技写作中。图表作文是用文字描述图表所表达的信息，要求考生对图表中的数据、图像所提供的信息加以分析理解，找出其变化规律，分析问题产生的原因或预测其发展趋势，从而得出正确结论或做出简短的评论。图表的种类很多，有条形图、线形图、饼状图等。图表中的文字说明提供了写作的重要线索。图表作文按提示要求一般写成说明文或议论文。

一、写作要求

① 认真观察，充分运用图表中所提供的信息资料进行写作。图表上方或下方的文字通常是其主题，而图表中的文字和说明实质上就是作文中的关键词。写作时注意文章整体结构的连贯性，恰当地运用转承词汇。

② 审读图表结构并仔细分析信息。选出最有意义的信息加以比较和对照。分辨其信息层次并按提示要求抓住问题本质，描述图表时要避免过多地引用图表中的数字，而要把列举的实例和数字结合起来进行论证。

③ 图表作文结构一般分为三段：第一段描述图表的客观概况并阐述主题；第二段对图表中最有意义或最重要的信息进行描述、归纳，或分析说明其原因；第三段得出结论或做出评论，有时提出解决问题的方法，有时预测发展变化和趋势。

二、作文示例及分析

举例

Directions:

For this part, you are allowed 30 minutes to write a composition of no less than 150 words on the topic Changes in People's Diet. Study the following table carefully and your composition must be based on the information given in the table. Write three paragraphs to

1) state the changes in people's diet in the past five years,

2) give possible reasons for the changes, and

3) draw your own conclusions.

You should quote as few figures as possible.

Year / Food	1986	1987	1988	1989	1990
Grain	49%	47%	46.5%	45%	45%
Milk	10%	11%	11%	12%	13%
Meat	17%	20%	22.5%	23%	21%
Fruits and vegetables	24%	22%	20%	20%	21%
Total	100%	100%	100%	100%	100%

这是一篇典型的图表作文。根据题目提供的情景纲要，作文应该主要议论人们在饮食结构方面的变化，说明可能产生这些变化的原因，并阐述对此的观点。

第一段的关键是说出图表所反映的变化。描述的信息是表格中显示的1986—1990年人们在饮食方面的变化。需要注意的是图表中数字太多，不可能全部论述，所以将主要数据表述清楚即可。如何分析和描述这些数字以说明其变化情况最重要。

第二段要求说明产生这些变化的原因。段落内容的阐述一定要紧紧围绕人们在饮食结构上产生变化的主要原因。

第三段按提纲要求写出合乎逻辑的结论。

审题时注意提纲中各要求之间的内在联系，先说明变化，再分析变化的原因，最后在分析上述变化原因的基础上写出这些变化将产生的结果。

参考范文

Changes in People's Diet

This table shows the changes in people's diet from the year 1986 to 1990. What looks beyond dispute is that great changes had taken place in the past five years. There was a general trend of decrease in the consumption of grain, but an increase in the consumption of some high protein, high energy food, such as milk and meat.

There are lots of reasons accounting for the phenomenon and I would like to explore a few of the most important ones here. Above all, after the reform and opening up and the strengthening of Chinese economy, people became rich, which enabled them to afford food with more nutrition. In addition, people began to lay emphasis on improving the structure of their diet and to learn more about diet. They not only paid attention to the quantity, but also the quality of what they ate.

According to the above-mentioned discussion, we can easily draw a conclusion that our society has been progressing and people have been living a better life than before. We are now able to get more delicious and nutritious food, thereby improving our health. It can be sure that a better life awaits us in the future.

【参考译文】

人们饮食结构的变化

该图表显示了 1986 年至 1990 年人们饮食的变化。毫无争议的是，在过去的五年里，人们的饮食发生了巨大的变化。谷物消耗有普遍下降的趋势，但一些高蛋白质、高能量食物的消耗有所增加，如牛奶和肉类。

解释这一现象的原因有很多，我想在这里说明一些最重要的原因。首先，改革开放后，国家经济实力的增强使人们变得富有，他们能够负担得起更多有营养的食物。此外，人们开始重视改善饮食结构，了解更多饮食相关的知识。他们不仅注重数量，而且注重食物的质量。

根据上述讨论，我们可以很容易地得出结论，我们的社会正在进步，人们的生活比以前更好。我们现在能够获得更美味和营养的食物，从而改善我们的健康。我们可以肯定，未来更好的生活在等着我们。

举例

Directions:

Write an essay based on the graphs below. In your writing, you should

1) describe the changes of the life expectancy and infant mortality in developing countries, and

2) explain the reasons for these changes.

You should write about 150 words on the ANSWER SHEET.

Health Gains in Developing Countries

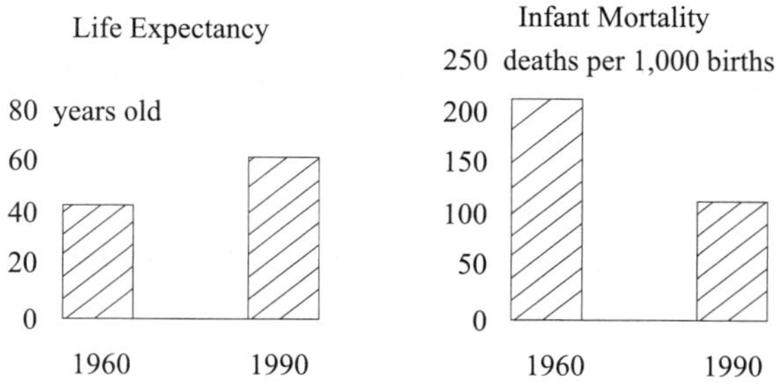

这是两个条形图。作文应按照题干要求在第一段介绍图表的信息。以图表所显示的数字为依据来描述 1960—1990 年这 30 年里发展中国家在人类平均寿命和新生儿死亡率方面所发生的变化。然

后在第二段中分析产生变化的原因，并展开论述。根据因果推理，产生这种结果的原因可以是多种多样的。我们在选取材料时，一定要选择最典型、最能说明问题的材料，这样内容才最具有说服力。比如，经济的发展、教育和医疗水平的提高，以及来自发达国家的援助，这些都是重要的原因。最后，在文章的结尾可以对未来做出预测：随着社会的发展，人们的生活会变得更加美好。

参考范文

Health Gains in Developing Countries

This graph shows us the changes in the life expectancy and infant mortality in developing countries between 1960 and 1990. We can see that the life expectancy in 1960 was about 40 years whereas in 1990, it increased to about 60 years. In the meantime, the infant mortality rate dropped from 200 deaths per 1,000 births to 100 deaths per 1,000 births.

There stands certain factors for the changes. First and foremost, thank to the strengthening of economy and the advances in science and medicine, people then were receiving better health care services than they used to, which played an important role in improving people's health conditions. Secondly, people were better off than in the past, which enabled them to attach much importance to their diet. At last, the government paid more attention to protecting the environment. More measures were taken to deal with the problem of pollution. All these were beneficial to people's health, which certainly prolonged their life expectancy.

In a word, the increase in life expectancy and the decrease in infant mortality were the result of multiple factors. I believe that as the country progresses, we will live a better life.

【参考译文】

发展中国家健康状况的改善

这张图表向我们展示了 1960 年至 1990 年发展中国家预期寿命和婴儿死亡率的变化。我们可以看到，1960 年的平均寿命大约是 40 岁，而在 1990 年，它增加到大约 60 岁。与此同时，婴儿死亡率从每千名新生儿中死亡 200 人下降到每千名新生儿中死亡 100 人。

这些变化有一定的因素。首先，由于经济的加强以及科学和医学的进步，人们得到了比以往更好的医疗保健服务，这在改善人们的健康状况方面发挥着重要作用。其次，人们过得比以前更好，这使他们非常重视自己的饮食。最后，政府更加重视保护环境，采取了更多措施来处理污染问题。所有这些都对人们的健康有益，这必然会延长他们的平均寿命。

总之，平均寿命的增长和婴儿死亡率的降低是多重因素作用的结果。相信随着国家的进步，我们会过上更好的生活。

举例

Directions:

Study the following graphs carefully and write an essay in at least 150 words.

Your essay must be written neatly on the ANSWER SHEET.

Your essay should cover these three points:

1) Effect of country's growing human population on its wildlife;

2) Possible reasons for the effect;

3) Your suggestions for wildlife protection.

The Ups and Downs of Population Growth

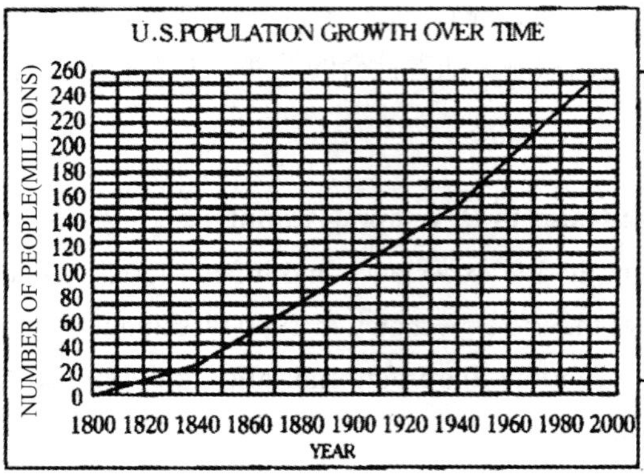

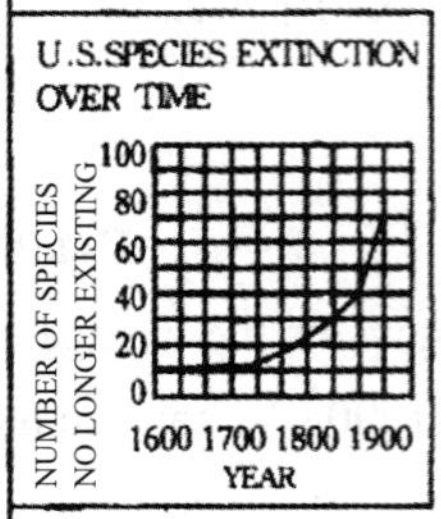

参考范文

The Ups and Downs of Population Growth

What keeps well-known is that the sharp increase of population and the extinction rate of wildlife species are experiencing a parallel trend. As is shown in the charts, in 1990, population in the U.S. reached an unprecedented level of 250 million, which was approximately 250 times of that of 1800. On the other hand, wildlife species disappeared from the country at an alarming rate: by 1900, about 70 wildlife species had been extinct in the U.S.

For one thing, in the last two centuries, as industrialization and man's thirst for material goods grew, the earth's natural covering of vegetation had been under constant encroachment, and the natural balance in the biological world was altered in a variety of ways. The rapid destruction of the tropical rain forests which are the ecosystems with the highest known species diversity on the earth had led to vast-scale habitat destruction. For another, overgrazing and pollution were also accountable for the high extinction of wildlife species, which had to fend for themselves in unfamiliar environments, and died out when they couldn't cope with the situation well.

To sum up, it is high time that we recognized the significance of biological diversity in all ecosystems. Population growth shall no longer go unchecked, and more natural habitats of wildlife species should be consciously restored.

【参考译文】

人口增长的起伏

众所周知，人口的急剧增长与野生动植物物种灭绝走势近乎平行。如图所示，1990 年，美国人口达到了前所未有的 2.5 亿，大约是 1800 年的 250 倍。另外，野生动植物物种正以惊人的速度从这个国家消失：到 1900 年，大约 70 种野生动物在美国灭绝了。

一方面，在过去的两个世纪里，随着工业化的发展和人类对物质产品需求的增加，地球上的自然植被被不断地侵蚀，生物界的自然平衡以各种方式发生改变。热带雨林是地球上已知生物多样性最高的生态系统，它的迅速破坏导致了大规模生物栖息地的破坏。另一方面，过度放牧和污染同样也是野生动植物物种大量灭绝的原因，它们不得不在不熟悉的环境中谋生，而当它们不能很好地适应这种情况的时候，它们就灭绝了。

总之，我们早该认识到生物多样性在整个生态系统中的重要性了。人们不能再放任人口增长，并且要有意识地恢复更多野生动植物的自然栖息地。

点评：本文是一篇满分作文。文章内容切题，条理清楚，大致发展脉络为：对图表所给信息进行描述→对数字信息进行小结→对造成这种现象的原因进行推测→提出自己的建议。完全符合题目的要求。文章内容表达精确、深刻，文字连贯，词汇准确多变，是一篇优秀的作文。

三、图表作文具体讲解

1. 第一段写法

根据以上范文分析，图表作文的第一段和图画作文的第一段很相似。图画作文的第一段是描述图画和总结寓意；图表作文的第一段则是描述图表和概括中心。它和图画作文比起来的优点是不会写跑题或偏题，因为数字传达的信息直接明了。

第一、二句话：用主语从句引出对图表的描述，需要注意的是描述图表时，只抓典型数据进行对比即可，其他数据只是陪衬，无须描述。典型数据一般都是最高、最低或首位数据，而且描述图表不要超过两句话。

下面是描述图表常用到的单词和句型。

（1）图表种类及概述法

泛指图表：graph/chart/diagram/illustration

饼状图：pie chart

条形图或柱状图：bar chart

线形图：line chart

表格：table

（2）描述图表数字变化的单词

增加：increase/rise/grow/expand/climb/soar/jump/rocket/ascend/accumulate/surge/swell

减少：decrease/fall/drop/decline/dive/plunge/reduce/descend/diminish/dwindle/shrink/go down/fall off/continue its downward trend/on the decline/on the slowdown

波动：fluctuate/rebound/undulate/wave

稳定：stable/stabilize

大幅度地：sharply/dramatically/markedly/remarkably/considerably/suddenly

慢慢地：slowly/slightly/modestly/gradually/moderately/gently

保持平稳：remain stable/steady/constant/the same/unchanged

（3）描述图表具体句型

Over the period from... to..., the... remained constant.

在……至……期间，……保持不变。

In the year between... and...

在……到……期间

In the 3 years spanning from 1995 to 1998...

从 1995 年到 1998 年这 3 年里……

The number of... remained steady/stable from (month/year) to (month/year).

……（年 / 月）至……（年 / 月），……的数量保持稳定 / 不变。

The number sharply went up to...

数字急剧上升至……

The percentage of... stayed the same between... and...

……至……期间，……的比率保持不变。

The figures peaked at... in (month/year).

数目在……（年 / 月）达到顶点，为……

The percentage remained steady at...

比率稳定维持在……

The percentage of... is slightly larger/smaller than that of...

……的比例比……的比例略高 / 低。

There is not a great difference between... and...

……与……之间的区别不大。

The graphs show a threefold increase in the number of...

该图表显示……的数目增加了三倍。

...decreased year by year while... increased steadily.

……逐年减少，而……稳步上升。

The figures/situation bottomed out in...

数字 / 情况在……达到底部。

The figures/situation reached the bottom/a low point/a trough.

数字 / 情况达到底部 / 低点 / 低谷。

A is... times as much/many as B.

A 是 B 的……倍。

A increased by...

A 增长了……

A increased to...

A 增长到……

There is an upward trend in the number of...

……的数量呈上升趋势。

A considerable increase/decrease occurred from... to...

从……到……，……急剧上升 / 下降。

From... to... the rate of decrease slowed down.

从……到……，下降速率减慢。

From this year on, there was a gradual decline/reduction in the..., reaching a figure of...

从这年起，……逐渐下降至……

be similar to...

与……相似

There are a lot of similarities/differences between... and...

……与……之间有许多相似 / 不同之处。

The difference between A and B lies in...

A 与 B 之间的差别在于……

...(year) witnessed/saw a sharp rise in...

……（年）……急剧上升。

第三句话：引出文章中心。

推荐句型：

The table/chart/diagram/graph shows (that)...

According to the table/chart/diagram/graph, ...

As (is) shown in the table/chart/diagram/graph, ...

As can be seen from the table/chart/diagram/graph/figures, ...

Figures/Statistics show (that) ...

It can be seen from the figures/statistics that...

We can see from the figures/statistics that...

It is clear from the figures/statistics that...

It is apparent from the figures/statistics/table/chart/diagram/graph that...

举例　2013 年英语（二）写作 Part B 第一段

Directions:

Write an essay based on the following chart. In your writing, you should

1) interpret the chart, and

2) give your comments.

You should write about 150 words on the ANSWER SHEET. (15 points)

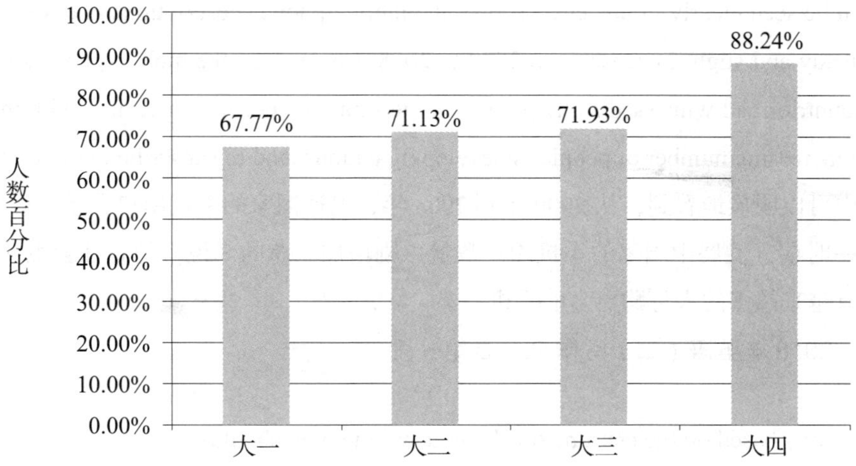

某高校学生兼职情况

What looks beyond dispute is that in the chart, there is a steady increase from 67.77% to 71.93%

for students holding temporary jobs from freshmen to juniors, while the percentage of seniors working part-time jumps to 88.24%.（用主语从句来描述图表，并且描述图表时只描述典型数据）The bar chart clearly reveals the statistics of students taking part-time jobs in a certain university.

如图所示，毫无疑问，从大一到大三，从事临时工作的学生比例从 67.77% 稳步上升到 71.93%。然而，大四做兼职的学生比例猛然上升到 88.24%。这个图表清楚地展示了某所大学学生做兼职的统计数据。

举例 2010 年英语（二）写作 Part B 第一段

Directions:

In this section, you are asked to write an essay based on the following chart. In your writing, you should

1) interpret the chart, and

2) give your comments.

You should write at least 150 words.

Write your essay on ANSWER SHEET 2. (15 points)

Mobile-phone subscriptions

(2000—2008)

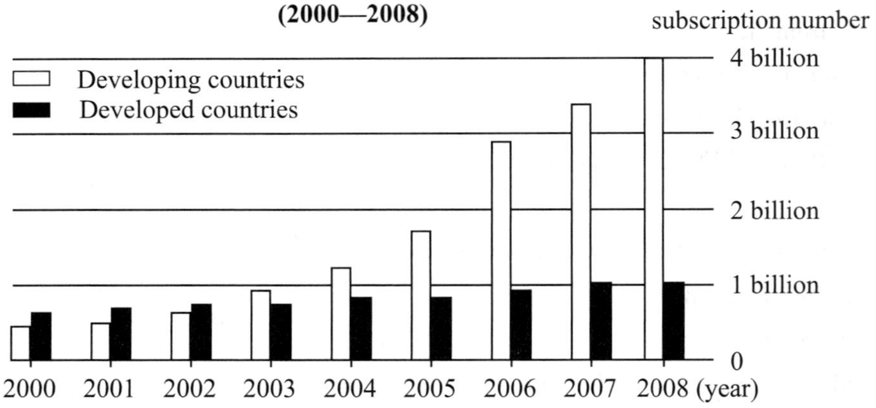

What can be seen clearly in this chart is that, the mobile-phone subscriptions in developed countries had have a steady and slight increase from 2000 to 2008. Conversely, the mobile-phone subscriptions in developing countries had witnessed a sharp jump in the same period. In conclusion, with the advance of social life, an increasing number of people in developing nations tend to subscribe to more cellphones.

从图表中可以明显地看到，从 2000 年到 2008 年，发达国家的手机用户数量在缓慢稳步增长。相反，在同一时期，发展中国家的手机用户数量急剧增加。总的来说，随着社会生活的发展，发展中国家会有越来越多的人订购更多的手机。

举例 2018 年英语（二）写作 Part B 第一段

Directions:

Write an essay based on the chart below. In your writing, you should

1) interpret the chart, and

2) give your comments.

You should write about 150 words on the ANSWER SHEET. (15 points)

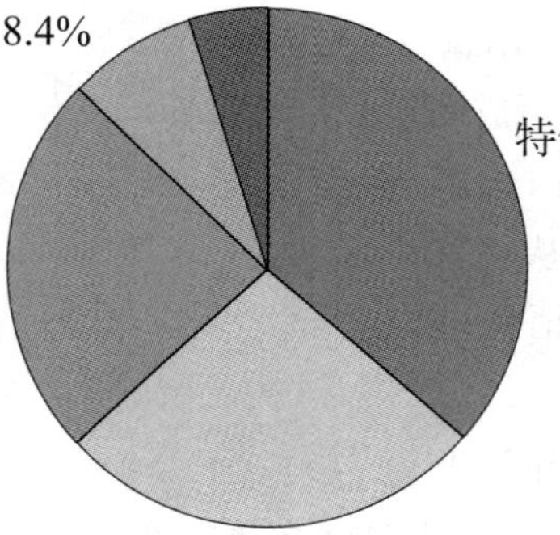

2017 年某市消费者选择餐厅时的关注因素

What can be seen clearly in the pie chart is that 36.3 percent of consumers, when having dinner in restaurants, regard specialties as a matter of prime importance. By contrast, it is surprising that only 8.4 percent of citizens care about the prices of their dishes. Apparently, the chart is trying to reveal to us that the price is no longer the main concern for quite a few national citizens.

从饼状图中，我们可以清楚地看到，36.3% 的消费者，在餐馆吃饭时，把特色视为一个至关重要的因素。相比之下，只有 8.4% 的市民关心菜肴的价格，这是令人惊讶的。显然，该图试图向我们揭示：价格不再是相当多的国民关心的主要问题。

2. 第二段写法

很显然，我们能够看出图表作文第二段同图画作文第二段一样都是分析原因，或这个问题产生的好处或害处。如果不好写原因分析，考生可以考虑举例，这点也同图画作文一样。并且我们前面讲了一些段落论述方式，比如引用名言、下定义和解释等，也可以考虑使用。

首句：引出原因分析

推荐句型：

The majority of people would agree that the issue has its deep roots as follows.

It is my belief that some reasons could account for such a phenomenon.

If proceeding unchecked, it will undoubtedly cause many problems.

On the surface of it, this may seem to be ridiculous, but if thinking again, we will be able to point out some reasons.

It is superficially plausible, but when subjected to analysis, it really has its fundamental reasons.

If we let this situation continue as it is, we do not know what will happen about people's relationships in the future.

You may criticize for/blame for...（不好的现象，比如说不诚实）, but the causes/roots of this problem/phenomenon go far deeper.

It is not an easy task to find the reasons for the complicated phenomenon.

There stand at least two reasons, I think, for the phenomenon of...

Recognizing a problem, on the other hand, is the first step in finding a solution.

第二句：具体论述

推荐句型：

not only... but also...（最好写成倒装）

the evidence that... manifests that...

although 引导的让步状语从句

which 引导的非限制性定语从句

the more... the more...

if 引导的虚拟语气（反面论证）

举例　2013 年英语（二）写作 Part B 第二段

It is to clarify the subject that I would like to point out certain points.（强调句型引出原因分析）To begin with, although part-time employment has the potential to negatively affect college students' studies, it can benefit their academic careers.（第一个原因用 although 引导的让步状语从句）What is more, it can help students understand their preferences better or to "test out" a possible career direction. Last but not least, the evidence that companies will give preference to those with real-world experience indicates that part-time jobs become quite necessary for the students who are leaving the campus.（第三个原因用同位语从句）

为了更清晰地描述这个题目，我想指出几个要点。首先，尽管兼职工作对高校学生的学业有潜在的负面影响，但是也对他们的学术生涯有好处。其次，它可以帮助学生更好地理解他们的喜好或者"尝试"可能的职业方向。最后，企业将优先考虑那些有社会经验的学生，这一事实表明，对于即将离开学校的学生来说，兼职工作变得非常必要。

举例　2010 年英语（二）写作 Part B 第二段

The issue, when subjected to analysis, really has its fundamental reasons.（借用第二段首句推荐句型，略有改变。）The primary reason is that developed countries not only have a limited number of populations but also most of them are well-educated. Therefore, the spreading of the mobile-phone service is efficient and soon the market is saturated. Furthermore, the lower the prices of cellphones become, the more subscribers there will exist in developing nations, which has been widely accepted.（the more... the more... 句型，后面加了一个 which 引导的非限制性定语从句）In the end, the developing countries have a large population demanding for mobile services although they cannot afford quite expensive ones.（最后一个理由是 although 引导的让步状语从句）

细心分析下，这个问题确实有着深刻的原因。首先，发达国家的人口不但有限而且他们受过良好教育。所以手机服务的普及是很有效率的，而且市场很快就饱和了。其次，手机的价格越低，发展中国家的订购量就越大，这点是人们普遍认同的。最后，尽管发展中国家的公民买不起太贵的手机，但是他们有着很大的需求量。

举例　2018 年英语（二）写作 Part B 第二段

To clarify the phenomenon thoroughly, some factors must be pointed out here. The most essential one seems that with the favorable policy of nearly thirty years, Chinese economy has been developing fast. Under such conditions, society has become more stable and harmonious. People have become wealthier. As a result, more Chinese are inclined to ignore the price of products. Another element is that people had been satisfied with the existing state of affairs and reluctant to move forward in the past. However, such situations, years later, become the other way round. They want to keep up with the times and have more communications. Thus, more people would like to have dinner in restaurants with their friends.

为了彻底阐明这一现象，这里必须指出一些因素。最重要的是，在近三十年的惠民政策下，中国经济发展迅速。在这样的条件下，社会变得更加稳定、和谐，人们更富有了，所以越来越多的中国人倾向于忽视产品的价格。另一个原因是，人们过去安于现状。但多年后，这种情况变得恰恰相反。人们想与时俱进，渴望更多的沟通，所以，更多的人想在餐馆与朋友一起吃饭。

3. 第三段写法

该段一般用于总结和预测趋势，用三句话就可以论述清楚。

首句：总结句

推荐句型：

Under no circumstances could we fail to attach importance to the issue of...

It is about time to pay much attention to the issue of...

So severe/essential/conspicuous is the issue of... that it should catch our attention.

第二句话：具体措施可以用一句话或两句话来概括，太长会显得文章结构不够完美，写作方法与图画作文一样。

采取具体方案的主体一般如下。

（1）政府

推荐句型：

People's awareness must be heightened through education and publicity.

We should appeal to the authorities to make strict laws to control...

Authorities, in coordination with the press, are obliged to...

（2）企业或家庭

推荐句型：

It is quite necessary that responsible companies should restrain themselves from doing sth.

Elders cannot have failed to educate their kids to do sth.

It is quite urgent that elders should inspire their children to do sth.

（3）个人

推荐句型：

Chinese citizens are expected to enhance their awareness that sth. is an indispensable part for the construction of a harmonious society.

We should cultivate the awareness that sth. is of great significance to us.

My major could be applied to call on the masses to do sth.

尾句

预测趋势或呼吁，如果是呼吁，则仍然同图画作文尾句。但是图表作文也可以预测趋势。

推荐句型：

If the tendency continues as it is, there will be more... doing sth.

If an increasing number of... did sth., sth. would happen.

It is by analyzing the trend in the past that we may forecast that the growth tendency will continue.

By observing the data in the past, we may forecast that...

In light of the statistics given above, we can safely predict that...

举例 2013 年英语（二）写作 Part B 第三段

It is necessary for university students to get part-time jobs.（论点）Therefore, authorities should inspire more students to walk out of campus.（措施）If students are able to effectively manage their time and secure a part-time position in a field related to their studies or interests, the job will certainly exert a positive impact.（预测趋势）

大学生是有必要做兼职工作的。因此，一些部门应该鼓励更多的学生走出校园。如果学生们能有效管理自己的时间，找到一个符合自己专业或兴趣的兼职岗位，那么做兼职工作必定是有益的。

举例 2010 年英语（二）写作 Part B 第三段

Consequently, with the improvement of their life, more citizens in developing nations could afford cellphones. Companies producing phones might lower the cost further to make more people benefit from it. If the trend continues, more citizens in developing countries will lead a convenient and comfortable life.

因此，随着生活水平的提高，更多发展中国家的公民买得起手机了。生产手机的公司可以进一步降低成本以使更多人受益。如果这种趋势继续的话，更多的发展中国家的公民会过上方便和舒适的生活。

举例 2018 年英语（二）写作 Part B 第三段

If the trend continues, more and more people will enjoy a high-quality life. However, it is advisable for the public to consume rationally, avoiding extravagance and waste. In conclusion, a booming economy will wait for us in the near future.

如果这种趋势继续下去，越来越多的人会享受高质量的生活。然而，公众应该理性消费，避免铺张浪费。总之，在不久的将来，等待我们的是一个繁荣的经济体。

第六章

考研英语写作话题汇总

第一节　应用文写作话题

1. 推荐信

Directions:

You are asked to write a letter of recommendation for Mary who wants to study for the master's degree under the supervision of Prof. Smith who was once your supervisor in your graduate study.

Write a letter to Prof. Smith in about 100 words.

Do not sign your own name at the end of your letter. Use "Li Ming" instead.

参考范文

Dear Prof. Smith,

It is a great pleasure to write to you again. This time I am to recommend Mary to you. She wants to pursue her study for the master's degree under your supervision.

Mary, one of my classmates in Chongqing University, was one of the most excellent students in our university because she managed to get A grades in almost all subjects. After graduation, she had worked in a biological company for three years, during which she had accumulated considerable practical experience.

I hope that Mary's intelligence, diligence and rich experience make her have a great chance to continue her study under your direction. Therefore, I recommend her to you with no reservation.

Wish you good health.

Faithfully yours,

Li Ming

【参考译文】

敬爱的史密斯教授：

每逢再次给您写信，我总是很开心，这封信是为了向您推荐玛丽，她想继续学习，在您的指导下获得硕士学位。

玛丽是我在重庆大学的一个同班同学，她是我们大学最优秀的学生之一，因为她几乎所有课程的成绩都是优秀。毕业后，她在一家生物公司工作了三年，这极大地增加了她的实践经验。

我希望她的智慧、勤奋和丰富的经验能让她拥有一次在您的指导下继续学习的好机会。因此我毫无保留地把她推荐给您。

祝您身体健康。

您真诚的，

李明

Directions:

Suppose one of your friends will visit your hometown. Write a letter in about 100 words to make a suggestion to him/her.

Do not sign your own name at the end of the letter. Use “Li Ming” instead.

参考范文

Dear my friend,

I am glad to hear that you are going to my hometown, Yunnan, for travel. Therefore, I’m eager to recommend a certain tourist attraction to you—Jade Dragon Snow Mountain.

To begin with, the accommodation there is quite convenient since there are quite a lot of private hotels with hospitable hosts. Then for your convenience, you can hire a guide who will help you prepare some necessities such as foods and facilities. Most importantly, the fantastic scenery there will make you forget all your worries and enjoy the peaceful and pure nature.

I wish you a great pleasure and an unforgettable memory in Yunnan. If there is anything I can do for you, just call me.

Yours ever,

Li Ming

【参考译文】

亲爱的朋友：

我很高兴获悉你要去我的家乡——云南旅游。因此，我很想给你推荐一个旅游景点——玉龙雪山。

首先，那里的住宿非常方便，因为那里有很多私人旅馆，且店主都热情好客。为了你的方便，你可以雇一个导游来帮你准备一些必需品，比如食物和设备。最重要的是，那里神奇的景色会让你忘掉所有烦恼，并让你享受平静、纯洁的自然。

最后，我希望你在云南能有一段快乐、难忘的记忆。如果我能帮上忙，请联系我。

你永远的朋友，

李明

2. 建议信

Directions:

Suppose one of your friends is going to choose a major for her university study. Write a letter in about 100 words to make a suggestion for her.

Do not sign your name at the end of the letter. Use “Li Ming” instead.

参考范文

Dear Xiaowei,

I am glad to know that you are going to enter college. It is my great pleasure to give you some suggestions.

As to the ideal major, the most suitable for you is Teaching Chinese to Speakers of Other Languages. For one thing, with the development of national economy and the deepening of communication among countries, there will be a sustaining need for Chinese teachers around the world. For another, you have a strong interest in Chinese language, history and culture, which is indispensable to the making of a Chinese teacher.

In the end, if you really follow my suggestions, you should try to make friends with students from different places, especially foreigners. Furthermore, English should never be ignored on campus.

Best wishes!

Yours ever,

Li Ming

【参考译文】

亲爱的小薇：

我很高兴知道你要上大学，我非常乐意给你一些建议。

至于理想的专业，最适合你的就是汉语国际教育专业。一方面，随着国家经济的发展以及国际交流的加深，世界各地对汉语教师的需求将会持续增加。另一方面，你对中国的语言、历史和文化有着浓厚的兴趣，这对成为一名中文教师是必不可少的。

最后，如果你真听从我的建议，你应该尽量和来自不同地方的学生交朋友，尤其是留学生。此外，大学里要永远重视英语学习。

祝你好运！

你永远的朋友，

李明

3. 求职信

Directions:

Write a letter in about 100 words to a high school to apply for an English teaching position.

Do not sign your own name at the end of your letter. Use “Li Ming” instead.

参考范文

Dear Sir or Madam,

I am a senior from the Department of English in Beijing Normal University. I am writing the letter to apply for the position of English teacher that you recently have advertised in the newspaper.

First and foremost, I, being interested in English teaching, have been a top student through all the four academic years, which is shown in my enclosed resume. During my college, I once taught English in a high school for half a year. In addition, I am pretty considerate and approachable. And most importantly, I enjoy communicating with teenagers. In the end, my girlfriend lives in the city where your school is located, so I will undoubtedly find a job there. For the reasons given above, I venture to apply for the position in your school.

If I am favored with an interview, I will be extremely grateful. Please contact me at any time. Thank you for your consideration.

Yours sincerely,

Li Ming

【参考译文】

亲爱的先生或女士：

我是北京师范大学英语系的一名大四学生。我写这封信是为了申请贵校最近在报纸上刊登过的英语教师的职位。

首先，我对英语教学感兴趣，在大学四年里，我一直都是一名优秀的学生，这些都附在了我的简历里。在大学期间，我曾在一所高中教过半年英语。此外，我很体贴，平易近人。最重要的是，我喜欢和青少年交流。最后，我的女朋友住在贵校所在的城市，所以我一定会在那里找一份工作。基于以上理由，我冒昧申请贵校的职位。

如果我能得到面试的机会，我会非常感激。请随时与我联系，谢谢您的考虑。

您真诚的，

李明

4. 感谢信

Directions:

Teachers' Day is coming. Write a letter to one of your teachers and show your appreciation to him/her, and then tell him/her how to reward his/her love in about 100 words.

Do not sign your own name at the end of the letter. Use "Li Ming" instead.

参考范文

Dear Mr. Liu,

Teachers' Day is coming. I am one of your students who admire you a lot. I just want to show my great appreciation to you for your assistance.

Maybe you've forgotten that rainy day when I felt so bad because I failed in the College English Test Band 4. So many people passed me but nobody turned back to solace me. At that time, you came with an umbrella. I remember clearly that you just put your hand on my shoulder, and then you told me with a slow tune: "Failure makes one wiser; Pain makes one stronger." I was stricken by your words. Quickly, by working hard, I passed the exam with a high grade.

At last, I will be a teacher just like you and treat my students in your manner. Wish you good health.

Yours truly,

Li Ming

【参考译文】

尊敬的刘老师：

教师节就要到了，我是您的学生之一，我很钦佩您。我写这封信是为了感谢您对我的帮助。

也许您已经忘了那个下雨天，当时我感觉很糟糕，因为我没有通过英语四级考试。很多人从我身旁经过，但是没有人回头安慰我。这时，您带着伞来了。我清楚地记得您把手放在我的肩膀上，然后缓慢地告诉我："失败使人明智；痛苦使人强大。"您的话使我深受感动。通过努力，我很快就以高分通过了考试。

最后，我将成为一名像您一样的老师，以您的方式对待我的学生。祝您身体健康。

您真诚的，

李明

5. 致歉信

Directions:

Suppose you cannot attend your friend's wedding ceremony as expected for some reasons. Write a letter in about 100 words to make an apology to her.

Do not sign your own name at the end of the letter. Use "Li Ming" instead.

参考范文

My dear friend,

How are you getting on with your life these days? I am writing the letter, directly speaking, to ask for your forgiveness for my not being able to attend your wedding ceremony tomorrow as I have promised.

Some accidents happened yesterday. My father was sent to hospital because he had a sudden heart attack. I got the call from my aunt just now. As you see, my father has lived alone since my mother passed away ten years ago. Although there are two elder brothers in the same village, they are busy earning money without much time and energy to take care of my pitiful father. So I have to go home without any delay. It is so urgent that no time could be spared to explain to you face to face.

I really regret that I cannot give you my sincere congratulations on the spot. However, best wishes to you and your will-be husband. I do feel terribly sorry. Please forgive me.

Yours truly,

Li Ming

【参考译文】

亲爱的朋友：

你最近过得怎么样？坦率地说，我写这封信是为了请求你的原谅，因为我明天不能如约去参加你的婚礼了。

昨天发生了一些事情。我的父亲被送到了医院，因为他心脏病突然发作了。我刚才接到我姑妈打来的电话。正如你所知，自从我的母亲十年前去世后，我的父亲就独自生活。尽管我的两个哥哥和父亲在一个村庄，但他们忙于赚钱，没有时间和精力照顾我可怜的父亲。所以我不得不立即回家。这件事情太紧急了，我没有时间当面和你解释。

我真的很遗憾不能当场给你真诚的祝福，但向你和你未婚夫致以最好的祝福。我真的很抱歉，请原谅我。

你真诚的，

李明

6. 通知

Directions:

Write a notice in the name of the Students' Union to inform students of a speech contest in about 100 words.

参考范文

NOTICE

The Students' Union has decided to hold an English speech contest to welcome freshmen. It will be held on July 28. In the contest, the maximum time of each participant is ten minutes. Besides, seven professors in English major will be invited as judges. Of course, the prize is also so attractive that you will get a cellphone if you win the first prize in the contest. The results will be announced in public immediately.

All participants are required to hand in their request forms by the end of June. In the end, welcome to take part in the activity. If you have any problem, just call us at 136 × × ×, or email us at × × ×@163.com.

Students' Union

【参考译文】

通知

学生会决定举办一场英语演讲比赛来欢迎新生。比赛将于7月28日举行，每位参赛者的最长演讲时间为十分钟。此外，七位英语专业的教授受邀担任评委。当然，奖品也很有吸引力，如果你在演讲中获得第一名，你将会得到一部手机。比赛结果会当场公布。

所有参赛者必须在六月底前递交申请表格。最后，欢迎大家参加本次活动。如有任何问题，请致电136 × × ×，或发邮件至 × × ×@163.com。

学生会

7. 备忘录

Directions:

Write a memo in about 100 words on behalf of the Students' Union to call on students to join in the volunteer activities of supporting education in remote areas.

参考范文

TO: All students of Chongqing University

FROM: Students' Union

DATE: June 20, 2019

SUBJECT: Volunteer Activities of Supporting Education in Remote Areas

At the end of the semester, we plan to organize meaningful activities of supporting education in remote areas, which are about in Sichuan and Guizhou provinces. Activities are scheduled on June 20, 2019, which include imparting kids knowledge, going to their homes to know about their living conditions and letting them know the importance of endeavors.

It is regarded as a good opportunity to show our love and know more about the living environment in remote areas. Fifty volunteers are needed. If you are willing and have time to take part in our activities, please come to the office of the Students' Union on the third floor of Yifu Building.

【参考译文】

收文人：重庆大学全体学生

发文人：学生会

日期：2019 年 6 月 20 日

主题：支持偏远地区教育的志愿活动

在本学期结束之际，我们计划组织一场有意义的活动，即支持偏远地区的教育发展，地点是在四川省和贵州省。这个活动定在 2019 年 6 月 20 日。活动包括教孩子们知识，去他们家中了解他们的生活情况，以及让他们知道努力的重要性。

这是一次展示我们的爱心、了解更多关于偏远地区的生活环境的好机会。我们需要 50 名志愿者。如果你愿意并有时间参加我们的活动，请到逸夫楼三楼学生会办公室报名。

8. 简历

Directions:

Suppose you are going to graduate from the university. Write a resume in about 100 words to apply for a job.

Do not use your own name. Use “Li Mei” instead.

参考范文

RESUME

Personal Data

Name: Li Mei

Sex: Female

Major: English

Date of Birth: June 26, 1990

Place of Birth: Zhoukou City, Henan Province

Telephone: 136 × × ×

Email: LiMei@163.com

Hobbies: Listening to music, reading and dancing

Foreign Languages: English and Japanese

Objective: To work as a teacher in a high school

Education

2008—2012	Studying at Shanghai University	Bachelor of English
2005—2008	Studying at Zhoukou No. 1 High School	
2002—2005	Studying at Zhoukou No. 7 Middle School	

Work Experience

2009 Teaching in New Oriental Training School

Special Skills and Technical Qualifications

Professional skills in English teaching

TEM-8 certificate

【参考译文】

简历

个人信息

姓名：李梅

性别：女

专业：英语

生日：1990 年 6 月 26 日

出生地：河南省周口市

电话：136×××

电子邮箱：LiMei@163.com

爱好：听音乐、阅读及跳舞

外语：英语、日语

目标：高中教师

教育经历

2008—2012　在上海大学学习　　　英语学士学位

2005—2008　在周口第一高级中学学习

2002—2005　在周口第七中学学习

工作经历

2009　　　在新东方培训学校任教

特殊技能和技术资格

英语教学职业技能

英语专业八级证书

9. 投诉信

Directions:

Suppose you have found something wrong with the electronic dictionary that you bought from an online store the other day. Write an email to the customer service center to

1) make a complaint, and

2) demand a prompt solution.

You should write about 100 words on ANSWER SHEET 2.

Do not sign your own name at the end of the letter. Use "Zhang Wei" instead.

Do not write the address.

参考范文

Dear Sir or Madam,

I am a customer who bought an electronic dictionary from your online store. Now, I write the letter to tell you that there exist certain flaws in the dictionary.

Firstly, when I received it, I found that its surface had been scratched, so I supposed it had been used or at least been unpacked, which made me feel upset. Secondly, some of the keys on the keyboard do not work properly. Under these circumstances, I feel that you did not keep your promise posted on the homepage of your online store.

I strongly request that effective measures should be taken to solve my problem. I will appreciate it very much if you can either exchange a new one for me or refund my money in full. I am looking forward to hearing from you soon.

Sincerely yours,

Zhang Wei

【参考译文】

亲爱的先生 / 女士：

我在贵公司网店买了一本电子词典。我写信是为了告诉您这本词典存在一些问题。

首先，当我收到它时，我发现它的表面已被划坏，所以我猜想它可能被使用过，或至少被人打开过，这让我感到很失望。其次，键盘上的一些按键不能正常使用。鉴于这种情况，我认为您没有遵守在网站主页上许下的承诺。

我强烈要求贵公司采取有效的措施来解决我的问题。不管是给我换一本新的，还是给我全额退款，我都会很感谢。希望尽早收到您的来信。

您真诚的，

张伟

第二节　短文写作话题

本部分内容不分英语一和英语二。原因有二，其一，考研英语大纲英语一和英语二都明确规定会考图画图表作文；其二，有些图画作文也可能通过图表作文考查。比如英语一通过图画考过两次网络对我们生活的影响。英语二 2020 年通过图表考查了网络在我们生活中的作用。此处重点关注的是“话题”，而不是考查的形式——图画和图表。最后，我们前面已经细致讲解过图画和图表作文的具体写法，除了第一段描述图画和图表不同，其他部分大同小异。

一、人生哲理类

1. 诚信

Directions:

Write an essay based on the following table. In your essay, you should

1) describe the table briefly,

2) explain its intended meaning, and

3) give your comments.

You should write about 150 words on the ANSWER SHEET.

	遵守诚信道德，不能欺骗别人	可以欺骗对方，但只是为了保护自己隐私而不是想伤害别人	网络是虚拟的，谁也看不见，欺骗很正常	说不清楚
人数（人）	111	242	92	5
百分比	24.67%	53.78%	20.44%	1.11%

某高校对大学生网络诚信现状调查

参考范文

According to the table, 53.78 percent of youngsters on campus argue that they can cheat others just for their personal benefits. At the same time, 20.44 percent of them argue that cheating can be accepted as normal because Internet belongs to a virtual world. The chart, **in as obvious a manner as possible, aims at informing us of the significance of** honesty.

Definitely, no one can deny the importance of honesty. It is conducive to the harmony of human relationships. By being honest, we are more likely to win others' trust and support even when we do something wrong and reduce unnecessary doubt when we express ourselves. **To further illustrate it, I would like to take George Washington as an example.** When he was a boy, he chopped down a cherry tree and chose to tell his father the truth. He built an image of integrity and won respect and trust from his people later.

Under no circumstances could we ignore the importance of integrity. When stuck in an embarrassing situation, we should remind ourselves that dishonesty and deception can merely win short-term trust, and that only with honesty can we build a durable and steady relationship.

【参考译文】

根据表格，有 53.78% 的大学生认为为了个人的利益，他们可以欺骗别人。与此同时，20.44% 的人认为欺骗是正常的、可以接受的，因为互联网属于虚拟的世界。这张图表以尽可能明显的方式告诉我们诚实的重要性。

当然，没有人能否认诚实的重要性。诚实有助于人际关系的和谐。通过诚实待人，我们更有可能赢得别人的信任和支持，即便是我们做错了事情。当我们表达自己的时候，也能减少不必要的怀疑。为了进一步说明诚实的重要性，我想以乔治·华盛顿为例。当他还是一个小男孩时，他曾经砍倒了一棵樱桃树，却选择告诉他的父亲真相，后来他塑造了一个诚实的形象，赢得了人民的尊敬和信任。

在任何情况下，我们都不能忽视诚信的重要性。当我们陷入尴尬的境地时，我们应该提醒自己，撒谎和欺骗只能赢得短期的信任。只有通过诚实，我们才能建立一个持久和稳定的关系。

2. 努力

Directions:

Study the following picture carefully and write an essay in which you should

1) describe the picture,

2) interpret the meaning of the picture, and

3) make your comments.

You should write 160-200 words neatly on the ANSWER SHEET.

参考范文

At the first glance, the caricature shows a sharp contrast—a young man, with heart and soul, is struggling to study in front of the table. On the contrary, another one is half-hearted when he is pretending to read a book. **It tells us that** we have to make strenuous efforts whenever we want to be successful in a particular field. How can a person achieve his ultimate goal without continuous practice and attempts?

There are numerous cases around us to list. However, the most suitable one is about mountaineering. Nobody is a born mountain climber. He can only become a skilled one after countless injuries. The scenery at the mountaintop is fantastic, but the road to the summit is always rough, full of hardships and dangers. Isn't scientific research the same? Countless sleepless nights and thousands of failures seem to be a normal part of a scientist's life. Only a few of them can make great scientific breakthroughs, and these a few people are the most persevering.

If a person intends to live an idle life, and waits for God to put something in his hands, he will achieve nothing but poverty. As university students, we should know clearly that there's no such thing as a free lunch in the world. Only by hard endeavors can dreams be achieved.

【参考译文】

乍一看，这幅漫画构成鲜明的对照。一个年轻人全心全意地在桌前学习。相反，另一个在心不在焉地假装看书。它告诉我们，只要我们想在某一特定领域取得成功，就必须付出艰苦的努力。没有不断的实践和尝试，一个人怎么会达成他的最终目标呢？

我们周围有很多案例可以列举。然而，最适合的是登山运动。没有人是天生的登山手，人们只有在受过无数次伤之后才能成为一个熟练的登山好手。山顶的风景很美，但通往山顶的道路总是崎岖不平，充满了艰难险阻。科学研究不也一样吗？无数的不眠之夜、成千上万甚至更多次的失败是科学家的家常便饭。只有少数人能在科学上取得重大突破，而这些少数人都是最坚韧不拔的。

所以在我看来，如果一个人打算过一种无所事事的生活，等待上帝把东西放在他的手中，他将一无所有，只有贫穷。作为大学生，我们应该清楚地知道，世界上没有免费的午餐，只有通过艰苦的努力才能实现梦想。

3. 欲速则不达

Directions:

Study the following picture carefully and write an essay in which you should

1) describe the picture,

2) interpret the meaning of the picture, and

3) make your comments.

You should write 160-200 words neatly on the ANSWER SHEET.

参考范文

What can be found in the cartoon is that a farmer with a hat on his head, standing in the field on a hot day and sweating, is pulling up seedlings to help them grow. **The picture does reflect a thought-provoking social phenomenon**—things need to develop but helping them grow can never be beneficial. It can only hinder their growth and even kill them.

Almost every Chinese is quite familiar with the story. Actually, in the general routine of study and career, we should follow the law of nature. It is understandable for us to dream of quick success and then take immediate actions to turn it into reality, but we cannot be too hasty. There existed a well-known writer in Japan who once said, "Success needs time, which means a process instead of a moment matter." If all teenagers and youngsters are in a hurry, quality will always suffer, making it more difficult for them to achieve the aim.

Up to now, we come to understand the meaning of the old saying "Haste makes waste" better. We should break our great plan into small parts, analyze the features of each part and carry it out step by step. When we follow the natural pace of development, success will be in our hands. When water flows, a channel is formed.

【参考译文】

在这幅漫画中可以看到的是，在一个炎热的日子里，一个农民头上戴着一顶帽子，站在田地里汗流浃背，正在拔高树苗以帮助它们生长。这幅图确实反映了一个发人深省的社会现象——事情需要发展进步，但帮助它们生长永远不会有好处。这只能阻碍它们成长，甚至杀死它们。

几乎每个中国人都对这个故事很熟悉。事实上，在日常的学习和工作中，我们应该遵循自然规律。我们梦想迅速成功，然后立即采取行动把它变成现实，这是可以理解的，但我们不能操之过急。日本曾经有一位著名的作家说过："成功需要时间，这是一个过程，而不是一瞬间的事情。"如果所有的青少年总是匆匆忙忙，质量就会受到影响，这就使得他们很难达成目标。

现在我们可以更好地理解"欲速则不达"这句老话的含义。我们应该把伟大的计划分解成小的部分，分析每个部分的特点，并逐步实施。当我们遵循自然的发展速度时，我们就会取得成功。这就叫水到渠成。

4. 困难

Directions:

Study the following picture carefully and write an essay in which you should

1) describe the picture,

2) interpret the meaning of the picture, and

3) give an example.

You should write 160-200 words neatly on the ANSWER SHEET.

参考范文

What can be seen in the cartoon is that a man both young and timid, sitting on the ground with a frightened expression, is faced with a big word "difficulty". **The message conveyed in the picture seems to be that** difficulties are really scary for quite a few young people.

Conquering the fear can actually bring huge benefits. One of my intimate friends' story can really be **a typical case in point**. He was a teacher in a middle school years ago, **but** the job was not his favorite. **In fact,** what he really wanted was to be a lawyer, but to become a lawyer is extremely difficult. **After days of consideration**, he resigned from the school bravely, losing his admirable status as a teacher at last. It was through his hard endeavors that his dream to be a lawyer came true. **The story, as can be seen, strikes us that difficulties will be good opportunities if we face them bravely.** So just try what you want. If the young just wait because they are afraid of troubles, what will happen to them? They can achieve nothing throughout their life.

So what can we do when facing challenges and frustrations? For one thing, responsible schools should encourage their students to face difficulties bravely which are quite necessary for their growth. **Then as a brave sea swallow, I just want to say, let the storm become more violent.**

【参考译文】

从漫画中可以看出，一个胆小的年轻人满脸恐惧地坐在地上，面对着一个巨大的词语“困难”。这个图片传达的信息是，很多年轻人害怕困难。

战胜恐惧其实能带来巨大的好处。我一个好朋友的故事就是典型的例子。几年前他是一名中学教师，但那份工作不是他最喜欢的。事实上，他真正想要的是成为一名律师，但是成为律师十分困难。经过几天的考虑，他勇敢地辞去了学校的职务，最终失去了令人羡慕的教师职位。正是通过他的努力，他当律师的梦想得以实现。正如我们所看到的，这个故事告诉我们，如果我们勇敢面对困难，那困难便会成为机会。如果年轻人害怕麻烦，都在等待，他们会怎么样呢？他们一生都将一事无成。

那么我们在面对挑战和挫折的时候又能做些什么呢？一方面，负责任的学校应该鼓励学生勇敢地面对困难，这些困难是成长所必要的。另一方面，作为一只勇敢的海燕，我只想说，让暴风雨来得更猛烈些吧！

5. 自信

Directions:

Write an essay of 160-200 words based on the following drawing. In your essay, you should

1) describe the drawing briefly,

2) explain its intended meaning, and then

3) support your view with an example/examples.

You should write neatly on ANSWER SHEET 2.

参考范文

What can be obviously seen is that in the picture, there is a sharp contrast between the thoughts of the goalkeeper and the ball player. The former exaggerates the goal and minimizes himself in his mind while the latter exaggerates the goalkeeper. Actually, both the goalkeeper and the goal are just in normal size. **The picture does reflect a thought-provoking social phenomenon—confidence should be deemed strikingly important by the majority of human beings.**

Difficulties, undoubtedly, are in the pathway of everyone. To overcome them, we must at first make correct judgment on the situation, which is based on confidence, courage and rational thinking. For example, when I was in the middle school, our school basketball team once played against another team which was very famous in our city. Every player in our team felt that the only result would be our team's failure. As a result, we didn't even make any preparations beforehand. Of course, the result was—our failure. One year later, we met the same team in a match again. This time, our teacher inspired us with confidence and hope. Then, we made a detailed plan and we practiced a lot, and out of everybody's imagination, we finally won. So confidence, as the picture and my example reflect, is the first step to success.

In conclusion, if we want to succeed in handling the difficult things, we must have confidence in ourselves, judge the situation rationally and be courageous enough to keep trying. Besides, the elderly should educate their kids, letting them know the necessity of a good mentality.

【参考译文】

从这幅图中明显可以看出，守门员和球员的想法形成鲜明的对比。前者放大了球门，在心里贬低自己，而后者却放大了守门员。事实上，守门员和球门的尺寸都很正常。这幅图确实反映了一个发人深省的社会现象——自信，大多数人应该意识到它是极其重要的。

毫无疑问，每个人都会遇到困难。要克服这些困难，首先我们必须基于信心、勇气和理性的思考对形势做出正确的判断。比如，当我在初中的时候，我们学校的篮球队和另一个在我们城市非常有名的球队比赛，我们队中的每个人都觉得唯一的结果就是我们队失败。因此，我们事先都没有做任何准备。结果当然是我们失败了。一年后，我们在一场比赛中再次遇到了那支球队。这一次，老师用信心和希望激励我们。然后我们制定了一个详细的计划，并且进行大量练习，出乎每个人的想象的是，最终我们赢了。因此，正如这幅图和我的例子所反映的，自信是成功的第一步。

总之，如果我们想成功地解决困难的事情，就应该自信、理性地判断形势，并有足够的勇气不断尝试。此外，年长者应该教育孩子们，让他们知道良好心态的必要性。

6. 压力

Directions:

Study the following picture carefully and write an essay of 160-200 words.

Your essay should meet the requirements below:

1) describe the picture, interpret its meaning, and

2) point out the implications in our life.

Your essay must be written clearly on the ANSWER SHEET.

参考范文

It is the vivid cartoon that presents us a sharp contrast between two different kinds of attitudes people hold in face of stress. The former is defeated by some misfortunes or crises when confronted with difficulties, but the latter optimistically fights against such events, sitting easily on the mountain of stress. Pressure, indeed, should be deemed as a motive instead of an adverse factor.

In the face of adversity, the optimist takes a positive attitude. **A case in point is** Frank, one of my friends, whose fate sounds so legendary. He never gives up in his life. If something goes wrong, he acts quickly, reaching out for advice, forming a new plan of action, and looking for solutions. He will think that he is much better than the facts would justify—and more often than not, that is what keeps him alive and active, as evidenced in many successful medical treatments. He actually recognizes that stress is nothing but a natural part of his routine life. What determines our choice of "being negative" or "being optimistic", indeed, will be our attitudes towards life, not the stress itself.

If we hold an optimistic attitude, we can change the current situations and walk on a wider road. Maybe boys and girls in our contemporary society can well be involved in numerous frustrations to develop a good mentality. **Only by realizing the strong points of stress can we overcome them confidently and achieve great success.**

【参考译文】

这幅生动的图片呈现给我们的是人们在面对压力时持有的两种形成鲜明对比的不同态度。前者在遇到困难时被一些不幸和危机打败，而后者则乐观地与这些事情抗争，轻松地坐在压力大山上。事实上，压力应该被当成动力，而不是不利因素。

面对逆境，乐观主义者采取积极的态度。举个例子，我的一个朋友叫弗兰克，他的命运听起来很传奇，但他在生活中从来没有放弃过。如果出现问题，他会迅速采取行动，寻求建议，寻找解决方案，并制定新的行动计划。他会认为自己比事实证明的要好得多——这通常正是他能保持活力的原因，许多成功的医学治疗案例都证明了这一点。事实上，他认识到压力只是他日常生活中很自然的一部分。决定我们选择“消极”还是“积极”的是我们对生活的态度，而不是压力本身。

如果我们保持乐观的态度，我们可以改变现状，走在一条更宽广的道路上。也许在我们当代社会，男孩和女孩可以在更多的挫折中练就一个好的心态。只有认识到压力的优点，我们才能自信地克服它们，取得巨大成功。

7. 合作

Directions:

Study the following picture carefully and write an essay to

1) describe the picture,

2) interpret its meaning, and

3) give your comments.

You should write 160-200 words neatly on the ANSWER SHEET.

参考范文

What can be seen in the cartoon is that a few individuals who represent all the partners in an organization, sitting in a long boat, are rowing together in a competition. **The purpose of the drawer, in my judgment, is to show that teamwork really plays an essential role in our career and study.**

Why do many people believe so? There exist quite a few reasons here. Undoubtedly, it is teamwork that keeps us continually doing something valuable and admirable in spite of difficulties and discouragements. Besides, cooperating with others not only makes us full of energy to face the coming challenges and competitions but also offers us the foundation for the coming success. **Maybe the most suitable example to validate the idea is as follows**. A person who is assigned various assignments along the production lines will make a mess just because no one can be proficient in all the things. Only by cooperating with others can we put our capacities into full play and can we be winners in the society.

It is, therefore, necessary that measures should be adopted to be cooperative. **For one thing**, we should be sensible enough to accept other people's opinions and suggestions. For another, it demands us to be active in taking a tougher job and always helpful and honest to other people. **Only through these manners can we complete jobs rapidly and effectively.**

【参考译文】

从这幅漫画可以看出，在一个组织中，代表所有人的几个人坐在一条长船上，在比赛中一起划船。在我看来，这幅漫画是为了表明团队合作在我们的职业和学习中确实起到了至关重要的作用。

为什么很多人对此深信不疑呢？有很多原因。毫无疑问，团队合作会使我们不断地做一些有价值和令人尊敬的事情，尽管会遇到困难和挫折。此外，与他人合作不仅让我们充满活力地去面对未来的挑战和竞争，而且为我们未来的成功奠定了基础。下面可能是验证这个想法最合适的例子。一个人被分配到生产线上做各种工作，他会搞得一团糟，因为没有人能精通所有的事情。只有通过与他人合作，我们才能充分发挥最大的能力，并成为社会的赢家。

因此，必须采取措施来进行合作。一方面，我们应该明智地接受别人的想法和建议。另一方面，它要求我们积极地接受一份更艰难的工作，经常乐于助人，诚信待人。只有通过这些方式，我们才能迅速、有效地完成工作。

8. 幸福、快乐

Directions:

Study the following picture carefully and write an essay to

1) describe the picture,

2) interpret its meaning, and

3) give your suggestions as to the best way to find happiness.

You should write 160-200 words neatly on the ANSWER SHEET.

参考范文

What looks quite self-evident in the picture is that a handsome young man is contemplating the true meaning of happiness. **The symbolic meaning keeps so conspicuous that what on earth happiness is.** Is it making more money, wining true love, or being in good health?

It is happiness that seems difficult to define. Those who have a relatively easy and comfortable life are sometimes depressed. Nevertheless, we may also have friends who have suffered a great deal but generally remain happy. **The best case is my uncle who** has always suffered a lot in his life. Although he was born in a poor family, he still felt satisfied because there were his beloved families around him; then in the middle-age, he lost his wife who died of a serious disease. Still my uncle is not defeated and bravely leads a delightful life. His famous words are that if you want to be happy, you will be.

Happiness, in my judgment, proves an attitude. It lies in the effort to be happy. People sometimes go to extremes and frantically pursue money, power and social status, which are all symbols of success but they are not always the elements of happiness. Perhaps if one really wants to possess happiness, he should just enjoy his current situation.

【参考译文】

从这幅图中，我们可以很明显地看出，一个既年轻又英俊的男孩正在思考幸福的真正含义。图画的象征意义如此引人注目，幸福究竟是什么呢？是赚更多的钱、赢得真爱，还是拥有健康的身体？

幸福似乎很难定义。那些生活相对安逸的人有时会感到沮丧。然而，我们也可能有朋友遭受了很大的痛苦，但总是很快乐。最好的例子是我叔叔，他生活中一直在吃苦头。他出生在一个贫穷的家庭，但他仍然感到满足，因为他爱的家人在他身边；然后在中年，他失去了身患重疾的妻子。然而我的叔叔并没有被打败，他勇敢地过着快乐的生活。他的名言是“如果你想快乐，你就会快乐”。

依我判断，幸福是一种态度。幸福在于为幸福而奋斗。人们有时会走极端，疯狂地追求金钱、权力和社会地位，这些都是成功的象征，但并非永远都是幸福的要素。也许，如果一个人真的想拥有幸福，他就应该享受当下。

9. 诚实

Directions:

Study the following drawing carefully, and write an essay in which you should

1) describe the drawing,

2) interpret its meaning, and

3) support your view with examples.

You should write 160-200 words neatly on the ANSWER SHEET.

参考范文

What is portrayed in the cartoon is that a celebrity in the television, looking rather wise and knowledgeable, is making false advertising. To make matters worse, he contends that advertisements have to be exaggerated. **The drawing mirrors a common social phenomenon which is really thought-provoking.** Honesty in business really plays an essential role in the process of sales.

There exists strong evidence showing that integrity should be the uppermost in our thoughts. Otherwise, our society is bound to deteriorate. In everyday life, humans suffer instead of enjoying the civilization and happiness of modern society because the society is filled with dishonesty and deception. **The most typical case here is about** unhealthy foods which have done harm to our bodies or even killed many innocent kids. If the current situation were not regulated or limited, human beings would pay a heavy price in the near future.

We must take counter-measures to settle the issue so as to ensure a healthy society for all. Most importantly, laws must be established to punish those who misbehave in terms of credibility severely. Besides, as law-abiding citizens, we should refuse dishonesty in business from now on.

【参考译文】

这幅漫画所描述的是，电视里一个看起来很聪明和博学的名人正在做虚假广告。更糟的是，他认为广告就得夸张。这幅画反映了一个很普遍、很发人深省的社会现象。商业诚信在销售过程中起着至关重要的作用。

有力的证据表明，在我们的思想中，诚信应该是最重要的。否则，我们的社会必定会恶化。在日常生活中，因为现代社会充满了谎言和欺骗，人们非但没有享受文明和幸福，反而在遭受痛苦。这里最典型的例子就是，不健康的食物对我们的身体有害，甚至杀死了许多无辜的孩子。如果不对目前的情况加以管理和限制，人类将在不久的将来付出沉重的代价。

为确保所有人生活在一个健康的社会中，我们必须采取应对措施来解决这个问题。最重要的是，必须制定法律来严惩那些在诚信方面行为不端的人。此外，作为一个守法的公民，我们应该从现在开始拒绝商业欺诈行为。

10. 目标

Directions:

Study the following drawing carefully and write an essay in which you should

1) describe the drawing,

2) interpret its meaning, and

3) support your view with examples.

You should write 160-200 words neatly on ANSWER SHEET 2.

终点又是新起点

参考范文

What looks quite self-evident in the cartoon is that a boy who is heavily sweating, running on annular tracks, has reached the finishing line which is also a new beginning. **Though this picture looks simple, the meaning behind proves quite far-reaching**—if one tends to make constant progress, he will never rest on laurels but keep forging ahead.

Such stimulating stories are not rare, yet the following one about Picasso is definitely typical. As a well-known artist, he greatly influenced the path of 20th-century art. But what impresses me most is not the notable success he achieved but his enterprising spirit. Besides the title of "the greatest artist of the 20th century", he is claimed as the youngest artist in the world because he unremittingly pursued and explored new styles of painting all his life. After producing his most famous post-impressionist style, he later developed many other styles. Even at the last moment of his life he was producing a new painting.

So there is never destination in one's life. What we, as youngsters on campus, can do is to pursue our dreams and keep moving in face of any difficulties. **That is the only way to make our lives brilliant and glorious.**

【参考译文】

从在这幅漫画中可以明显地看到，一个汗流浃背、在环形跑道上奔跑的男孩，已经到达终点，继而又开始新的征程。虽然这幅图看起来很简单，但背后的意义很深远——如果一个人总是不断进步，那他一定会继续前进，而不是故步自封。

这样令人振奋的故事并不少见，而下面关于毕加索的故事绝对是典型的。作为一位著名的艺术家，他的作品对 20 世纪的艺术道路产生了重大的影响。但给我印象最深的不是他所取得的显著成就，而是他的进取精神。除了"20 世纪最伟大的艺术家"名号，他还被称为世界上最年轻的艺术家，因为他一生都在不懈地追求和探索新的绘画风格。在创作了他最著名的后印象派风格之后，他又发展了许多其他风格，甚至在生命的最后一刻，他还在创作一幅新画。

所以人生旅途没有终点。作为年轻的大学生，我们应该做的是追逐梦想，并且面对任何困难都要坚持前行。这就是使我们的生活灿烂辉煌的唯一途径。

二、社会热点话题

1. 环保

Directions:

Write an essay of 160-200 words based on the following drawing. In your essay, you should

1) describe the drawing briefly,

2) explain its intended meaning, and

3) give your comments.

You should write neatly on the ANSWER SHEET.

参考范文

What looks quite worrying is that in the cartoon, sadly, a bird that has lost its home, standing on an ax which has been used to cut down the trees, is looking around the barren forest and shedding tears. **The purpose of the picture is to remind us that** environmental protection, **is exceedingly necessary**.

To clarify the issue, I would like you to share my views. As is known to us, such misconduct including cutting trees or destroying meadow lands will cause serious consequences. In the first place, there remains no doubt that lack of environment protection awareness will destroy the ecosystem of all creatures, with the result that our descendants may be deprived of the opportunities of enjoying the pleasure of being in contact with the real nature. In the second place, the environmental protection awareness is a mirror of national civilization while people's deeds are the reflection of national morality. So, the climate of immorality will be established if we let the worrying situation go unchanged.

In my opinion, we should get moving to stop the disturbing trend and raise standards of morality. What's more, to retrieve the worrisome situation entails our government's legal measures against the misdeeds, our media's publicity of the concept of environment protection and everyone's endeavors. **All in all, we should bear in mind that only when everyone establishes the notion of environment protection can we make the earth better and more sustainable.**

【参考译文】

在这幅漫画中，令人担忧的是一只失去了家的鸟悲伤地站在被用来砍树的斧子上，环顾着光秃秃的森林，并且流下了眼泪。这幅图提醒我们保护环境是非常必要的。

为了阐明这个问题，我将分享一些观点。众所周知，像砍树、破坏草地这些行径会导致严重的后果。首先，毫无疑问，缺乏环保意识会破坏所有物种的生态系统，从而导致我们的后代丧失享受和大自然亲近的机会。其次，环保意识是国家文明程度的一面镜子，人们的行为是国家道德水平的反映。所以，如果令人担忧的情况没有改变，不道德的风气将会产生。

在我看来，我们应该采取行动，阻止这种不利的趋势并且提高人们的道德标准。此外，为了改变这种令人担忧的情况，政府需要立法，抵制错误的行为，媒体需要对环境保护概念做宣传，以及每个人都要为之努力。总之，我们应该牢记在心，只有我们每个人建立了环保意识，才能使我们的地球变得更好以及更能可持续发展。

2. 教育

Directions:

Write an essay of 160-200 words based on the following pictures. In your essay, you should

1) describe the pictures briefly,

2) interpret the meaning, and

3) give your comments.

You should write neatly on the ANSWER SHEET.

与其只提要求，不如做个榜样

参考范文

What could be seen clearly is that in the left cartoon, "Son, go and study hard!" shouts the father who is watching TV alone, sitting on the couch and smoking. The boy actually can't focus on his homework at all. While **in the right one**, both the father and the boy are concentrating on their work. **The symbolic meaning is quite obvious**—the actions of parents speak louder than their words.

A great majority of people might agree that the issue has its deep roots as follows. The primary element is that parents indeed play important roles in the growth of their children. Parents can teach children by setting good examples in their daily life. If parents fail to meet their requirements, how can they ask their children to do so? **Moreover**, in children's view, their parents are always perfect, and they usually follow suit, especially when they're young. So it's of great significance to set good examples for children. Just as an old saying in China goes, parents are surely the most suitable teachers in the life of their kids.

In conclusion, it is high time to place great importance on the way parents educate kids. Parents cannot just tell their children what to do, but instead they should set good examples. Only in this manner can children feel that they're respected and can handle matters according to their parents' requirements.

【参考译文】

在左边这幅漫画中，我们可以清楚地看到，"儿子，你给我好好学习！"一个坐在沙发上抽烟、独自看电视的父亲说道。那个男孩实际上一点儿也不能集中精力写作业。但在右边的漫画中，父亲和儿子都在集中精力做事。其象征意义非常明显，即父母的行为重于语言。

很多人都会认为这个问题有如下所示的深刻根源。最重要的因素是，父母确实在孩子的成长过程中扮演着重要角色。在日常生活中，父母能通过树立良好的榜样来教育孩子。如果父母自己达不到他们对孩子的要求，他们怎么能要求孩子这么做？此外，在孩子看来，他们的父母总是完美的。父母做什么，他们就会跟着学，尤其是他们还年轻的时候。所以，为孩子树立良好的榜样非常重要。就像中国的一句古语所说，父母无疑是孩子一生中最好的老师。

总之，是时候重视父母教育孩子的方式了。父母不能只告诉孩子应该做什么，他们也应该自己做出良好榜样。只有用这种方法，孩子们才能感觉到他们受到了尊重，并且能根据父母的要求处理问题。

3. 房价

Directions:

Write an essay based on the following chart. In your essay, you should

1) interpret the meaning of the chart, and

2) give your comments.

You should write about 150 words on the ANSWER SHEET.

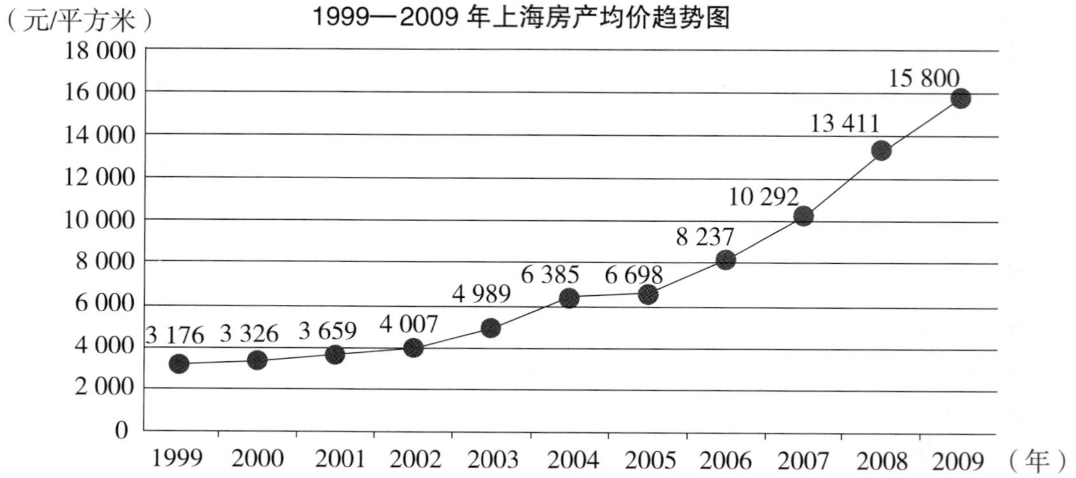

参考范文

In the simple chart, the price of housing estate in Shanghai rocketed to 15,800 RMB per square in 2009, **which leaves a deep impression on readers simply because it took only a decade. This chart, as a matter of fact, desires to draw our attention towards the issue of** real estate industry, **which has been brought into the limelight for a long time**.

If we let this situation continues as it is, we will never know what will happen to the real estate industry **in the future**. Nowadays, our real estate industry has experienced such an unprecedented boom that all of us begin to consider it as too hot in one way or another. The average price has been soaring for quite a few years. In some big cities, it seems to be out of control—it has been nearly impossible for the common local citizens to afford a satisfactory apartment in the downtown area. Consequently, how to create a healthier and more reasonable property market has been a problem of great importance. If the price continues to soar, what will happen in the future? More Chinese will lead a stressful life.

I believe, among all the possible measures, the following ones are the most appropriate. In the first place, the legislators should establish a series of policies so as to curb speculation and thus keep the price of houses at a reasonable level. In the second place, more economically affordable housing should be built so as to relieve the burden of common citizens. **Only through the joint efforts can China**

realize the healthy development of housing market.

【参考译文】

图表显示，只用了 10 年时间，上海房价迅速增长到 15 800 元每平方米，这给读者留下了深刻的印象。事实上，这个图表想要唤起我们对房地产业问题的关注，这个问题已经被关注很长时间了。

如果我们让这种情况继续下去，我们不知道房地产业将来会发生什么。现在，我们的房地产业经历了空前的繁荣，以至于我们所有人都认为它在某种程度上太热门了。房子平均价格在几年之内猛增。在一些大城市，它看起来已经失控——对普通市民来说，在市中心买一套舒适的住宅几乎是不可能的。因此，如何建立一个更健康、更合理的房地产市场已经是非常重要的问题。如果房价继续增长，将来会发生什么？更多中国人会过上“压力山大”的生活。

在所有可能的措施中，我相信下面的这些是最合适的。首先，立法者应该制定一系列政策来抑制投机行为，从而把房价维持在一个合理的水平。其次，应该建造更多的经济适用房，来减轻普通市民的负担。只有通过共同的努力，中国才能实现房地产市场的健康发展。

4. 孩子教育

Directions:

Study the following pictures carefully and write an essay in which you should

1) describe the two pictures,

2) interpret their meanings, and

3) point out the reasons for such a phenomenon.

You should write 160-200 words neatly on the ANSWER SHEET.

父亲和儿子的生活

参考范文

In the vivid cartoon, there is a sharp contrast between the father and the son. In the former picture, the old father is working hard in the field, bending over and sweating heavily. **On the contrary, in the latter one**, his son is squandering money on social contact, food and daily facilities. **The art works are to draw our attention to the issue of** hardship of the elderly and ease of the young.

The reasons for this phenomenon, in my judgment, come down to one essential point—failure of both family and school education. For one thing, quite a lot of Chinese parents spoil their children. All parents' love for children is the same, but the difference is in the way of showing it. Many parents hope that their children will have a bright future, which, in their eyes, means key universities, hot majors, good salaries and so on. So they try their best to satisfy their children's demands instead of teaching them to struggle for future with their own hands. For another, centering on exam marks, schools also fail, to a large extent, to impart moral standards to the students, especially the conception of self-reliance and hardwork.

So it is urgent that the phenomenon described in the pictures above should be relieved. For one thing, a reform in our current education system is not only necessary but also urgent. Besides, for a young adult, it is quite necessary to know the uneasy life of our parents. **So should not all the conscientious Chinese pay attention to the issue?**

【参考译文】

在这幅生动的漫画中，父亲和儿子之间存在着鲜明的对比。在前一幅图中，老父亲正在田野里辛勤工作，弯着腰、大汗淋漓。相反，在后一幅图中，他的儿子把钱浪费在社交、食物和日常所需的设备上。这两幅图是要引起我们对老年人的艰辛和年轻人的安逸的关注。

根据我的判断，造成这种现象的原因归结为一个根本问题——家庭教育和学校教育的失败。一方面，相当多的中国父母溺爱孩子。所有父母对孩子的爱都是一样的，但表现出来的方式却不同。很多家长太希望孩子有一个光明的未来，在他们看来，这意味着重点大学、热门专业、高工资等。所以他们尽量满足孩子们的要求，而不是教他们用自己的双手为未来奋斗。另一方面，以考试成绩为中心的学校教育在很大程度上也未能向孩子们传授道德标准，尤其是自力更生和艰苦奋斗的观念。

因此，迫切需要消除上面图片中描述的现象。一方面，当前教育体制的改革不仅是必要的，而且是迫切的。此外，对于一个年轻人来说，了解我们父母生活的不易是很有必要的。难道不是所有有良知的中国人都应该关注这个问题吗？

5. 社会公德

Directions:

Study the following picture carefully and write an essay in which you should

1) describe the picture,

2) give the reasons of such a phenomenon, and

3) list possible solutions.

You should write 160-200 words neatly on the ANSWER SHEET.

“嘘，能小声点吗？”

参考范文

What can be found clearly in the cartoon is that a middle-aged man is talking loudly on the phone as if he were the only person in the waiting room. **At this very moment**, the passengers sitting beside him are feeling quite annoyed. The lady is dropping off because she is exhausted. **The picture has revealed a current social phenomenon that** social ethics are not followed in public.

We cannot help asking why quite a few people behave in such a way. On the one hand, they have been brought up in such a way as to only take their own interests into consideration whenever anything arises, which is by no means what parents and teachers expect, but this is largely the consequence of today’s education. Although years of teaching in class and family may tell them how to do, real life practice may be more influential. On the other hand, they have been brought up in such a way as not to take rules and regulations seriously. Therefore, in their belief, rules and regulations only restrain those silly people, and the violation of them can be exciting—they just want to show off even at the cost of others' benefits.

It is to relieve the current situation that all of us have a long way to go. First, teachers and parents should act in such a way to teach children to take others into consideration whenever they take action. Second, the authorities should severely punish those who violate rules and regulations. **It is high time that we fought for the end of the undesirable phenomenon of social ethics.**

【参考译文】

从这幅漫画中可以清楚地看到，一个中年人打电话时大声说话，好像他是候车室里唯一的一个人。此时此刻，坐在他旁边的乘客感觉很烦恼。由于劳累，女士在打瞌睡。这幅图揭示了当前的一种社会现象，即人们在公共场合不遵守社会公德。

我们不禁要问，为什么很多人的行为都是这样的？一方面，他们在成长过程中，在任何情况下都只会考虑自己的利益，这绝不是父母和老师的初衷，但这在很大程度上是当今教育的后果。尽管多年的学校和家庭教育可能会告诉他们怎么做，但现实生活中的实践可能会更有影响力。另一方面，他们在成长过程中不认真对待规章制度。因此，在他们看来，规章制度只约束那些愚蠢的人，而不遵守规则令人兴奋——即使牺牲别人的利益也要炫耀自己。

为了缓解当前的局面，我们都有很长的路要走。首先，教师和家长应教育孩子在行动时考虑他人。其次，有关部门要严惩违反规章制度的人。是时候为结束这种社会公德的负面现象而奋斗了。

6. 大学生就业

Directions:

Study the following chart carefully and write an essay in which you should

1) describe the chart,

2) analyze the reasons why it is difficult for university graduates to find a job, and

3) point out the possible ways to solve the problem.

You should write about 150 words neatly on the ANSWER SHEET.

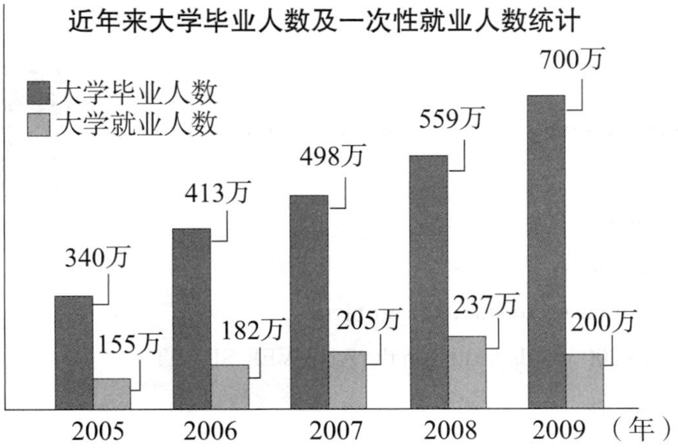

参考范文

What a worrying problem current graduates are facing! As is shown in the bar chart, the number of graduates, from the year of 2005 to 2009, rocketed to 7 million. **On the contrary**, the youngsters who can seek employment successfully, **as is shown in the chart**, grew slowly from 1.55 million to 2 million. **It is clear that the author of the chart wants to draw our attention to the difficulty** university graduates have in finding jobs.

There are many elements that can account for the phenomenon. In the first place, the enrollment expansion of universities and colleges has resulted in a great increase in the number of graduates every year, which has exceeded the increase of positions in the job market. What makes things worse is that quite a lot of students like to choose those hot majors when they enter the university and to look for jobs in big developed cities when they graduate. So it is even more difficult for them to find a suitable job. If the trend continues, what will happen to graduates in the future? They might lose hopes in their life.

The society and graduates, from my point of view, need to make joint efforts to handle this problem. On one hand, the society should continue to focus on economic development so as to provide more employment opportunities for graduates. On the other hand, students on campus really should spend more time and energy on their majors. Only in this way can we create a healthy job market.

【参考译文】

现在毕业生面临着一个多么令人担忧的问题啊！正如条形图所示，从 2005 年到 2009 年，毕业人数猛增到 700 万人。相反，能找到工作的年轻人，如图所示，从 155 万人缓慢增长到 200 万人。很明显，图画的作者想让我们关注大学毕业生就业的困难。

出现这个现象的原因有很多。首先，高校扩招导致每年毕业生人数大幅增加，超过了就业市场岗位的增长。更糟糕的是，相当多的学生在进入大学时喜欢选择那些热门的专业，毕业后喜欢在发达的大城市找工作。所以他们更难找到合适的工作。如果这一趋势继续下去，未来的毕业生会怎么样呢？他们可能会失去生活的希望。

在我看来，社会和毕业生需要携手共同努力处理这一问题。一方面，社会要继续关注经济发展，为毕业生提供更多的就业机会。另一方面，校园里的学生真的应该在他们的专业上花更多的时间和精力，只有这样我们才能创造一个健康的就业市场。

7. 虚假产品

Directions:

Study the following drawing carefully and write an essay in which you should

1) describe the drawing,

2) analyze the reasons, and

3) point out the possible ways to solve the problem.

You should write 160-200 words neatly on the ANSWER SHEET.

参考范文

The cartoon effectively draws our attention to a hot social phenomenon—fake products. In the caricature, a man who is about to buy new home appliances, holding a magnifying glass, is watching the product to see whether it is authentic or fake. **Obviously, the message conveyed in the picture is that** fake products have become exceedingly widespread in our daily life.

To clarify such a phenomenon, I would like to point out three arguments. To begin with, under modern conditions, fake products are not only quite cheap but also rather easy to be available for all people, so why bother to buy the authentic ones? In addition, the evidence that quite a few dishonest businessmen manage to make more money by illegal behavior indicates that there will be more counterfeit products flooding into our society and life. At last, there is little doubt that the lack of national supervision seems to be an indispensable factor. The less authorities interrupt such illegal action, the more pervasive those matters keep.

So what could we do when facing these fake products? For one thing, responsible governments should encourage people to buy authentic products. At the same time, the government should try to praise those honest sellers in public so that more people can learn from them. **Then as a law-abiding youngster, I just want to say,** refuse counterfeit products from now on.

【参考译文】

这幅漫画有效地吸引了我们对社会热点现象——假冒伪劣产品的关注。在漫画中，一个拿着放大镜准备买新的家用电器的人正在看产品，看它是真的还是假的。显然，图片中传达的信息是，假冒伪劣产品在我们的日常生活中变得非常普遍。

为了阐明这种现象，我想指出三个点。首先，在现代条件下，假货不仅很便宜，而且对所有的人来说都很容易买到，那么为什么还要买真货呢？此外，有证据表明，相当多的奸商通过非法行为赚了更多的钱，这意味着将会有更多的盗版产品充斥着我们的社会和生活。最后，毫无疑问，缺乏国家的监督似乎是不可或缺的因素。政府越少地干预此类非法行为，这些问题就越普遍。

那么面对这些假冒伪劣产品我们该怎么办呢？首先，负责任的政府应该鼓励人们购买正版商品，并公开表扬诚实商家的行为，这样更多的人会向他们学习。然后，作为一个守法的青少年，我只想说，从现在起拒绝盗版。

8. 电子商务、网购

Directions:

Study the following drawing carefully and write an essay in which you should

1) describe the drawing,

2) give your comments about the phenomenon, and

3) point out the possible trend.

You should write 160-200 words neatly on the ANSWER SHEET.

参考范文

What is subtly demonstrated in the above drawing is that in front of a desktop sits a fashionable lady who is staring at the screen and addicted to online shopping. As far as the lady concerned, it is cheap and convenient to shop online. However, she does not aware that there are scams behind online shopping. **The picture does reflect a thought-provoking social phenomenon.**

This picture reminds us that utmost attention should be paid to shopping online, which has exerted profound impact on people's daily life. Of course, e-commerce does have its own advantages. It can save us a lot of time and we can buy products everywhere we want as long as we can surf the Internet. However, online trading is by no means without its disadvantages. **Firstly**, the quality of products cannot be guaranteed. Online shoppers can only look at the pictures, so they cannot distinguish the quality of products. **Secondly**, online payment may reveal the user's personal information, which might be used by hackers, resulting in unnecessary economic losses. **Finally**, indulging in online shopping can also affect the emotional communication with family and friends.

In a word, it may be an inevitable trend that online shopping becomes more and more popular, so we must pay attention to protecting our personal information when shopping online. **At the same time**, we should learn to consume rationally and avoid blind and excessive consumption.

【参考译文】

上面这幅画巧妙地展示了一位时尚的女士正盯着屏幕，沉迷于网上购物。对这位女士而言，网上购物既便宜又方便。然而，她不知道网上购物背后有骗局。 这幅画确实反映了一种发人深省的社会现象。

这幅画提醒我们，应该高度重视网上购物，这对人们的日常生活产生了深远的影响。当然，电子商务确实有自己的优势。它可以让我们节省很多时间，只要可以上网，我们就可以在任何地方购买我们想要的产品。然而，网上交易绝不是没有缺点的。首先，产品质量没有保障，网购者只能看图片，因此他们不能分辨出产品质量的好坏。其次，网上付款有可能会泄露用户信息，从而被黑客利用，导致不必要的经济损失。最后，沉迷于网购还会影响与亲朋好友的感情交流。

总之，网上购物越来越受欢迎可能是一种不可避免的趋势，因此我们必须在网购时注意保护个人信息。与此同时，我们应该学会理性地消费，避免盲目和过度消费。

9. 城市化进程

Directions:

Study the following picture carefully and write an essay in which you should

1) describe the picture,

2) list the advantages and disadvantages of urbanization, and

3) draw your conclusion.

You should write 160-200 words neatly on the ANSWER SHEET.

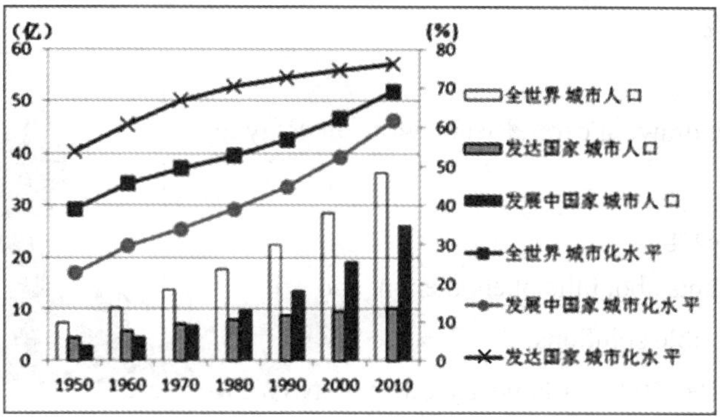

参考范文

What can be seen in the chart is that, from 1950 to 2010, the speed of urbanization in developed nations almost keeps steady, with only a little increase. By contrast, the same process in developing countries is on sharp ascent, from about 22 percent to 62 percent in 60 years. In addition, the number of people in cities in developing countries also rocketed from 1950 to 2010. **The data vividly clarify a truth that** more citizens in poorer nations have moved to big cities.

I firmly believe that although urbanization may bring a series of unfavorable consequences, **the advantages of urbanization are more than its weak points.** First, when an increasing number of farmers flood into cities, there are more citizens devoted to the construction of metropolis, which may be in turn beneficial to inhabitants there. In addition, it becomes an international trend to have more people live in the city although it may be ignored by many people. Last but not least, rural laborers, leaving their poor hometowns, can not only find high-salary jobs but also make their kids share the same education with their peers there.

All in all, urbanization **brings more benefits than problems**. The present society is experiencing great changes. **What we should do is to** welcome those people from rural areas and **think deeply how to strike a balance between economic development and social harmony**.

【参考译文】

从图表中可以看出，从1950年到2010年，发达国家的城市化速度几乎保持稳定，略有增长。相比之下，发展中国家的这一进程正在急剧上升，60年来从22%左右上升至62%左右。此外，发展中国家的城市人口数量在1950年至2010年间也飞速增加了。这些数据生动地阐明了一个事实，即更多贫穷国家的公民倾向于搬到大城市。

我坚信，虽然城市化可能会带来一系列不利的后果，但城市化的优点大于其缺点。首先，当越来越多的农民涌入城市时，更多的公民就会投身于大都市的建设，这反过来可能对当地居民有利。此外，尽管大多数中国人可能会忽视这一点，但更多的人居住在城市已成为一种国际趋势。最后，离开贫困家乡的农村劳动力不仅可以找到高薪工作，还可以让他们的孩子享受和当地同龄人同样的教育。

总之，城市化带来的好处多于其带来的问题。当今社会正发生巨大的变化。我们应该做的是欢迎从农村来的居民，并深入思考如何实现经济发展与社会和谐之间的平衡。

10. 保护传统文化

Directions:

Study the following drawing carefully and write an essay in which you should

1) describe the drawing,

2) give your comments about the phenomenon, and

3) point out the possible solutions.

You should write 160-200 words neatly on the ANSWER SHEET.

参考范文

What looks beyond dispute is that the poor historic building is shedding tears, shouting "SOS" for help because it is being destroyed by humans and stolen by robbers. **The picture does reflect a thought-provoking social phenomenon.** Traditional cultural heritage, from my perspective, should be protected imperatively.

To clarify the phenomenon thoroughly, I would like to point out certain arguments. To start with, quite a few people hold that Chinese traditional culture is of little use in modern society and it has failed to meet the needs of social development. What is more, Chinese traditional culture is facing an unprecedented challenge. With the rapid advance of communication among different nations, rich and colorful culture from foreign countries has distracted people's attention. Under such conditions, few people can resist the temptation of foreign culture. **Now, we have to ask ourselves a question: if there are no ancient buildings or articles, what can be left to our offspring in the future?**

So urgent is the current situation that something should be done rapidly and effectively. Firstly, a large-scale education campaign should be launched to inform the public of the importance of protecting our Chinese traditional culture. Additionally, Chinese traditional culture needs to adjust to the rapid development and the growing demand of society. **As a young man, I just desire to say: refuse the damage to cultural heritage from now on.**

【参考译文】

无可争议的是，这座可怜的历史建筑正在落泪，大喊着“救命”，因为它正在被人破坏，遭强盗抢劫。在我看来，这确实反映了一种发人深省的社会现象。传统文化遗产，在我看来，应该受到必要的保护。

为了彻底阐明这种现象，我想指出一些要点。首先，相当多的人认为中国传统文化在现代社会中用处不大，不能满足社会发展的需求。此外，中国传统文化面临着前所未有的挑战。随着国际交流的迅速发展，来自外国的丰富多彩的文化分散了人们的注意力。在这样的情形下，很少有人能抵御外来文化的诱惑。现在，我们得扪心自问了：如果没有古建筑和古物品，我们将来会为后代留下什么呢?

当前形势十分紧迫，我们必须迅速、有效地采取措施。首先，要开展大规模的教育活动，使公众认识到保护中国传统文化的重要性。此外，中国传统文化还需要适应社会的快速发展和人们日益增长的需求。作为一个年轻人，我只想说：从现在开始拒绝破坏文化遗产的行为。

11. 私家车、交通

Directions:

Study the following drawing carefully and write an essay in which you should

1) describe the drawing,

2) give your comments about the phenomenon, and

3) point out the possible solutions.

You should write about 150 words neatly on the ANSWER SHEET.

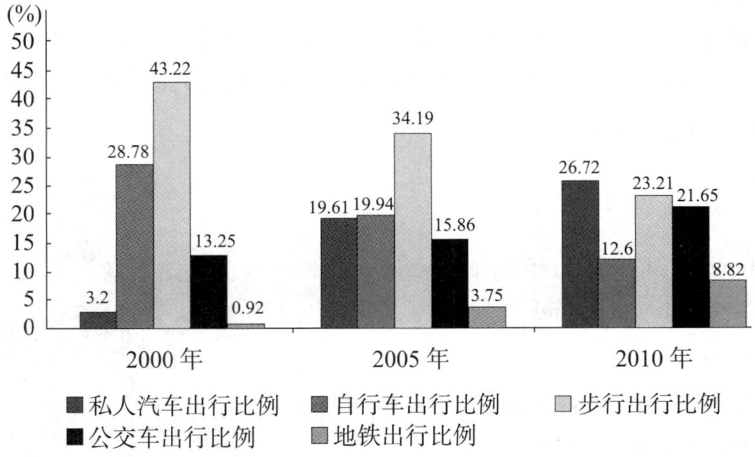

北京市出行结构的变化

参考范文

What can be seen in the bar chart is that the share of trip by private car, from the year of 2000 to 2010, accumulated by 23.52 percent dramatically. By contrast, the share of going out on foot, in the same period, shrank to 23.21 percent sharply. **The purpose of the graph is to present readers a worrying issue**—private cars have been used by more and more Chinese citizens.

Why should private cars be restricted? There exist quite a few elements here. The primary factor seems that cars contribute to air pollution. The more private cars exist in the street, the dirtier the already contaminated atmosphere will become. **Furthermore**, these autos have been a terrible threat to the heavy traffic in the city. If more cars appear in busy streets, there will be more traffic jams, which is really a hazard to all of us. **Finally**, the evidence that cars consume a large amount of fuel manifests that oil resources, as a typical non-renewable material, will be used up rapidly. **All these facts lead to only one conclusion**: confining the ever-growing number of cars.

Consequently, private cars **must be discouraged in metropolis**. As responsible citizens, we have to say "No" to private cars so as to have fresher air. Besides, auto factories can develop mass transit to take place of private cars. **All in all, it is about time to focus on** the limitation of private cars.

【参考译文】

从条形图中可以看出，从 2000 年至 2010 年，私家车的出行比例大幅增长了 23.52%。相比之下，同期步行外出的比例锐减至 23.21%。图画想向读者呈现一个令人忧虑的现象——越来越多的中国公民使用私家车。

为什么私家车应该受到限制呢？这里有很多原因。主要原因似乎是汽车造成的空气污染。街道上的私家车越多，被污染的空气就越脏。此外，这些汽车对城市拥挤的交通造成了可怕的威胁。如果在繁忙的街道上出现更多的汽车，将会造成更严重的交通堵塞，这会对我们所有人造成影响。最后，汽车消耗大量燃料，作为一种典型的不可再生能源，石油资源将被迅速消耗。所有这些事实都指向一个结论：限制不断增长的汽车数量。

因此，在大都市里，不应该鼓励使用私家车。作为负责任的市民，我们必须对私家车说“不”，这样才能有更新鲜的空气。此外，汽车厂家可以发展公共交通来取代私家车。总而言之，现在是时候关注限制私家车的问题了。

12. 养宠物

Directions:

Study the following picture carefully and write an essay of 160-200 words in which you should

1) describe the picture,

2) suggest ways to control dogs in public places, and

3) give your own comments on it.

You should write neatly on the ANSWER SHEET.

参考范文

What can be seen in the ridiculous drawing is that a lady who looks quite fashionable is holding a cute dog, walking in the neighborhood. On the contrary, a man behind her feels so upset about the polluted ground by the pet. What a nuisance! **The cartoon, in as obvious a manner as possible, manifests that plentiful attention should be paid to the issue of** raising pets.

There exists a mountain of evidence showing that pets should be confined. First and foremost, although having a pet around the house may reduce the loneliness of senior citizens, they may do harm to their neighbors and strangers in the community. Subsequently, pets have definitely become a major cause of environmental pollution. The more frequently these little animals haunt in the street or village, the worse our living conditions will get. In the end, what must be pointed out is that pets especially dogs enjoy barking and making a lot of noise at midnight, which may influence inhabitants' sleep. **So if more families own these little animals without any confinement, a dim and gloomy future will be waiting for us.**

To sum up, effective measures should be taken to deal with the problem. In the first place, the local government is supposed to launch a campaign telling dog owners to pick up the dog poop after their dogs. Secondly, the dog owners who leave their dog's mess on the streets deserve to be fined heavily. **Only through these actions can citizens co-exist with cute and loyal animals.**

【参考译文】

从这幅滑稽的漫画中可以看出，一位看起来相当时髦的女士正牵着一只可爱的狗在附近散步。相反，她后面的那个人对被宠物“污染”过的地面感到很困扰。多么令人讨厌啊！这幅漫画以尽可能明显的方式表明，饲养宠物的问题应该引起足够的重视。

有大量证据表明，宠物应该受到限制。首先，尽管在家里养宠物可以减少老年人的孤独感，但它们可能会伤害到邻居和社区里的陌生人。其次，宠物已成为环境污染的主要原因之一。这些小动物越经常出没在街上或村庄里，我们的居住环境就越差。最后，必须指出的是，宠物，尤其是狗，喜欢在午夜吠叫，产生大量的噪音，导致邻居夜不能寝。因此，如果更多的家庭拥有这些小动物而不受任何限制，那么等着我们的可能是一个灰暗的未来。

综上所述，应该采取有效的措施来解决这个问题。首先，当地政府应该发起一场运动，让狗主人在他们的狗排便后捡起狗的排泄物。其次，那些把狗的排泄物留在街上的狗主人应该被处以重罚。只有通过这些行动，公民才能与可爱而忠诚的动物共存。

13. 性别歧视

Directions:

There has been a discussion recently on the issue in a newspaper about gender discrimination. Study the following picture carefully and write an essay of 160-200 words in which you should

1) describe the picture,

2) provide your own comments on it, and

3) give some solutions to it.

You should write neatly on the ANSWER SHEET.

参考范文

What looks beyond dispute in the cartoon is that a girl who may have just graduated from a university, wondering “why am I not given a job chance?”, is rejected by a company decisively and ruthlessly. **The artist’s intention is exceedingly clear**—He points out that there still exists prejudice and discrimination against women in our modern society.

The majority of women would agree that quite a few elements could account for this. In the first place, although some businesses are run completely by women, some people still cling to the perspective that many jobs done by men can hardly be finished by women, simply because they are not strong enough physically. In their eyes, women are the weaker sex—both physically and emotionally. Thus, women are only suited to the performance of domestic duties. And a woman’s place is within the protective environment of the home. Secondly, they believe that most of the world-famous scientists and statesmen are found to be males. Finally, they assert that the whole society seems to have always been dominated by men only. In a word, men should enjoy more rights than women.

All in all, there is little doubt that women are making outstanding contributions to the progress of modern society. For one thing, rules and regulations should be applied to limit the discrimination against females. For another, as a female, I just desire to say that catch the chance once you are qualified in a position.

【参考译文】

在这部漫画中，毫无争议的是，一个似乎刚大学毕业的女孩被一家公司坚决无情地拒绝了，她在想“为什么不能给我一个工作机会？”作者的意图非常明显——他指出，在我们的现代社会，仍然存在着对妇女的偏见和歧视。

大多数女性都认同，有相当多的因素可以解释这一点。首先，尽管有些企业完全由女性经营，但有些人仍然坚持认为许多由男性做的工作很难由女性完成，因为女性身体不够强壮。在他们眼中，女性无论在身体上还是在情感上都比较柔弱。因此，女性只适合履行家庭职责。女性的位置是在有保护性的家庭环境中。其次，他们认为世界上大多数著名的科学家和政治家都是男性。最后，他们断言整个社会似乎总是由男人主导。简言之，男人应该比女人享有更多的权利。

总之，毫无疑问，妇女对现代社会的进步做出了杰出的贡献。一方面，应当运用规章制度来限制对妇女的歧视。另一方面，作为一名女性，我只想说，一旦你胜任一个职位，就要抓住机会。

14. 献爱心

Directions:

Study the following picture carefully and write an essay of 160-200 words in which you should

1) describe the picture,

2) give your own comments on it, and

3) offer an example.

You should write neatly on the ANSWER SHEET.

参考范文

What looks quite obvious in the caricature is that an old lady with a walking stick is lying on the ground for some illness. Seeing this, a boy is rushing to lift her up as quickly as possible. **What a touching and positive picture! We can conclude that** with reasonable protective regulations, love keeps like a little lamp, which appears brighter in darker places.

It is to clarify my perspective that a typical case could be listed here. We should remember how Chinese people of all provinces responded to the call to help the victims of the earthquake in Sichuan Province. In the natural disaster, a sea of inhabitants lost their homeland and their family overnight and they felt extremely grieved and broken-hearted. At that moment, Chinese citizens, without any enforcement, jumped to rescue with foods, clothing and other daily necessities. Although all of those could not change the situation at that time, the natives still felt the love from strangers. **As is shown in the story, if human beings are selfish and indifferent, a dim and gloomy future will be awaiting them.**

The best way to show love, **to be frank, is to** help those who are in trouble no matter whether they are family members or complete strangers. Meanwhile, government should introduce proper laws to protect those who help others. **Only by these actions could a harmonious relationship be formed between individuals.**

【参考译文】

从这幅漫画中可以很明显地看出，一位拿着拐杖的老太太因病躺在地上。与此同时，一个男孩一看到就冲过去把她扶起。多么感人和正能量的图画呀！我们得出，有了合理的保护条例，爱就像一盏小灯，它在黑暗的地方更明亮。

为了阐明我的观点，这里可以举一个典型的例子。我们应该记住中国各省人民是如何回应帮助四川地震灾民的号召的。在这场自然灾害中，很多人在一夜之间失去了家园和家人，他们感到极度悲痛和心碎。那时，中国公民在没有任何强制的情况下，立即展开救援，给他们提供食物、衣服和其他日常用品。尽管所有这些都不能改变当时的状况，但当地人还是感受到了来自陌生人的爱。如故事所示，如果人是自私的、冷漠的，那么等待着他们的将是一个阴暗的未来。

坦率地说，表达爱的最好方式就是帮助那些有困难的人，不管他们是家人还是完全陌生的人。与此同时，政府应该出台适当的法律保护那些帮助他人的人。只有通过这些行动，才能在个体之间形成和谐的关系。

15. 节约

Directions:

Write an essay of 160-200 words based on the following drawing. In your essay, you should

1) describe the drawing briefly,

2) interpret its intended meaning, and

3) give your comments.

You should write neatly on the ANSWER SHEET.

参考范文

What looks quite apparent in the picture is that a boy, sitting in front of the table, is lifting a plate with the words “empty plate” on it after a meal. **Apparently, this picture emphasizes** the inheritance of the virtue of thrift.

To explain the phenomenon thoroughly, quite a few elements must be pointed out here. To begin with, with the rapid advance of economy, the material life of Chinese citizens becomes increasingly rich and their consumption ideas also change greatly. We cannot deny these facts, but we can never abandon the traditional virtue of our nation—thrift. In addition, compared with developed countries, our country has not become wealthy yet, so it is necessary to encourage frugality. If an extravagant trend is to be left unfettered, it will not only waste financial and material resources, but also damage Chinese traditional virtue or even impair the interests of our future generations.

It is about time that we began to address this issue. We must remember that China has always been a country which celebrates thrift and distastes waste. For one thing, the elderly should set good examples for their descendants. For another, as youngsters, we should keep in mind that “**waste is shameful, while thrift noble.**”

【参考译文】

从图中可以明显地看出，一个坐在桌子前的男孩在吃完饭后举起一个写着“光盘”的盘子。显然，这张照片强调了节俭美德的传承。

要全面地解释这一现象，就必须指出以下几点。首先，随着经济的快速发展，中国公民的物质生活日益丰富，消费观念也相应地发生了很大的变化。我们不能否认这些事实，但我们也绝不能抛弃我们国家的传统美德——节俭。此外，与发达国家相比，我们还不富裕，因此有必要鼓励节俭。如果奢侈浪费的趋势不加以限制，不仅会浪费财力和物质资源，还会损害中国传统美德，甚至损害我们后代的利益。

现在是我们开始解决这个问题的时候了。千万牢记中国一直是一个崇尚节俭、厌恶浪费的国家。一方面，长辈应该为他们的后代树立好榜样。另一方面，作为年轻人，我们要记住“浪费是可耻的，节俭是高尚的”。

16. 心理健康

Directions:

Write an essay based on the following chart. In your essay, you should

1) interpret the meaning of the chart, and

2) give your comments.

You should write about 150 words on the ANSWER SHEET.

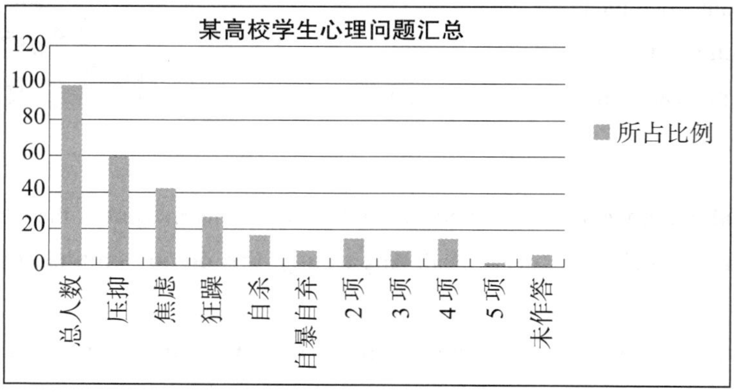

参考范文

As is exhibited in the bar chart, the issue of the students having psychological problems is greatly severe. To be specific, 60 percent of youngsters on campus are feeling depressed, which sounds extremely shocking. At the same time, there exist more than 15 percent of students tending to commit suicide. What a worrying truth!

I do believe that the following causes can account for the phenomenon. The primary one is that people in the modern world are confronted with great pressure from study and work. Because of being depressed for a long time, people will face some problems in mental health, which will pose a severe threat to them and have a negative effect on their daily life. To be a healthy person, mental health seems to be more important. Besides, from the social perspective, only when all citizens are in good health will the society have better work force with higher efficiency. Consequently our country will be able to harvest more fruits produced by its people.

So if you are confronted with any depression, just talk with your family and your friends. In addition, teachers and parents should pay attention to the psychological changes of youngsters and take timely actions. **Only with the joint efforts of their families and friends can the pressure of psychology be eliminated gradually.**

【参考译文】

如条形图所示，学生有心理问题的情况十分严峻。具体来说，校园里 60% 的年轻人感到压抑，这听起来非常令人震惊。同时，有超过 15% 的学生有自杀倾向，这是一个多么令人担忧的事实啊！

我坚信造成这种现象的原因如下。首先，现代社会里的人面临着巨大的学习压力和工作压力。因为长期处于抑郁状态，人们会面临心理健康方面的一些问题，这些问题对他们构成严重的威胁，对他们的日常生活产生负面影响。要成为一个健康的人，心理健康似乎更重要。此外，从社会的角度看，一个社会只有在全体公民身体健康的情况下，才会有更优秀的劳动力和更高的效率，才能够收获更多的人民生产的果实。

所以，如果你有任何压抑的情绪，你可以同家人和朋友交谈。此外，教师和家长应关注青少年的心理变化，并及时采取行动。只有在家人和朋友的共同努力下，心理压力才能逐渐消除。

17. 运动健身

Directions:

Write an essay based on the picture. In your essay, you should

1) interpret the meaning of the picture, and

2) give your comments.

You should write 160-200 words on the ANSWER SHEET.

参考范文

What looks quite apparent in the cartoon is that an elderly man and a little girl, although they are at different ages, are jogging happily side by side. There are also eight big Chinese characters nearby which mean "thousands of diseases can be cured by exercises." **The picture tries to catch our eyes and point out the truth that** doing sports is viewed as exceedingly indispensable in our daily life.

Undoubtedly, an increasing number of individuals agree that plentiful elements can support the viewpoint. The primary cause is that people with good health can work with full energy and confidence. Their progress in turn contributes to their health and happiness. On the contrary, a sick guy usually lacks the vigor and interest to act his role in life, which deprives him of many opportunities to become successful and happy. What is more, it is known that maintaining an active lifestyle should be one of our priorities in life. Only by taking care of ourselves can we stand a chance of being the kind of person we strive to be in the job, in our family and in our communities.

So it is high time for everyone to spare some time to exercise outside. First, do not always find excuses to avoid doing sports. Besides, eating less junk food and having a balanced diet is also a key step to remaining healthy for most people. Just as an old Chinese saying goes, health is the basis of happiness.

【参考译文】

从这幅漫画中可以明显地看出，一位老人和一位小女孩虽然年龄不同，却肩并肩快乐地慢跑。旁边还有八个大字："运动运动，百病难碰"。这幅画试图让我们注意到一个真相——运动在我们的日常生活中是非常必要的。

毫无疑问，越来越多的人会认同，有很多的理由可以支持上述观点。首先，健康的人可以充满活力和信心百倍地工作，他们的进步反过来也有助于他们的健康和幸福。相反，生病的人通常缺乏精力和兴趣去扮演他在生活中的角色，这剥夺了他许多成功和快乐的机会。而且人们都知道保持积极的生活方式应该是我们生活中的要事之一。只有照顾好自己，我们才有机会成为理想中的自己，无论是在职场、在家中还是在社会上。

所以现在是每个人抽出时间到外面活动的时候了。首先，不要总是找借口逃避运动。此外，少吃垃圾食品和均衡饮食也是大多数人保持健康的关键。正如中国的一句老话所说："健康是幸福的基础。"

18. 爱阅读

Directions:

Write an essay based on the following picture. In your essay, you should

1) interpret the meaning of the picture, and

2) give your comments.

You should write 160-200 words on the ANSWER SHEET.

书籍是人类进步的阶梯

参考范文

What can be seen clearly in the cartoon is that a boy is standing in front of piles of books which look like a stepladder, and the words below the picture read "books are the ladder of human progress." **So the implication of the picture is quite self-evident**: more books should be read to purify our minds and widen our horizons.

There are plentiful elements that account for the point. First and foremost, not only is the world changing rapidly in every field but also new experience and opinions appear day by day. However, you cannot experience all of these yourself. So reading books is the most effective way to keep pace with the advance of society. Besides, the more books one reads, the more thoroughly he can ensure a grasp of what he is interested in, **which has been widely accepted in public**. In the end, if a person is busy with his work and fails to read books including some masterpieces, he will become a dead-alive person without any thoughts or ideas.

So essential is reading that time should be spared for it. However, there exist as plentiful good books as bad ones. What readers can do is to separate good plants from wild weeds. Keep in mind "read more books, and read good ones."

【参考译文】

从漫画中可以清楚地看到，一个男孩站在一堆像梯子一样的书前，图片下面的文字写着："书是人类进步的阶梯。"因此，这幅图片的含义是不言而喻的：我们应该多读些书来净化我们的思想，开阔我们的视野。

很多因素可以支撑这一观点。首先，世界各个领域都在迅速变化，而且新的经验和观点每天都在出现。但是，你不能切身体会一切。读书是跟上社会进步的脚步的最佳方式。其次，一个人读书越多，就越能彻底地把握他感兴趣的东西，这点已被公众广泛接受。最后，如果一个人忙于自己的工作而没有阅读包括名著在内的书籍，他就会变成没思想或观点的行尸走肉。

阅读如此重要，我们应该花时间读书。然而，书籍良莠不齐。读者可以做的是分清良莠。请记住"多读书，读好书"。

第七章

习题大操练

第一节　改错练习

一、Jobs for Graduates

考生作文

As is know to all, nothing is more serious than the problem of job for graduates. This problem, which had a fairly bad effect on the speedy development of the modern society, left graduates throughout universities panic and confused. They no longer have a sense of safety.

What causes the problem? As far as I concerned, first and foremost, our government carried out a policy that absorbs more students from middle school into university. In the second, lot of courses which lock of creativity are set up unreasonably in university.

In my opinion, firstly, government should not take more students from middle school into university. Second, most of the courses should be set up reasonably in order to meet the market demands. Last but not least, all of the graduates should improve their abilities in study and in part-time jobs before graduate.

错误解析

Jobs for Graduates

As is [1] know to all, nothing is more serious than the problem of [2] job for graduates. This problem, which [3] had a fairly bad effect on the speedy development of the modern society, [4] left graduates throughout universities panic and confused. They no longer have a sense of safety.

[1] be + 动词过去分词为被动语态的结构，改为 known。

[2] 可数名词，后面加 s。

[3] 与前文时态一致，had 改为 has。

[4] 时态错误，left 改为 has left。

What causes the problem? As far as [5] I concerned, first and foremost, our government [6] carried out a policy that absorbs more students from [7] middle school into university. In the [8] second, [9] lot of courses which [10] lock creativity are set up unreasonably in [11] university.

In my opinion, firstly, [12] government should not take more students from [13] middle school into university. [14] Second, most of the courses should be set up reasonably in order to meet the market demands. Last but not least, all of the graduates should improve their abilities in study and [15] in part-time jobs before [16] graduate.

[5] As far as I am concerned 是固定搭配，加 be 动词。
[6] 此处应该用完成时态 has carried。
[7] 可数名词不能单独使用，改为 schools 和 universities。
[8] 改为 second place。
[9] 改为 lots of，固定搭配，意为"大量的"。
[10] 拼写错误，改为 lack。
[11] 改为 universities，应该为复数。
[12] 可数名词不能单独使用，前面加 the。
[13] 同样地，school 和 university 变成复数。
[14] 此处用副词，改为 Secondly。
[15] 表意错误，"提升学习能力，做兼职"，而不是"提升做兼职的能力"，in 改为 take。
[16] 介词后跟名词，改为 graduation。

总结 本篇作文最大的问题是名词单复数以及时态。写作时一定要细心，你以粗心为由，但是阅卷老师认为这是水平问题。

二、Occupying the Seat

考生作文

When it comes to occupy the seat, it become more serious than before. How to solve the problems, that is college to facing it.

However, things will change worse if we cannot deal with this seating occupy for the following reasons. Stresses are bringed by an increasing number of people, facilities are far from meeting the stuent's need and more and more students cannot learning things what they don't want it. For the students, they have too many shortcomings but they don't find them, such as bad habits, for scores and so on.

As far as I am concerned, stuents should cultivate their comprehensive characterises for working hard, and as for the another, I'm sure the government will be sattled in the future.

错误解析

Occupying the Seat

When it comes to [1] occupy the seat, it [2] become more serious than before. How to solve the [3] problems [4], that is college to facing it.

[1] to 为介词，介词后跟动词 ing 形式，改为 occupying。
[2] 改为 becomes/is becoming。
[3] 只有一个问题，改为 problem。
[4] 表达不清晰，改为 is what many colleges are faced with。句子前面的逗号删除。

However, things will [5] change worse if we cannot deal with this [6] seating [7] occupy for the following reasons. Stresses are [8] bringed by an increasing number of people [9], facilities are far from meeting the [10] stuent's need and more and more students cannot [11] learning things [12] what they don't want it. For the students, they have too many shortcomings but they don't find them, such as bad habits, [13] for scores and so on.

As far as I am concerned, [14] stuents should cultivate their comprehensive [15] characterises for working hard, and [16] as for the another, I'm sure the government will [17] be sattled in the future.

[5] 改为 get。
[6] 改为 seat。
[7] 改为 occupying。
[8] 改为 brought。
[9] 逗号改为句点，facilities 首字母大写。
[10] 改为 students' needs。
[11] 情态动词后用动词原形 learn。
[12] 定语从句，没有引导词，what 改为 that，同时去掉 don't 和 it。
[13] 表意不明。
[14] 改为 students，单词拼写问题。
[15] 单词拼写错误，应为 characteristics。
[16] 去掉 as 和 the。
[17] 改为 settle the problem。

总结　该生语法基础太薄弱了，需要加强语法练习。本文唯一的优点就是用英文完成了写作，但文章惨不忍睹。改动之后还是无法通读。

三、Reading Selectively or Extensively?

考生作文

Reading is a good habit, along with the development of society, knowledge is becameing more and more important, and the book provide everyono who reached with knowledge, so we must reading. On the one thing, we can found out many intreasting stories, which can make us happy. On the other thing, reading can give us many ideologies of life. Moreover, reading can make us stay away from the computer and TV-st, and keep our body healthy.

However, there is also some disadvantages for reading. Firstly, a few people would read some pornographic book. Secondly, if we don't assume the right proture in reading, our eyes will get hurt. Thirdly, we can't found out what we will found of we don't choice the useful and healthy book.

In my opinion. the reading is important, and the right way for reading is also important.

错误解析

Reading Selectively or Extensively?

Reading is a good habit [1] , along with the development of society, knowledge is [2] becameing more and more important, and the book [3] provide [4] everyono [5] who reached with knowledge, so we must [6] reading. [7] On the one thing, we can [8] found out many [9] intreasting stories, which can make us happy. [10] On the other thing, reading can give us many ideologies of life. Moreover, reading can make us stay away from the computer and [11] TV-st, and keep our body healthy.

However, there [12] is also some disadvantages for reading. Firstly, a few people would read some pornographic [13] book. Secondly, if we don't assume the right [14] proture in reading, our eyes will get hurt. Thirdly, [15] we can't found out what we will found of we don't choice the useful and healthy book.

In my opinion [16] . [17] the reading is important, and the right way for reading is also important.

[1] 逗号改为句点，后面 along 首字母大写。
[2] 用 become 的 -ing 形式 becoming。
[3] 主语是第三人称单数，谓语用 provides。
[4] 改为 everyone。
[5] 去掉 who reached。
[6] must 后跟动词原形，改为 read。
[7] 改为 For one thing。
[8] 改为 find。
[9] 拼写错误，改为 interesting。
[10] 改为 For another。
[11] 直接写 TV 就行了。
[12] 后面的名词为复数，改为 are。
[13] 改为 books。
[14] 拼写错误，应该是 posture（姿势）。
[15] 表意不明。
[16] 句点变逗号，标点符号错了也会扣分。
[17] the 去掉。

总结 应注意单词拼写、语法、大小写和文章结构等问题。

四、Reading Classics

考生作文

Ancient books, especially the classics, were worshipped by nearly every leaner for they not only illuminate but also further one's mind. What's more, it is obvious that books promote the spread of culture.

Unfortunately, a large number of people today fail to enjoy the classic. The cause of this situation is reasonably that society pours so much pressure to people especially junior students, professors, white-collar workers and doctors. With out enough time to rest, they can hardly have free time to read the book. Furthermore, even if they get free time, maybe on weekend, they are tend to relax themselves by doing something easily like listening to music, watching TV, playing games, or just sleeping. By brief, in such a fast-paced society, time turned to be so precious. It is hardly to accumulate time to enjoy the classics.

Facing the situation, the only thing we ingraduate do is to read them as many as possible.

错误解析

Reading Classics

Ancient books, especially the classics, were [1] worshipped by nearly every [2] leaner for they not only [3] illuminate but also [4] further one's mind. What's more, it is obvious that books promote the spread of culture.

Unfortunately, a large number of people today fail to enjoy the [5] classic. The cause of this situation [6] is reasonably that society pours so much pressure to people especially junior students, professors, white-collar workers and doctors. [7] With out enough time to rest, they can hardly have free time to read [8] the book. Furthermore, even if they get free time, maybe on weekend, they [9] are tend to relax themselves by doing something [10] easily like listening to music, watching TV, playing games, or just sleeping. [11] By brief, in such a fast-paced society, time [12] turned to be so precious. [13] It is hardly to accumulate time to enjoy the classics.

Facing the situation, the only thing we [14] ingraduate do is to read them as many as possible.

[1] worship 表示"崇拜某人",改为 respected/preferred。
[2] 拼写错误, leaner 改为 learner。
[3] 缺少宾语,应改为 illuminate one's life。
[4] 中式表达,改为 deepen one's thoughts。
[5] 改为复数 classics。
[6] 去掉 reasonably。
[7] 一个单词不要分开,改为 Without。
[8] the book 改为 books。
[9] 一句话中只有一个谓语动词,去掉 are。
[10] 改为 easy。
[11] In brief 为固定搭配,意为"简要来说"。
[12] 改为 has become,用现在完成时态。
[13] 表意不明。
[14] 改为 can。

总结 这篇作文语法错误较多,表达像中式英语,不够地道。

五、Travelling Abroad

考生作文

Recently, more and more citizens would like to travel abroad. As is shown in the graph, In 1995, 10,000 citizens travelled another countries. The number of people who travelled abroad rose nearly to 40,000 in 2000, and in 2005, the number increased sharply above 120,000.

There are many reasons to explain this change. First of all, with the fast develop of economic. The number of the rich has enlarged, they have enough money travel abroad. Furthermore, they like to travel abroad in order to communicated with foreign and join other cultures. The last but not the least, so many people start to study English, they travel abroad to improve their English and understand English culture history.

Many advantages as travelling abroad may bring to us, but as all coins have two sides, it also brings about many disadvantages. It will be best illustrated if given the following example: some visitors who travel abroad have aim. They want to living in that country and do not want to return. It is sharme for them. Consequence, if you like to travel abroad, you must pay more attention to it.

错误解析

Travelling Abroad

Recently, more and more citizens would like to travel abroad. As is shown in the graph, [1] In 1995, 10,000 citizens [2] travelled [3] another countries. The number of people who travelled abroad rose nearly to 40,000 in 2000, and in 2005, the number increased sharply [4] above 120,000.

There are many reasons to explain this change. First of all, with the fast [5] develop of [6] economic [7]. The number of the rich has enlarged, they have enough money travel abroad. Furthermore, they like to travel abroad in order to [8] communicated with [9] foreign and join other cultures. [10] The last but not the least, so many people start to study English, [11] they travel abroad to improve their English and understand [12] English culture history.

[13] Many advantages as travelling abroad may bring to us, but as all coins have two sides, it also brings about many disadvantages. It will be best illustrated if given the following example: some visitors who travel abroad have [14] aim. They want to [15] living in that country and do not want to return. It is [16] sharme for them. [17] Consequence, if you would like to travel abroad, you must pay more attention to it.

[1] 小写，改为 in。
[2] 不及物动词后接宾语要加介词，改为 travelled to。
[3] 改为 other。
[4] above 改为 to。
[5] 改为 development。
[6] 改为 economy。
[7] 句点改为逗号，The 首字母小写，enlarged 后用句号，they 首字母大写，并在 money 后面加 to。
[8] 改为 communicate。
[9] 改为 foreigners。
[10] 固定搭配是 Last but not least。
[11] they 改为 and。
[12] history 前面加 and。
[13] 改为 Travelling abroad may bring us many advantages。
[14] 改为 their aims。
[15] 改成 live。
[16] 改为 a shame（一种耻辱）。
[17] 改为 As a consequence 或 Consequently。

总结 这还像一篇作文，虽然读起来格外费力。

六、Reading

考生作文

When it comes to reading, everybody have inadividuls opinions. Some people think that we should read book setectively. There are some reason for read book selectively.

First, more and more books are published. It is impossible for us to read all the books. for the reason that our time and vigorous is limited. What's more, many book can poisonous to our mind, owning to the contents of those books including crime, violent, unheathly and so on.

The other people, who hold that reading widely is better, There are some reason for read book widely. First and foremost, reading books widely can extent our knowledge in all aspect. They believe that "to know more, to read more". Besides, if one man have many kinds of knowledge. He will have more chance to success.

错误解析

Reading

When it comes to reading, [1] everybody have inadividuls opinions. Some people think that we should read [2] book [3] setectively. There are some [4] reason for [5] read book selectively.

First, more and more books are published. It is impossible for us to read all the books [6] . for the reason that our time and [7] vigorous [8] is limited. What's more, many [9] book can [10] poisonous to our [11] mind, [12] owning to the contents of those books including crime, [13] violent, unheathly and so on.

[14] The other people [15] , who hold that reading widely is better, There are some [16] reason for read book widely. First and foremost, reading books widely can [17] extent our knowledge in all [18] aspect. They believe that [19] "to know more, to read more". Besides, if one man [20] have many kinds of knowledge [21] . He will have more chance to success.

[1] 改为 every individual has his own opinions。
[2] 可数名词不可单独使用，改为 books。
[3] 拼写错误，改为 selectively。
[4] 改为 reasons。
[5] 改为 reading books。
[6] 句点改为逗号，因为后面的内容是前面句子的状语。
[7] and 前后词性应保持一致，改为 vigor。
[8] 改为 are。
[9] 改为 books。
[10] 形容词前面加 be。
[11] 改为 minds。
[12] 拼写错误，owning 改为 owing，并且，owing to 引导状语时一般放句首，不放句末，改为 because of，前面的逗号去掉。
[13] 单词并列时前后词性应保持一致，改成名词 violence, unhealthy factors。
[14] The 去掉，other 首字母大写。
[15] 去掉第一个逗号和 who，第二个逗号改为句点。
[16] 改为 reasons for reading books。
[17] 改为 extend。
[18] 改为 aspects。
[19] 中式表达，改为 the more you read, the more you know。
[20] 改为 has。
[21] 句点改为逗号，He 首字母小写，chance 改为 chances，to 后面跟动词原形，success 改为 succeed。

总结 这篇作文基础性错误较多，学生需要加强语法知识。

第二节　英语（一）历年真题及参考范文

1. 2005 年写作真题及参考范文

Part A

Directions:

Two months ago you got a job as an editor for the magazine *Designs & Fashions*. But now you find that the work is not what you expected. You decide to quit. Write a letter to your boss, Mr. Wang, telling him your decision, stating your reason(s), and making an apology.

Write your letter with no less than 100 words. Write it neatly on ANSWER SHEET 2.

Do not sign your own name at the end of the letter; use "Li Ming" instead. You do not need to write the address. (10 points)

参考范文

Dear Mr. Wang,

I feel sorry to write this letter of resignation, but I have decided to resign from my current position as the editor of the magazine *Designs & Fashions*.

The reason is that I have found the work here is not what I have expected. Before I was appointed as the editor, I had assumed that my job would involve a lot of my expertise in art design. However, most of my working hours have been concerned with choosing the photos of women's and men's fashionable clothes and making advertisements for them. As the current job is contrary to my previous expectations and does not need my expertise, I cannot continue doing it.

I must apologize for any possible inconvenience this may have caused. I will appreciate it if you can accept my resignation.

Sincerely yours,

Li Ming

【参考译文】

亲爱的王先生：

我很抱歉写这封辞职信，但我已决定辞去我现在的《设计与时尚》杂志编辑的职位。

原因是我发现这个工作并不是我所期望的那样。在我被任命为编辑之前，我以为我的工作会涉及很多我在艺术设计方面的专业知识。但是，我的大部分工作时间都花在了挑选男女时装的照片和制作广告上。因为现在的工作与我以前的期望相反，而且不需要我的专业知识，所以我不能继续做了。

我对辞职所带来的任何不便深感抱歉。如果你可以接受我的辞职，我会很感激。

你真挚的，

李明

Part B

Directions:

Write an essay of 160-200 words based on the following drawing. In your essay, you should first describe the drawing, then interpret its meaning, and give your comments on it.

You should write neatly on ANSWER SHEET 2. (20 points)

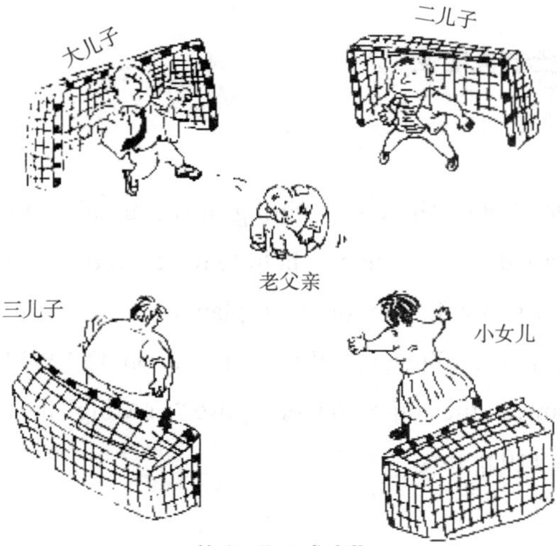

养老“足球赛”

参考范文

The vivid cartoon draws an analogy between a helpless old man's plight and a football match.

As we can see, there are four goals in the picture. In front of them are the eldest son, the second son, the third son and the youngest daughter respectively. The father is too old and senile to stand. My god! He becomes the football of the four mad players. Whenever the old man seeks support from one of his giant babies, that biological child just kicks him away like a football! This phenomenon is commonly seen in the society today, which has become a serious social problem. Many old people have undergone all sorts of hardships to raise their children. However, when the children have grown up, they consider the old as a burden and want to get rid of them.

In a word, this is indeed a sad story. These giant babies don't know the rules and morality of society. They have grown up physically, but they are extremely selfish and unhealthy mentally. The moral is that no matter what kind of person you have become in your adult life, you should never shirk your responsibility for supporting your own parents, which is an acknowledged virtue of human beings.

【参考译文】

这幅生动的漫画用足球赛来比喻一个无助的老人的困境。

正如我们所看到的，这幅画中有四个球门。球门前面分别是大儿子、二儿子、三儿子和小女儿。老父亲年老体衰，无法站立。天哪，他成了四个疯子运动员的足球！每当老人向他的一个巨婴寻求帮助时，那孩子就把他当成足球踢走。这种现象在当今社会很普遍，而且已经成为一个严重的社会问题。许多老人为抚养孩子经历了各种困难。然而，当孩子长大后，他们认为老人是一种负担，而且想摆脱他们。

总而言之，这的确是一个悲惨的故事。巨婴不懂社会规则和道德。他们虽人高马大，但极为自私，心理不健全。从道德上讲，无论你成年后变成什么样的人，你都不应该逃避赡养自己父母的责任，这是人类公认的美德。

2. 2006 年写作真题及参考范文

Part A

Directions:

You want to contribute to Project Hope by offering financial aid to a child in a remote area. Write a letter to the department concerned, asking them to help find a candidate. You should specify what kind of child you want to help and how you will carry out your plan.

Write your letter in no less than 100 words. Write it neatly on ANSWER SHEET 2.

Do not sign your own name at the end of the letter; use “Li Ming” instead.

Do not write the address. (10 points)

参考范文

Dear Sir or Madam,

I am writing to inquire about whether Project Hope can help me find a child in a remote area to whom I can offer the financial support.

The candidate should be a child about 10 years old who is unable to continue his or her education due to poverty. The records of the child’s grades and performance at school should indicate that he or she has the potential to be an outstanding student in the future.

I would like to offer the child my financial aid annually until he completes college education. The money will be used to cover the child’s tuition and books at school. In addition, I intend to establish a support program through the assistance of a local bank so that the child can receive the money regularly and conveniently.

I am looking forward to hearing from you.

Yours sincerely,

Li Ming

【参考译文】

亲爱的先生或女士：

我写信是想咨询希望工程能否帮助我在偏远地区找到一个我可以为其提供经济资助的孩子。

受资助者应是 10 岁左右的孩子，由于贫困无法继续接受教育。孩子的成绩单及其在校表现应表明他或她有将来成为优秀学生的潜力。

我愿意每年为孩子提供经济援助，直到他或她完成大学学业。这笔钱将用于支付孩子在学校的学费和书籍费用。此外，我打算通过当地银行的协助建立一个资助项目，以便孩子能够定期、方便地收到这笔钱。

期待收到您的回信。

您真挚的，
李明

Part B

Directions:

Study the following photos carefully and write an essay in which you should

1) describe the photos briefly,

2) interpret the social phenomenon reflected by them, and

3) give your point of view.

You should write 160-200 words neatly on ANSWER SHEET 2. (20 points)

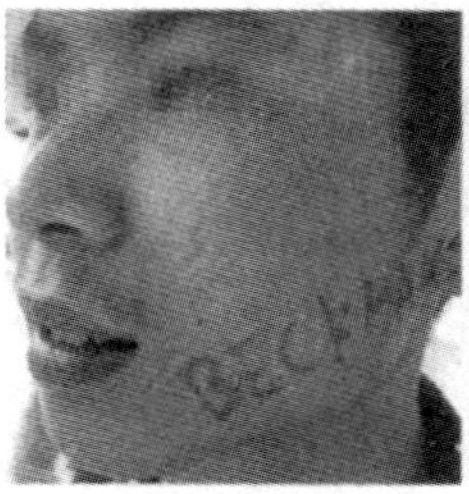

把崇拜写在脸上
注：Beckham（贝克汉姆）——英国足球明星。

花 300 元做个“小贝头”

参考范文

These two pictures reflect a common and serious issue in the world today, and that is the worship of celebrities among the young. In the left-hand picture, a man has proudly had David Beckham's name painted on his face. In the right-hand picture, a man can't wait to ask his barber to cut his hair in accordance with David Beckham's style in spite of the high cost of 300 RMB.

It is a common practice for the young to worship superstars as their idols. Most of them admire famous Chinese or foreign football players, actors, actresses and singers. They not only go to matches and watch TV serials and movies starred by the heroes or heroines in their eyes, but also spend a considerable amount of money imitating their idols in almost every aspect of their lives, such as their styles, glasses, clothes, shoes, etc.

It is certainly advisable for one to have his own role model. However, if one blindly follows others' footsteps without self-control, he will misunderstand the spirit of popular culture. Anyway, the purpose of popular culture is to enhance the quality of people's life. Young people should learn their role model's merits rather than their lifestyles.

【参考译文】

这两张照片反映了当今世界一个普遍而严重的问题，即年轻人对名人的崇拜。在左图中，一个男人得意地在脸上写了贝克汉姆的名字。在右图中，一名男子迫不及待地花费 300 元的重金要求他的理发师按照贝克汉姆的发型给他剪头发。

年轻人崇拜超级明星是一种普遍行为。他们中的大多数人都崇拜国内或者外国的足球运动员、演员和歌手。他们不仅去看比赛，看电视连续剧，看由他们心目中的男女英雄主演的电影，而且几乎在生活的每一个方面（如他们的风格、眼镜、衣服、鞋子等）都花费大量的金钱来模仿他们的偶像。

一个人有自己的榜样当然是可取的，但是如果一个人盲从他人，就会误解流行文化的精神。总之，流行文化的目的是提高人们的生活质量。年轻人应该学习他们榜样的优点，而不是他们的生活方式。

3. 2007 年写作真题及参考范文

Part A

Directions:

Write a letter to your university library, making suggestions for improving its service.

You should write about 100 words on ANSWER SHEET 2.

Do not sign your own name at the end of the letter. Use “Li Ming” instead.

Do not write the address. (10 points)

参考范文

Dear Sir or Madam,

I am a sophomore from the Department of Social Sciences in our university. The purpose of my letter, to be frank, is to offer my proposals for improving your service.

Our library should do its best to purchase the latest publications as well as make sure that it has a full set of classical and reference works in that libraries play a vital role in the education and entertainment. Another important facility I suggest to have is computers with internet access. Only in this way will the library expand its service to a larger number of readers.

In the end, I wish my suggestions could be considered thoroughly.

Best wishes!

Yours sincerely,

Li Ming

【参考译文】

亲爱的先生或女士：

我是我们大学社会科学系的一名大二学生。坦率地说，我写这封信是为了提出一些改进你们服务的建议。

我们的图书馆应该尽最大努力购买最新的出版物，并确保有全套的古典文学作品和参考文献，因为图书馆在教育和娱乐中发挥着至关重要的作用。另外应该提供可以联网的电脑这一重要设施。只有这样，图书馆才能为更多的读者服务。

最后，我希望我的建议能得到充分考虑。

愿您一切顺利！

您真挚的，

李明

Part B

Directions:

Write an essay of 160-200 words based on the following drawing. In your essay, you should

1) describe the drawing briefly,

2) explain its intended meaning, and then

3) support your view with an example/examples.

You should write neatly on ANSWER SHEET 2. (20 points)

参考范文

What can be obviously seen is that in the picture, there exists a sharp contrast between the thoughts of the goalkeeper and the ball player. The former exaggerates the goal and minimizes himself in his mind while the latter exaggerates the goalkeeper. Actually, both the goalkeeper and the goal are just in normal size. The picture does reflect a thought-provoking social phenomenon—confidence should be deemed strikingly important in our current society.

Difficulties, undoubtedly, are in the pathway of everyone. To overcome them, we must at first make correct judgment on the situation, which is based on confidence, courage and rational thinking. For example, when I was in the middle school, our school basketball team once played against another team which was very famous in our city. Every player in our team felt that the only result would be our team's failure. As a result, we did not even make any preparations beforehand. Of course, the result was—our failure. One year later, we met the same team in a match again. This time, our teacher inspired us with confidence and hope. Then, we made a detailed plan and practiced a lot, and out of everybody's imagination, we finally won. So confidence, as the picture and my example reflect, is the first step to success.

In conclusion, if we want to succeed in handling difficulties, we must have self-confidence, judge the situation rationally and be courageous enough to keep trying. Besides, the elderly should educate their kids, letting them know the necessity of a good mentality.

【参考译文】

从这幅图中可以明显看出，守门员和球员的想法存在着鲜明的对比。前者夸大了球门，在心里贬低自己，而后者却夸大了守门员。事实上，守门员和球门的尺寸都很正常。这幅图确实反映了一个发人深省的社会现象——人们应该意识到自信在当今社会是极其重要的。

毫无疑问，每个人都会遇到困难。要克服它们，首先我们必须基于信心、勇气和理性的思考对形势做出正确的判断。比如，我上初中的时候，我们学校的篮球队和另一个在我们城市非常有名的球队比赛，我们队中的每个人都觉得唯一的结果就是我们队失败。因此，我们事先甚至没有做任何准备。结果当然是我们失败了。一年后，我们在一场比赛中再次遇到了那支球队。这一次，老师用信心和希望激励我们。然后我们制订了一个详细的计划，并且进行大量练习，超乎每个人想象的是，我们最终赢了。因此，正如这幅图和我的例子所反映的，自信是成功的第一步。

总之，如果我们要成功地解决困难，我们应该自信、理性地判断形势，并有足够的勇气不断尝试。此外，年长者应该教育他们的孩子，让他们知道良好心态的必要性。

4. 2008 年写作真题及参考范文

Part A

Directions:

You have just come back from Canada and found a music CD in your luggage that you forgot to return to Bob, your landlord there. Write him a letter to

1) make an apology, and

2) suggest a solution.

You should write about 100 words on ANSWER SHEET 2.

Do not sign your own name at the end of the letter. Use “Li Ming” instead.

Do not write the address. (10 points)

参考范文

Dear Bob,

I am writing to make an apology to you for I was in such a great hurry that I forgot to return the music CD which I borrowed from you last week. Yesterday I came back home and I found it in my luggage. I am so sorry that you cannot listen to it at present.

The CD which I borrowed from you is made in Canada, so I believe you can find another one in your local store. How about you buy another CD by yourself and I pay for it? If you cannot find a similar one, I will send it back to you by post. And if there are any other solutions you like, please let me know.

I am sorry again for my carelessness. Looking forward to your early reply.

Yours sincerely,

Li Ming

【参考译文】

亲爱的鲍勃：

我写信是为了向你道歉，因为我太匆忙而忘了归还上周我向你借的音乐 CD。昨天我回到家，发现 CD 在我的行李里。我非常抱歉你现在没法听这张 CD 了。

你借给我的 CD 产自加拿大，所以我相信你能在当地的商店再买一个。你自己买一张 CD，然后我付钱怎么样呢？如果你不能找到相同的 CD，我会把这个给你邮寄回去。如果你有其他的解决方式，请告诉我。

我再次为我的粗心大意感到抱歉。希望尽快收到你的回信。

你真诚的，
李明

Part B

Directions:

Write an essay of 160-200 words based on the following drawing. In your essay, you should

1) describe the drawing briefly,

2) explain its intended meaning, and then

3) give your comments.

You should write neatly on ANSWER SHEET 2. (20 points)

你一条腿，我一条腿；
你我一起，走南闯北。

参考范文

As is vividly depicted in the picture, two disabled men are running fast through teamwork although each of them has only one leg. Obviously, it is teamwork that makes it possible for them to go anywhere they want.

Why do many people believe teamwork is important? There exist quite a few reasons. Undoubtedly, it is teamwork that keeps us continually doing something valuable and admirable in spite of difficulties and discouragements. Besides, not only does cooperation with others make us full of energy to face the coming challenges and competitions but also offers us the foundation for the coming success. Maybe the most suitable example to validate the idea is as follows. A person who is assigned various jobs along the production lines will make a mess just because no one can be proficient in all things. Only by cooperating with others can we put our capacities into full play and can we be winners in the society.

So it is necessary that measures should be adopted to be cooperative. For one thing, we should be sensible to accept other people's opinions and suggestions. For another, it demands us to be active in taking a tougher job and always be helpful and honest to other people. Only through these manners can we complete jobs rapidly and effectively.

【参考译文】

图中生动地描绘了两个残疾人通过合作跑得很快，尽管他们每个人只有一条腿。显然，正是团队合作使他们有可能去任何想去的地方。

为什么很多人认为合作很重要呢？这里有很多原因。毫无疑问，尽管会遇到困难和挫折，但正是团队合作使我们不断地做一些有价值的和令人钦佩的事情。此外，与他人合作不仅使我们充满活力以面对未来的挑战和竞争，也为我们未来的成功奠定了基础。也许下面的例子最适合验证这个观点。一个人在生产线上被分配了各种工作，他会搞得一团糟，因为没人可以精通所有的事情。我们只有通过与他人合作，才能充分发挥自己的能力，并成为社会的赢家。

因此，采取合作的措施是必要的。一方面，我们应该明智地接受他人的想法和建议。另一方面，它要求我们要积极地接受一份更艰难的工作，经常乐于助人、诚信待人。只有通过这些方式，我们才能迅速、有效地完成工作。

5. 2009 年写作真题及参考范文

Part A

Directions:

Restrictions on the use of plastic bags have not been so successful in some regions. "White Pollution" is still going on.

Write a letter to the editor(s) of your local newspaper to

1) give your opinions briefly, and

2) make two or three suggestions.

You should write about 100 words on ANSWER SHEET 2.

Do not sign your own name at the end of the letter. Use "Li Ming" instead.

Do not write the address. (10 points)

参考范文

Dear Editor,

I am a university student. I am writing this letter to you in order to give some opinions about restraining the usage of plastic bags in our local area.

I have observed that many local residents are in favor of using plastic bags and many salesmen are still attracting their regular customers by giving complimentary plastic bags. However, in order to cope with the worsening global warming, a substitute of plastic bags should be made and accepted by customers. In addition, local authorities are supposed to make relative laws against such misconduct.

I will appreciate it if you can take my suggestions into consideration. I am looking forward to hearing from you soon.

Yours sincerely,

Li Ming

【参考译文】

亲爱的编辑：

我是一名大学生，我写这封信给你，是为了表达我对当地禁止使用塑料袋的一些看法。

据我观察，当地许多居民赞成使用塑料袋，而且许多销售商仍然通过提供免费塑料袋来吸引他们的老客户。但是，为了解决日益恶化的全球变暖问题，我的建议是制造一种为客户所接受的塑料袋替代品。此外，地方政府应该制定相关法律来制止这种错误行为。

如果你能认真考虑我的建议，我将不胜感激。我期待尽快收到你的来信。

你真挚的，

李明

Part B

Directions:

Write an essay of 160-200 words based on the following drawing. In your essay, you should

1) describe the drawing briefly,

2) explain its intended meaning, and then

3) give your comments.

You should write neatly on ANSWER SHEET 2. (20 points)

网络的“近”与“远”

参考范文

It looks conspicuous in the cartoon that quite a few adults and children, sitting in their respective rooms, are surfing the Internet crazily. Indeed, the caricature reflects a popular phenomenon: heavy use of the Internet has influenced the relationships among individuals deeply.

There are many reasons accounting for this issue. Firstly, with the rapid development of society, advance in office equipment has been made, which has led to the improvement of the working means of many people. Therefore, many people are required to be proficient in the operation of computers. Some even become addicted to the Internet. Secondly, the Internet enmeshes the world so that people assume they can gain various information on it without stepping out of their rooms. Thirdly, a lot of unhealthy contents are easily obtained on the Internet. At the same time, some fascinating movies and games could attract a host of teenagers and youngsters.

So frankly speaking, this social phenomenon is a double-edged sword. It has both positive and negative impacts on the whole society. It is universally accepted that the Internet offers many benefits to humans. Some young men, on the opposite, spend most of their time on computers, which will lead them into poor health. So what we can do is to curb its weak points and promote its merits.

【参考译文】

从这幅漫画中可以很明显地看到，相当多的成年人和儿童坐在各自的房间里疯狂地上网。事实上，漫画确实反映了一个普遍的现象：互联网的过度使用深深地影响了人与人之间的关系。

有大量的原因来解释这个问题。第一，随着社会的快速发展，办公设备的不断进步使许多人的工作方式得到了改善。因此，许多人必须熟练操作计算机。有些人甚至对互联网上瘾。第二，互联网将世界连成一个网，这样人们就可以在不走出房间的情况下获得互联网上的各种信息。第三，许多不健康的内容很容易在网上找到。同时，一些引人入胜的电影和游戏也能吸引大批青少年。

所以坦率地说，这种社会现象是一把双刃剑。它对整个社会既有积极的影响，也有消极的影响。人们普遍认为互联网给人类带来了许多好处。相反，一些年轻人把大部分时间都花在电脑上，这会导致他们健康状况变差。因此，我们能做的就是抑制它的弱点，发扬它的优点。

6. 2010 年写作真题及参考范文

Part A

Directions:

You are supposed to write for the Postgraduates' Association a notice to recruit volunteers for an international conference on globalization. The notice should include the basic qualifications for applicants and other information which you think is relevant.

You should write about 100 words on ANSWER SHEET 2.

Do not sign your own name at the end of the notice. Use "Postgraduates' Association" instead. (10 points)

参考范文

NOTICE

Do you want to have a good opportunity to practice yourself? Come and join us. We are recruiting volunteers for an international conference. To begin with, applicants should have Chinese nationality, a strong professional spirit, cheerful personality and be aged under 35. In addition, candidates must have outstanding skills in English listening comprehension and the ability to speak Chinese and English fluently. Finally, students with academic backgrounds are preferred.

Those postgraduates who are interested in taking part in it may sign up at the monitors of their classes before Feb. 1, 2010. Everybody is welcome to join us.

Postgraduates' Association

【参考译文】

通知

你想有一个锻炼自己的好机会吗？来加入我们吧。我们正在为一个国际会议招募志愿者。首先，申请人应具有中国国籍、强烈的职业精神、开朗的性格，且年龄在 35 岁以下。其次，申请人必须具备出色的英语听力理解能力和流利的中英文口语能力。最后，有相关专业经验的学生优先考虑。

有兴趣参加的研究生可以在 2010 年 2 月 1 日前到各班班长那里报名。欢迎大家加入。

研究生协会

Part B

Directions:

Write an essay of 160-200 words based on the following drawing. In your essay, you should

1) describe the drawing briefly,

2) explain its intended meaning, and

3) give your comments.

You should write neatly on ANSWER SHEET 2. (20 points)

文化"火锅"，既美味又营养

参考范文

What can be seen clearly in the cartoon is a hot pot with numerous ingredients in it, including so many domestic and alien cultures such as Buddha, Kungfu and Shakespeare. It seems that the hot pot tastes very delicious because of the rich nutrition of the multicultural elements.

The picture, in as obvious a way as possible, characterizes the function of cultural exchanges. Since China has opened its door widely to the outside world, many people from different countries have been deeply fascinated by Chinese culture. They accept and love Chinese culture as a whole. In addition, Chinese culture should be well shared with foreigners who have shown their enthusiasm towards China. Meanwhile, Chinese people are also exposed to foreign cultures when more foreigners come to this oriental country. In this way people from various nations will be able to acquire better understanding of each other and live peacefully in this world.

In my opinion, the culture of every nation is a kind of precious heritage, and belongs to the whole mankind. With economic globalization, the blending of different cultures has become an inevitable trend. Both China and the Western world are no longer isolated from each other. The more culture people know about, the more beneficial it will be to the global villagers.

【参考译文】

我们可以从这幅漫画中清楚地看到一个有着众多成分的火锅，其中包含了如此多的国内外文化，如佛、功夫和莎士比亚。火锅看起来非常美味，因为有营养丰富的多元文化元素。

这幅画以尽可能明显的方式强调了文化交流的作用。自从中国对外开放以来，许多来自不同国家的人深深地迷恋着中国文化。他们接受和热爱整个中国文化。此外，应该与对中国表现出热情的外国人分享中国文化。同时，当更多的外国人来到这个东方国家时，中国人也会接触到外国文化。这样，世界各国人民就能够更好地相互了解，和平地生活在这个世界上。

在我看来，每个国家的文化都是一种宝贵的遗产，它属于全人类。随着经济全球化的发展，不同文化的融合已成为必然趋势。中国和西方国家不再彼此孤立。人们了解的文化越多，就越有利于地球村的居民。

7. 2011 年写作真题及参考范文

Part A

Directions:

Write a letter to a friend of yours to

1) recommend one of your favorite movies and

2) give reasons for your recommendation.

Your should write about 100 words on ANSWER SHEET 2.

Do not sign your own name at the end of the letter. Use “Li Ming” instead.

Do not write the address. (10 points)

参考范文

Dear friend,

It is a great pleasure to write to you again. The purpose of my letter is to recommend a fantastic movie to you. Its name is *2012.*

Firstly, you cannot imagine how terrific the story is. It tells about the doomsday on which the world becomes ruins and everyone feels painful, and it manages to make us feel true love ultimately. In addition, the hero in the movie looks so brave and persistent that I believe you will like him.

I hope that you will enjoy the movie.

Best wishes!

Yours truly,

Li Ming

【参考译文】

亲爱的朋友：

很高兴再次给你写信。我写这封信的目的是向你推荐一部科幻电影——《2012》。

首先，你无法想象这个故事有多么精彩。它讲述了在世界末日，整个世界都毁了，每个人都感到非常恐慌，而且它使我们在最后时刻感受到了真爱。另外，电影中的男主人公看起来十分勇敢和坚强，所以我相信你会喜欢他的。

希望你喜欢这部影片。

祝你好运！

你真挚的，

李明

Part B

Directions:

Write an essay of 160-200 words based on the following drawing. In your essay, you should

1) describe the drawing briefly,

2) explain its intended meaning, and

3) give your comments.

You should write neatly on ANSWER SHEET 2. (20 points)

旅程之“余”

参考范文

What an impressive cartoon it looks! Two youngsters sitting on the boat are throwing rubbish into the lake, with all kinds of garbage floating on the surface. Clearly, we can deduce from the picture that with the rapid advance of tourism, environmental contamination is becoming increasingly serious in modern society.

To analyze the issue, I am going to point out some elements here. To begin with, the faster national economy develops, the worse our environment is likely to become, which is universally acknowledged. Then the truth that bright stars and moon cannot be seen anymore by citizens manifests that something should be done to put an end to such a phenomenon. In the end, if the current situation continues and everyone fails to pay attention to it, what would happen? Human beings might evaporate from the earth.

So grave is the pollution that something must be done to solve the issue. For one thing, people should know the importance of the clean environment to their personal lives. For another, kids should be educated to protect our common homeland so as to have a clean sky and green grassland.

【参考译文】

这是一幅多么令人印象深刻的漫画啊！两个坐在船上的年轻人正往湖里扔垃圾，各种各样的垃圾漂浮在水面上。从图中可以明显推断出，随着旅游业的快速发展，现代社会的环境污染正变得日益严重。

为了分析这个问题，我会在这里指出一些要点。首先，国民经济发展越快，我们的环境就可能越差，这是共识。此外，市民不再看得见明亮的星星和月亮的事实表明，应该采取一些措施来制止这种现象。最后，如果当前的形势继续下去，而且我们每个人都不去关注它，会发生什么呢？人类可能会从地球上消失。

污染太严重了，我们必须采取措施来解决这个问题。一方面，人们应该知道清洁的环境对个人生活的重要性。另一方面，人们应该教育孩子们来保护我们共同的家园，让我们拥有洁净的天空和碧绿的草地。

8. 2012 年写作真题及参考范文

Part A

Directions:

Some international students are coming to your university. Write them an email in the name of the Students' Union to

1) extend your welcome and

2) provide some suggestions for their campus life here.

You should write about 100 words on ANSWER SHEET 2.

Do not sign your own name at the end of the letter. Use "Li Ming" instead.

Do not write the address. (10 points)

参考范文

Dear friends,

I, on behalf of the Students' Union, write this letter to welcome you to our university.

For the first few days, you will find everything on our campus is quite different, fresh and alien. Therefore, after arriving, you can take full advantage of every opportunity to communicate with us directly to enhance the understanding of each other. In addition, the climate in Beijing is considerably different from that in your hometown, but you will soon get accustomed to living here. Finally, I hope to accompany you and introduce some special and unique campus characteristics and cultures to you so as to let you understand our college life better.

We shall strive to make your visit as pleasant as possible by providing the best service as well as support for you. All of our students are looking forward to your early coming eagerly.

Yours sincerely,

Li Ming

【参考译文】

亲爱的朋友们：

我代表学生会写这封信欢迎你们来我们学校。

在最初的几天里，你们会发现我们校园里的一切都非常与众不同、新鲜和陌生。因此，抵达后，你们可以充分利用每一个机会，直接与我们沟通，以增进相互之间的了解。另外，北京的气候与你们家乡的气候大不相同，但你们很快就会习惯住在这里。最后，我希望能陪同你们，向你们介绍一些独特的校园特色和文化，让你们更好地了解我们的大学生活。

我们将努力为你们提供最好的服务和帮助，使你们的访问尽可能愉快。我们所有的学生都迫不及待地期待着你们早日到来。

你真挚的，
李明

Part B

Directions:

Write an essay of 160-200 words based on the following drawing. In your essay, you should

1) describe the drawing briefly,

2) explain its intended meaning, and

3) give your comments.

You should write neatly on ANSWER SHEET 2. (20 points)

参考范文

What looks beyond dispute is that two men stand in the middle with quite different expressions when facing the same situation. One feels gloomy after the water has run out while the other feels lucky. How impressive this drawing seems to be in depicting that optimism plays a key role in the general routine of daily life!

Although numerous cases can account for my perspective, the following one is the most favorable here. My grandparents have three children including two daughters and a son. When their children were so young, my grandpa worked in a remote town and failed to help my grandma take care of the three kids. But she never complained about life and took on all kinds of nasty and boring jobs in order to raise her three kids. Eventually, young babies became strong and mature and had their own jobs. The story vividly tells us the truth that our attitude rather than the situation itself determines how we feel.

So if most of us feel negative in the harsh reality, we will definitely have a gloomy future. Everyone is bound to encounter hardships and difficulties in life. We should keep an optimistic attitude towards any hardship. Just as a famous figure puts it, it is our attitude that has changed everything in our life.

【参考译文】

很明显，面对相同的情况，中间站着两个表情迥异的人。看到水洒了，一个人感到沮丧，而另一个人感到幸运。这幅图画深刻描绘了乐观主义在日常生活中起到的重要作用。

尽管有许多案例可以解释我的观点，但下面的例子在这里非常合适。我的爷爷奶奶有三个孩子，包括两个女儿和一个儿子。在他们的三个孩子还小的时候，爷爷在一个偏僻的城镇工作，不能帮奶奶照顾三个孩子。但是她从来不抱怨生活，为了养活三个孩子，她做了各种又脏又累的工作。最终，年幼的孩子变得强大而成熟，有了自己的事业。这个故事生动地告诉我们一个事实，那便是我们对事物的态度决定了我们的感受，而并非所发生的情况本身。

所以，如果我们大多数人在严酷的现实中感到消极，我们肯定会有一个黯淡的未来。生活中每个人都会遇到困难和挫折，我们应该保持乐观的态度来渡过难关。正如一位著名人物所说，正是我们的态度改变了我们生活中的一切。

9. 2013 年写作真题及参考范文

Part A

Directions:

Write an e-mail of about 100 words to a foreign teacher in your college, inviting him/her to be a judge for the upcoming English speech contest.

You should include the details you think necessary.

You should write neatly on the ANSWER SHEET.

Do not sign your own name at the end of the e-mail. Use “Li Ming” instead.

Do not write the address. (10 points)

参考范文

Dear Professor Smith,

I am a senior from the Department of English in our university. I am writing the letter in order to invite you to be a judge for the English speech contest.

This contest, as a matter of fact, will be held on the second floor in the theater on this Sunday morning, and it will start at nine o’clock sharp. There will be four other judges, and you will work together to mark the final results. After the contest, we will have a party in the evening and we wish that you will enjoy it.

I am looking forward to a favorable reply at your earliest convenience. Your prompt attention to my letter would be highly appreciated.

Yours sincerely,

Li Ming

【参考译文】

亲爱的史密斯教授：

我是我们大学英语系的一名大四学生。我写这封信是为了邀请您担任英语演讲比赛的评委。

事实上，本次比赛将于本周日上午在剧院二楼举行，9 点准时开始。还有另外四位评委，你们将一同评判最终成绩。最后，比赛结束后，我们将在晚上举行一个聚会，我们希望您能喜欢。

期待您方便的时候能尽早给我答复。如果您能及时关注我的来信，我将不胜感激。

您真挚的，

李明

Part B

Directions:

Write an essay of 160-200 words based on the following drawing. In your essay, you should

1) describe the drawing briefly,

2) interpret its intended meaning, and

3) give your comments.

You should write neatly on the ANSWER SHEET. (20 points)

选　择

参考范文

What can be seen clearly in the cartoon is that a sea of undergraduates, standing on the road with four branches, are facing different choices such as hunting for jobs, going abroad, pursuing higher degrees, or starting their own business. This picture sends a clear message to readers about the far-reaching significance of sensible choices.

The most favorable reason to explain my viewpoint is that the more sensibly graduates choose the direction of development, the higher efficiency can be achieved in both their life and career, which is what many hard-working human beings fail to pay attention to. As a writer who had gained great reputation ever said: "Sometimes, choices are more important than hard endeavors." So if they know the significance of choices and think clearly before taking any action, they can save more time and make steady and further development.

Some departments in universities should help graduates understand their own advantages and disadvantages before they leave the campus. In addition, as youngsters, university students should think it over and be responsible for their choices. In the end, once they make a prudent option, they should be persistent till their dreams come true.

【参考译文】

从这幅漫画中可以清楚地看到，一大群本科毕业生站在有四个分支的路上，面临着不同的选择，比如找工作、出国、追求更高学历或创业。这幅图向读者传达了一个明确的信息，即明智选择的深远意义。

解释我的观点的最好的理由是，毕业生选择发展方向越明智，他们就越能高效地生活和工作，对于这一点，有许多勤劳的人没有注意到这个问题。曾经有一位享有盛誉的作家说过："有时候，选择比努力更重要。"所以，如果人在行动之前都想清楚选择的重要性，就可以节省更多的时间，稳步而深入地发展。

大学里的一些部门理应帮助毕业生在离开校园前了解自己的优缺点。此外，作为年轻人，大学生应该仔细考虑，并对自己的选择负责。最后，一旦做出谨慎的选择，就要坚持下去，直到实现自己的梦想。

10. 2014 年写作真题及参考范文

Part A

Directions:

Write a letter of about 100 words to the president of your university, suggesting how to improve students' physical condition.

You should include the details you think necessary.

You should write neatly on the ANSWER SHEET.

Do not sign your own name at the end of the letter. Use "Li Ming" instead.

Do not write the address. (10 points)

参考范文

Dear Mr. President,

I am one of the senior students in our university. I am writing the letter to provide some conducive suggestions on how to improve the students' physical condition.

First of all, it is widely accepted that youngsters on campus have more free time, most of which is used to surf the Internet or watch movies. So it is time for the school to consider offering some physical education classes. That is to say, they have to be forced to do exercise at the beginning. Then, with these classes, some competitions could be held on campus such as basketball competitions and swimming contests.

I hope that you will carefully take my suggestions into consideration. I am looking forward to your reply.

Yours respectfully,

Li Ming

【参考译文】

尊敬的校长：

我是我们大学的一名大四学生。我写这封信的目的是提供一些关于如何改善学生身体状况的建议。

首先，人们普遍认为，校园里的年轻人有更多的空闲时间，但是大多数时间被用来上网或看电影了。所以现在是校方考虑开设体能课的时候了。也就是说，学生们一开始会被强制锻炼。然后，通过这些课程，可以在校园内开展一些比赛，如篮球赛和游泳比赛。

我希望您能认真考虑我的建议。期待您的答复。

您真挚的，

李明

Part B

Directions:

Write an essay of 160-200 words based on the following drawing. In your essay, you should

1) describe the drawing briefly,

2) interpret its intended meaning, and

3) give your comments.

You should write neatly on the ANSWER SHEET. (20 points)

相 携

参考范文

As is vividly depicted in the left part of the drawing, thirty years ago, there stood a delicate mother, holding the tiny hand of a lovely girl. With time flying, the little girl who has already grown into a gorgeous lady is supporting her old mother as illustrated in the picture on the right. We are informed that accompanying may be the best gift.

There are quite a few reasons which can account for the intended meaning. To begin with, it is a Chinese tradition to respect the elderly and take care of the young, which has been widely accepted by the public. In addition, the evidence that senior citizens have struggled to create better living and working conditions for posterity manifests that they should be supported by their offspring when they retire. The last factor that I have to point out here is that without diligence and endeavor of the past generations, we could by no means enjoy the current prosperity and happiness.

As a consequence, it is so crucial to respect parents and spend time with them. The essential action, obviously, is to educate kids to honor the elderly. Apart from this, youngsters should go back to see their parents frequently in spite of busy jobs. In the end, just as an old saying has put it, "Filial piety is the most important of all virtues."

【参考译文】

左图生动地描述了三十年前，一位精致的母亲，牵着一个可爱女孩的小手。而右图则说明，随着时间的飞逝，小女孩已经长成一位优雅的女士，正在搀扶着她的老母亲。我们认识到：陪伴可能是最好的礼物。

有很多原因可以解释我的看法。首先，尊老爱幼是被公众广泛接受的中国传统。此外，老年人努力为子孙后代创造更好的生活和工作条件，这一事实表明，当他们退休时应该得到后代的赡养。我在这里必须指出的最后一个原因是，如果没有过去几代人的勤奋和努力，我们绝不能享受现在的繁荣和幸福。

因此，尊重和陪伴父母是非常重要的。很显然，最重要的行动就是从小教育孩子要尊重老人。除此之外，尽管工作繁忙，年轻人理应经常回去看望父母。最后，就像一句老话所说：“百善孝为先”。

11. 2015 年写作真题及参考范文

Part A

Directions:

You are going to host a club reading session. Write an email of about 100 words recommending a book to the club members.

You should state reasons for your recommendation.

You should write neatly on the ANSWER SHEET.

Do not sign your own name at the end of the letter. Use “Li Ming” instead.

Do not write the address. (10 points)

参考范文

Dear friends,

As the next reading session is scheduled to be launched in two days, it’s a great honor for me to take this opportunity to recommend you a book—*The Road Less Traveled.*

There are two reasons for my recommendation. First, it is a book about how to be spiritually healthy. It has been a best-seller of psychology category for nearly 30 years. Second, the principles the author described in the book stand the test of time and have especially high value in modern times when an increasing number of people are suffering from emotional problems.

I believe reading such a classical book written by an authoritative writer will produce a far-reaching and thought-provoking effect on all club members.

Yours faithfully,

Li Ming

【参考译文】

亲爱的朋友们：

下一次的读书会将在两天后举行，我很荣幸有机会给你们推荐一本书——《少有人走的路》。

我推荐这本书有两个理由。第一，这本书是有关如何保持心理健康的，近三十年来一直是心理学类的畅销书。第二，作者在书中描述的原理经受了时间的考验，而且在现代社会，当越来越多的人遭受情感问题时，这些原理具有特别高的价值。

我相信阅读一本权威作者所写的如此经典的作品，将会对我们所有俱乐部成员产生发人深省的深远影响。

你真诚的，
李明

Part B

Directions:

Write an essay of 160-200 words based on the following picture. In your essay, you should

1) describe the picture briefly,

2) interpret its intended meaning, and

3) give your comments.

You should write neatly on the ANSWER SHEET. (20 points)

手机时代的聚会

参考范文

The simple caricature not only attracts the eyes but also captures the heart. The four youngsters who may be intimate friends, sitting in front of the table served with dishes, are fiddling with their cellphones with heart and soul without any communication with each other. The message conveyed in the picture seems to be that heavy use of cellphones is so serious nowadays and it's time to pay attention to it.

In order to find a solution, the first step is to analyze the root causes. The primary element I would like to point out is that not only does heavy use of cellphones exert great influence on our health but also wastes too much precious time of teenagers and youngsters. Another factor is that, the more frequently kids surf the Internet with cellphones, the worse their performance will become, which leaves teachers and parents quite a deep impression. In the end, if the tendency continues, the grave consequence will be easy to be predicted—the users of cellphones will look like mummies and consequently, their actions will be slow. How horrible it sounds!

For my part, I think more time should be spared to accompany our families and friends face to face instead of just sitting and staring at the cold screen. Besides, kids should be kept from being addicted to surfing the Internet. All in all, the Internet looks like a two-edged sword. What we could do is to avoid its shortcomings and make use of its strong points.

【参考译文】

这幅简单的漫画不但吸引人的眼球，而且抓住了人的心。四个年轻人可能是亲密的朋友，他们坐在摆好菜的桌子前，却在心无旁骛地玩着手机，彼此没有任何交流。图片中传达的信息似乎是：如今，滥用手机的现象如此严重，是时候关注这个问题了。

第一步是分析根源并找到对策。我要指出的一个重要原因是，滥用手机不仅会对我们的健康产生巨大影响，而且浪费了青少年太多宝贵的时间。另一个原因是孩子们使用手机上网的频率越高，他们的表现就越差，这给教师和父母留下了很深的印象。最后，如果这种趋势继续下去，可怕的后果将很容易被预测到——手机用户可能看起来像木乃伊，行动缓慢。这听起来多么可怕啊！

在我看来，我们应该腾出更多的时间来与家人和朋友面对面地交流，而不只是坐着，盯着冰冷的屏幕。此外，应该阻止孩子们沉迷于上网。总而言之，互联网就像是一把双刃剑。我们所能做的就是避免其缺点，利用其优点。

12. 2016 年写作真题及参考范文

Part A

Directions:

Suppose you are a librarian in your university. Write a notice of about 100 words, providing the newly-enrolled international students with relevant information about the library.

You should write neatly on the ANSWER SHEET.

Do not sign your own name at the end of the notice. Use "Li Ming" instead.

Do not write the address. (10 points)

参考范文

NOTICE

To all international students,

Do you want to be acquainted with the services of the library in our university? Then, please pay attention to the following information. By the way, I'm a librarian here.

To begin with, there exist a sea of books and magazines covering not only all the majors and subjects, but also many extra-curricular reading materials. So if you need something, please do not hesitate to refer to materials you need. In addition, the library opens every day, from 9:00 am to 10:00 pm. In the end, if you cannot fully understand Chinese at the very start and fail to find what you want, please go upstairs. There is a machine waiting there to help you.

Welcome to the library! If you have any problem, please let me know.

Yours sincerely,

Li Ming

【参考译文】

通知

所有留学生们：

想了解我们大学图书馆的服务吗？那么，请注意以下相关信息。顺便告知一下，我是图书管理员。

首先，图书馆里有很多书籍和杂志，不仅涵盖了所有的专业和科目，而且还有许多课外阅读材料。所以如果你需要什么，请毫不犹豫地来查阅你需要的材料。此外，图书馆每天上午 9:00 至晚上 10:00 开放。最后，如果你一开始不能完全理解汉语，找不到你想要的材料，请上楼，那里有一台机器会给你提供帮助。

欢迎来到图书馆，如果你有任何问题，请告诉我。

你真诚的，
李明

Part B

Directions:

Write an essay of 160-200 words based on the following pictures. In your essay, you should

1) describe the pictures briefly,

2) interpret the meaning, and

3) give your comments.

You should write neatly on the ANSWER SHEET. (20 points)

与其只提要求，不如做个榜样

参考范文

What could be seen clearly is that in the left cartoon, “Son, go and study hard!” shouts the father who is watching TV alone, sitting on the couch and smoking. The boy actually can’t focus on his homework at all. While in the right one, both the father and the boy are concentrating on their work. The symbolic meaning is quite obvious—the actions of parents speak louder than their words.

A great majority of people might agree that the issue has its deep roots as follows. The primary element is that parents indeed play important roles in the growth of their children. Parents can teach children by setting good examples in their daily life. If parents fail to meet their requirements, how can they ask their children to do so? Moreover, in children’s view, their parents are always perfect, and they usually follow suit, especially when they’re young. So it’s of great significance to set good examples for children. Just as an old saying in China shows, parents are surely the most suitable teachers in the life of their kids.

In conclusion, it is high time to place great importance on the way parents educate kids. Parents cannot just tell their children what to do, but they should set good examples. Only in this manner can children feel that they’re respected and can handle matters according to their parents’ requirements.

【参考译文】

在左边这幅漫画中，我们可以清楚地看到，“儿子，你给我好好学习！”一个坐在沙发上抽烟、独自看电视的父亲说道。那个男孩实际上一点儿也不能集中精力写作业。但在右边的漫画中，父亲和儿子都在集中精力做事。其象征意义非常明显，即父母的行为重于语言。

很多人都会认为这个问题有着如下所示的深刻根源。最重要的因素是，父母确实在孩子的成长过程中扮演着重要角色。在日常生活中，父母能通过树立良好的榜样来教育孩子。如果父母自己达不到他们对孩子的要求，他们怎么能要求孩子这么做呢？此外，在孩子看来，他们的父母总是完美的。父母做什么，他们就会学样，尤其是在他们还年轻的时候。所以，为孩子树立良好的榜样非常重要。就像中国的一句古语所说，父母无疑是孩子一生中最好的老师。

总之，是时候重视父母教育孩子的方式了。父母不能只告诉孩子应该做什么，而应该自己做出良好榜样。只有用这种方法，孩子们才能感觉到他们受到了尊重，并且能根据父母的要求处理问题。

13. 2017 年写作真题及参考范文

Part A

Directions:

You are to write an email to James Cook, a newly-arrived Australian professor, recommending some tourist attractions in your city. Please give reasons for your recommendation.

You should write neatly on the ANSWER SHEET.

Do not sign your own name at the end of the email. Use “Li Ming” instead.

Do not write the address. (10 points)

参考范文

Dear Prof. James Cook,

Welcome to China. I am honored to write this letter to recommend you some tourist attractions in Shanghai.

To begin with, I have to mention the Bund, which has almost become the symbol of Shanghai. It extends from Jinling Road in the south to the Waibaidu Bridge over the Suzhou Creek in the north. Every year it attracts tens of millions of tourists all over the world. What’s more, Yu Garden is another famous tourist spot because of its Chinese traditional design and over 400 years’ history. I am sure you will like them.

I wish your visit here joyful and fruitful and I will be happy to escort you during your stay here.

Yours sincerely,

Li Ming

【参考译文】

敬爱的詹姆士·库克教授：

欢迎到中国来！很荣幸给您写信，向您推荐几个上海的旅游景点。

首先，我不得不提到外滩，这几乎已成为上海的标志，它南起金陵路，北至苏州河上的外白渡桥，每年吸引着无数来自世界各地的游客。另外，豫园也是一处非常著名的景点，它有着中国传统设计和超过 400 年的历史。我相信你一定会喜欢它们。

希望您旅途愉快、收获满满。在此期间我会很开心地一直陪着您。

您真挚的，
李明

Part B

Directions:

Write an essay of 160-200 words based on the following pictures. In your essay, you should

1) describe the pictures briefly,

2) interpret the meaning, and

3) give your comments.

You should write neatly on the ANSWER SHEET. (20 points)

“有书”与“读书”

参考范文

What is clearly presented in the first painting is that although there exist so many books on the bookshelf, the boy is only proud of possessing them. By contrast, another boy in the second picture is determined to finish reading 20 books this year. Simple as the cartoons look, the implication we can get from them is that action speaks louder than words.

To clarify my perspective, I would like to tell a famous Chinese fable, the hero of which is an old man named Yu Gong. There, as almost every Chinese knows, existed an immense mountain in front of his house. Because of the inconvenience brought by the mountain, he had the dream of removing it. When he really tried to do it, all his relatives and neighbors laughed at him, saying that “the mountain is so giant that it is impossible to get rid of”, but he didn’t give up. He believed that “where there is a will, there is a way.” Finally, after several generations’ endeavor, the mountain was eventually removed. From this, we can see that, if one just has a dream but never takes actions, he will by no means achieve glories in his short life.

Consequently, it is time to pay attention to the importance of action. For one thing, as a youngster, once we have a dream, just do it without hesitation. For another, kids should be encouraged to do what they want instead of just waiting. Finally, we should keep it in mind that “keep on moving, and glories can be achieved sooner or later.”

【参考译文】

在第一幅画中可以清楚地看到，尽管一个男孩的书架上有那么多书，但他仅仅以拥有书为骄傲。相比之下，第二幅画中的另一个男孩决心一年读完 20 本书。虽然漫画看起来很简单，但我们可以从中得出的寓意是：行动胜于言语。

为了阐明我的观点，我想讲一个中国著名的寓言，寓言的主人公是一个叫愚公的老人。几乎每个中国人都知道，在他家前面有一座巨大的山。因为大山带来的不便，他梦想着把这座山搬走。当他真的这么做的时候，他所有的亲戚邻居都嘲笑他，说："这座山太大了，要搬走它是不可能的"，但他没有放弃。他相信"有志者，事竟成"。最终，经过数代的努力，山终于被搬走了。从这个故事中我们可以看出，如果一个人只是有梦想却从未付诸行动，他绝不会在短暂的一生中获得辉煌的成就。

因此，是时候重视行动的重要性了。一方面，作为一个年轻人，一旦我们有了梦想，就要毫不犹豫地去实现梦想。另一方面，应该鼓励孩子做他们想做的事情，而不仅仅是等待。最后，我们要记住"不断前进，辉煌的成就迟早会来到"。

14. 2018 年写作真题及参考范文

Part A

Directions:

Write an email to all international experts on campus, inviting them to attend the graduation ceremony. In your email, you should include the time, place and other relevant information about the ceremony.

You should write about 100 words neatly on the ANSWER SHEET.

Do not use your own name at the end of the email. Use "Li Ming" instead. (10 points)

参考范文

Dear Experts,

I am the chairman of Students' Union. I am writing the letter to invite you to attend the graduation ceremony.

To begin with, the activity will be held on the playground next Monday afternoon, which will be a fine day according to the weather report. In addition, there will be a variety of programmes such as dancing and singing. So I believe that you will enjoy them. What's more, some gifts are to be sent to express our gratitude for your attendance.

At last, we are sincerely waiting for your reply and eager for your attendance.

Yours truly,

Li Ming

【参考译文】

尊敬的专家们：

我是学生会主席。我写这封信是为了邀请你们参加毕业典礼。

首先，活动将于下周一下午在操场举行，根据天气预报，周一将是晴天。此外，届时会有各种各样的节目，如舞蹈和唱歌。我相信你们会喜欢的。另外，我们会送一些礼物给你们，以感谢你们的出席。

最后，我们真诚地等待你们的答复，并期待你们的出席。

最真挚的，

李明

Part B

Directions:

Write an essay of 160-200 words based on the picture below. In your essay, you should

1) describe the picture briefly,

2) interpret the meaning, and

3) give your comments.

Write your answer neatly on the ANSWER SHEET. (20 points)

选课进行时

参考范文

It can be clearly seen from the picture that a boy, who is selecting courses, is confused about how to choose a better course. He is considering whether to choose the courses which are easy to pass, with little homework and higher scores, or to choose those that contain new knowledge, but hard to pass, and focus more on innovation.

As far as I am concerned, I will choose the latter ones. The reasons can be listed as follows. First of all, as the pace of urban life accelerates and the pressure of competition continues to increase, college students are facing fierce competition. Thus those courses which are full of advanced knowledge are of great advantage, because by learning these, our horizon can be broadened and our knowledge can be enriched. In addition, courses which focus more on creativity can help us become more competitive among peers. At last, an increasing number of companies have focused their attention on innovative ability and comprehensive quality of job seekers. There is no doubt that those who have a wide range of knowledge and innovative ability are closer to success after graduation.

In a word, it is necessary for us to choose courses in a reasonable way. We young people are the hope of our country, and we have the responsibility to study hard, cultivate innovative ability, and improve overall quality.

【参考译文】

从图片中可以清楚地看到，一个正在选课的男孩对如何选择更好的课程感到困惑。他正在考虑是选择容易通过、作业少、分数高的课程，还是选择那些包含新知识，但难以通过的更注重创新的课程。

就我而言，我会选择后者。原因如下。首先，随着城市生活节奏的加快和竞争压力的持续增加，大学生们面临着激烈的竞争。因此，这些充满先进知识的课程是非常有利的，因为通过学习这些课程，我们的视野得以拓宽，我们的知识得以丰富。此外，更注重创造力的课程可以让我们在同龄人中更有竞争力。最后，越来越多的公司将注意力集中在求职者的创新能力和综合素质上。毫无疑问，那些拥有广泛知识和创新能力的人在毕业后更接近成功。

总之，我们必须合理地选择课程。作为年轻人，我们是国家的希望，我们有责任好好学习，培养创新能力，提升综合素质。

15. 2019 年写作真题及参考范文

Part A

Directions:

Suppose you are working for the "Aiding Rural Primary Schools" project of your university. Write an email to answer the inquiry from an international student volunteer, specifying the details of the project.

You should write about 100 words on the ANSWER SHEET.

Do not use your own name in the email; use "Li Ming" instead. (10 points)

参考范文

Dear friend,

I am a staff member of the project of "Aiding Rural Primary Schools". Now I feel honored to interpret the details about the activity to you.

Our primary task, to begin with, is to teach those poor children English. Obviously, English keeps so essential that many countries are introducing it into their primary school curricula. With the help of the language, one can improve himself a lot. However, those kids in rural primary schools fail to have opportunities to learn it well. Therefore, it is quite necessary for us to help them. In addition, each of you can make intimate friends with those boys and girls. You may live in their houses, understanding their life more deeply and communicating with them.

In the end, thanks for your participation. If you have any suggestions, please do not hesitate to tell us.

Yours sincerely,

Li Ming

【参考译文】

亲爱的朋友：

我是“支援乡村小学”项目的一位成员。现在，我很荣幸能够为你介绍此次活动的细节。

首先，我们的首要任务就是给那些贫困的孩子上英语课。显而易见，许多国家都很重视英语，把英语课纳入小学的课程。有一门外语的帮助，我们可以大幅度提升自己。然而，乡村小学的孩子都没有机会学好英语。因此，对我们来说，帮助他们学好英语是很有必要的。此外，你可以跟孩子们成为好朋友，还可以住在他们家里，更深入地了解他们的生活，更好地与他们沟通。

最后，感谢你的参与。如果你有任何建议，请及时告诉我们。

你真挚的，
李明

Part B

Directions:

Write an essay of 160-200 words based on the picture below. In your essay, you should

1) describe the picture briefly,

2) interpret the implied meaning, and

3) give your comments.

Write your answer on the ANSWER SHEET. (20 points)

途中

参考范文

What catches our eyes in the cartoon is that a seemingly exhausted adult with a depressed look is saying "I feel worn out. I give up." when he is climbing a hill. But his counterpart is smiling to him and passionately encouraging him "please don't, we will continue after having a rest for a while."

The meaning of the painting proves quite conspicuous: persist in your dream even if the road is tough. A case in point is Ma Yun, a well-known celebrity in China. He had been an English teacher in Zhejiang Province before he engaged in e-commerce. It was he that started the country's first e-commerce website in 1998. In just six years, it became the leader in the field, serving well over 50,000 member traders in 200 countries or regions, with an annual business turnover amounting to about $10 billion. "The first few years were pretty good for us," he recalled. "In 2001 and 2002, however, the so-called 'Internet bubble' exploded and because of that, staying alive became our top concern." Despite the adversity, Ma Yun did not give up his ambition of turning the company into the greatest of its kind in the world.

Therefore, persistence plays a key role in the glories of all citizens. On the one hand, ambitious teenagers and youngsters can well be inspired by themselves to continue facing difficulties. On the other hand, as an undergraduate in modern society, I just want to say, "Unlimited scenery on the top of the mountain."

【参考译文】

这幅漫画很吸引我们眼球的是，一个看上去很疲劳的成年人，一脸沮丧，在他登山时，他说："累了，我不爬了。"可是，另一个登山的人对他笑了笑，并且热情地鼓励他："别呀！休息一下再接着爬。"

这幅图清晰明了地表达了它的含义：即使困难重重，也要坚持梦想。比如说，马云在中国是一个人尽皆知的名人，他从事电商之前，曾经在浙江省教英语。他在 1998 年创办了中国的第一个电商网站，仅用了六年的时间，它就成了中国电子商业的龙头，服务于 200 个国家和地区的 5 万多名贸易商人，年收入营业总额达到了 100 亿美元。他声称："前面这几年我们的发展都挺好的，然而，在 2001 和 2002 年爆发了所谓的'互联网泡沫'，正因如此，生存下去成了我们的首要任务。"尽管困难重重，马云也没有放弃他的抱负——把公司变成全球电子商务行业最棒的公司。

因此，坚持对于所有人的成功都很重要，一方面，雄心勃勃的青少年可以因此而鼓励自己去面对困难。另一方面，作为一个现代大学生，我想说："无限风光在顶峰。"

16. 2020 年写作真题及参考范文

Part A

Directions:

The Students' Union of your university has assigned you to inform the international students about an upcoming singing contest. Write a notice in about 100 words.

Write your answer on the ANSWER SHEET.

Do not use your own name in the notice. (10 points)

参考范文

NOTICE

Dear international students,

Do you want to make more friends and improve your singing ability? Then, come to join us now.

The singing contest, according to our plan, will be held in the auditorium on 12 April. More than 120 university students from various departments have signed up for the activity. In addition, you can perform on the stage in Chinese or in your native languages, which will prove a good opportunity to show your culture and yourself. Subsequently, girls and boys, at the end of the contest, will be invited to play games in the auditorium. I'm absolutely sure that you will enjoy it.

Welcome to join us. If you have any questions, please call us at 132×××.

Students' Union

【参考译文】

告示

亲爱的留学生们：

你们想结交更多的朋友，提高歌唱能力吗？那么，现在就加入我们吧。

根据计划，歌唱比赛将于 4 月 12 日在大礼堂举行。来自各系的 120 多名大学生报名参加了这次活动。此外，你们可以在舞台上用中文或你们的母语表演，这将是一个展示你们的文化和你们自己的好机会。随后，在比赛结束时，大家将被邀请在大礼堂里玩游戏，你们肯定会喜欢的。

欢迎加入我们。如果你们有任何问题，请致电 132 × × × 与我们联系。

学生会

Part B

Directions:

Write an essay of 160-200 words based on the pictures below. In your essay, you should

1) describe the pictures briefly,

2) interpret the implied meaning, and

3) give your comments.

Write your answer on the ANSWER SHEET. (20 points)

习 惯

参考范文

What looks beyond dispute in the left cartoon is that a girl doing her homework intently is saying to herself "I won't stop being worried until I finish it as soon as possible." But in the right one, a boy who is sitting in the chair comfortably is thinking "I will never begin until it is down to the wire on my project." The meaning behind keeps quite conspicuous—good habits especially self-discipline should be cultivated by teenagers and youngsters.

It is the following example about my uncle that seems the most typical although numerous examples exist in everyday life. My uncle had been a civil servant in a small town. In fact, the job was not his favorite, and what he really wanted was to be a professor of a certain university. After quitting his position, he spent at least 10 hours studying different subjects of postgraduates' examination each day, never giving up even when confronted with stresses from his family and his friends. He always finished what needed to be done as soon as possible during that time and never postponed his plan. At last, it was through his hard endeavors that the dream to be a professor came true. The story, as can be seen, strikes us that self-discipline sometimes really means great change.

So if a teenager or a youngster fails to be self-restraint, he may achieve nothing until the end of his life. Parents ought to help their kids to manage their time reasonably. In addition, various measures should be taken to confine our lazy behavior, for we know the more self-restraint we are, the more excellent we will become.

【参考译文】

显而易见，左图中是一个专心做作业的女孩在对自己说："尽早完成才放心。"而右图中，一个舒适地坐在椅子上的男孩心想："不到最后不动手。"图画背后的意义很明显——青少年应该培养好习惯，尤其是自律。

尽管在日常生活中有很多这样的例子，但下面这个关于我叔叔的故事是最典型的。我叔叔在一个小镇当过公务员。事实上，这份工作并不是他最喜欢的，他真正想做的是成为大学教授。辞职后，他每天至少花 10 个小时学习研究生考试的不同科目，即使面对来自家人和朋友的压力，他也从不放弃，他总是尽早完成应该做的事情，从未推迟过自己的计划。最后，通过艰辛的努力，他成为一名教授的梦想实现了。正如我们所看到的，这个故事告诉我们自律有时真的意味着巨大的改变。

因此，如果青少年都不能自制，那他直到生命结束都可能会一事无成。家长应该帮助他们的孩子合理安排时间。此外，我们应该采取各种措施来约束我们的懒惰行为，因为我们知道越是自我约束，我们就会变得越优秀。

17. 2021 年写作真题及参考范文

Part A

Directions:

A foreign friend of yours has recently graduated from college and intends to find a job in China. Write him or her an email to make some suggestions.

You should write about 100 words on the ANSWER SHEET.

Do not sign your name at the end of the letter. Use "Li Ming" instead.

Do not write the address. (10 points)

参考范文

Dear my friend,

I am glad to hear that you have graduated from college. My letter, to be honest, is to give you some suggestions about your future job in China.

When the idea occurs to me, the first city you might like to stay, I think, is Beijing, the capital of China, because the natives are open-minded, hospitable, and inclusive. Consequently, you will feel comfortable working there. In addition, you could look for the relevant employment information about your major on the internet first. Therefore, when you arrive, you will find the company with a goal in mind. Hope you can take my suggestions into consideration.

In the end, welcome to China and make necessary preparations in advance. I am waiting for your reply.

Yours truly,

Li Ming

【参考译文】

亲爱的朋友：

得知你大学毕业了，我很高兴。老实说，我写这封信是给你一些关于你未来在中国工作的建议。

知道这件事的时候，我想到的是，你最喜欢居住的城市可能是中国的首都北京，因为当地人思想开放，热情好客，包容。因此，你在那里工作会感到舒服。此外，你可以先在网上查找有关你专业的就业信息。因此，当你到达时，你会带着明确的目标去找公司。希望你能考虑我的建议。

最后，欢迎来到中国，并提前做好必要的准备。期待你的答复。

你真诚的，

李明

Part B

Directions:

Write an essay of 160-200 words based on the following drawing. In your essay, you should

1) describe the drawing briefly,

2) explain its intended meaning, and then

3) give your comments.

You should write neatly on the ANSWER SHEET. (20 points)

参考范文

What could be seen clearly in the cartoon is that a little as well as cute boy, wearing opera costume, looks like the Monkey King, a classic character Chinese are familiar with. He is talking with his father, "Many classmates consider that learning an opera is not interesting." In contrast, his father replies, "You enjoy it. That is enough."

Funny and simple as the picture looks, it indeed implies profound meaning. First of all, in an era of cultural diversification, it is of great importance to make one's own choice. However, what is disturbing is that some young people rarely develop this pattern of thinking and behavior when they are under pressure from their peers. Secondly, as indicated by the hobby and taste issues, youngsters tend to be influenced by the comments of others, instead of following their favorite lifestyle. In fact, it is self-confidence in their own option that these young people lack. Lastly, without independent thinking, it is almost impossible to stimulate people's interest in fields such as art and culture, let alone exercise their freedom of choice.

As a consequence, so indispensable is self-confidence in our life that they should be developed consciously especially among kids and teenagers. On the one hand, parents should respect their children's choices instead of laughing at them. On the other hand, as university students, we should spend more time to understand ourselves and find out our strengths, which is helpful in our future career and life. In the end, just as Shakespeare put it, "Learning must be in line with one's own interests in order to benefit".

【参考译文】

漫画中可以看到一个可爱的小男孩，他穿着戏剧服装，打扮得像美猴王——中国人都很熟悉的一个经典角色。他正在和他的父亲交谈，"许多学生认为学习戏剧不好玩。"相反，他的父亲回答说，"你喜欢它，这就足够了。"

图片看起来有趣而简单，但它确实传达了一种深刻的意义。首先，在一个文化多元化的时代，做出自己的选择是非常重要的。然而，令人不安的是，一些年轻人在同龄人的压力下，很少有这种思维和行为模式。其次，正如业余爱好和品味问题所表明的那样，年轻人容易受到他人评论的影响，而不是遵循他们最喜欢的生活方式。事实上，这些年轻人缺乏的是对自己选择的自信。最后，如果没有独立的思考的能力，几乎不可能激发人们对艺术和文化等领域的兴趣，更不用说行使他们选择的自由了。

因此，在我们的生活中，自信是不可或缺的，人们应该有意识地培养自信，特别是儿童和青少年。一方面，父母应该尊重孩子的选择，而不是嘲笑他们。另一方面，作为大学生，我们应该花更多的时间来了解自己，找到自己的优点，这对我们未来的职业和生活是有帮助的。最后，正如莎士比亚所说，"学习必须符合自己的兴趣才能受益。"

18. 2022 年写作真题及参考范文

Part A

Directions:

Write an email to a professor at a British university, inviting him/her to organize a team for the international innovation contest to be held at your university.

You should write about 100 words on the ANSWER SHEET.

Do not use your own name in the email; use "Li Ming" instead. (10 points)

参考范文

Dear Sir or Madam,

I am Li Ming, the leader of the Student Union of XX University. I sincerely hope you can spare some time to organize a team for our global innovation competition.

The contest, a rather competitive one, is due on June 15, three months from now, when there will be ten groups, four people in each one, from universities around the globe taking part in it. I am sure it would be a great success if you can give us some instructions on how to pick team members.

I am looking forward to your reply.

Yours faithfully,

Li Ming

【参考译文】

亲爱的先生或女士:

我叫李明，是 XX 大学的学生会主席。我真诚地希望您能抽出时间组织一个团队，来参加我们的全球创新大赛。

这场竞赛，定于 3 个月后的 6 月 15 日举行，届时将有 10 支（每支队伍 4 人）来自世界各高校的队伍参加，竞争将会相当激烈。如果您能给我们一些关于如何挑选团队成员的指导，我相信本场竞赛将会取得巨大成功。

期待您的回复。

您真诚的，

李明

Part B

Directions:

Write an essay of 160–200 words based on the picture below. In your essay, you should

1) describe the picture briefly,

2) interpret the implied meaning, and

3) give your comments.

Write your answer on the ANSWER SHEET. (20 points)

参考范文

Many a time have we heard from students arguing about the usefulness of participating in lectures, just as depicted in the cartoon. The girl in the left voices a negative opinion on campus speeches written in the bulletin board, which are unrelated to her major, while the other girl believes that there may exist some kind of enlightenment from those lectures.

What can be inferred from the picture is thought-provoking. Both sides of this academic activity, namely the scholar and the students, should reflect on themselves. Is the content too tedious or abstruse to understand? Or does the problem lie in the fact that students do not realize the importance of those seemingly irrelevant lectures? From my point of view, I tend to attribute this phenomenon to students. It is the lack of long-term vision for their career development that leads to this short-sighted choice of not willing to spare time for lectures on general topics. Should they gain a better understanding of correlation between different disciplines or the competitiveness of labor market, be it for advancing knowledge of their own majors, or just making themselves more competitive, they would enter for the lectures without any hesitation.

To conclude, campus lectures are necessary and beneficial for students in any major.

【参考译文】

我们曾多次听到学生们争论参加讲座是否有用，就像这幅漫画所描述的那样。左边的女孩对公告栏上写的与自己专业无关的校园演讲表达了负面的看法，而另一个女孩认为这些演讲可能有某种启发。

从这幅图中可以推断出的信息是发人深省的。这一学术活动的双方，即学者和学生，都应当反思自己。其内容是否太过乏味或晦涩难懂？还是说问题在于学生没有意识到那些看似不相干的讲座的重要性？在我看来，我倾向于把这种现象归因于学生。正是因为他们对职业发展缺乏长远的眼光，才导致他们短视，不愿意花时间去听非专业性话题的讲座。如果他们能更好地了解不同学科之间的相关性或劳动力市场的竞争力，无论是为了提高自己的专业知识，还是仅仅为了让自己更有竞争力，他们都会毫不犹豫地参加讲座。

总之，校园讲座对任何专业的学生都是必要且有益的。

第三节　英语（二）历年真题及参考范文

1. 2010 年写作真题及参考范文

Part A

Directions:

You have just come back from the U.S. as a member of a Sino-American cultural exchange program. Write a letter to your American colleague to

1) express your thanks for his/her warm reception;

2) welcome him/her to visit China in due course.

You should write about 100 words on ANSWER SHEET 2.

Do not sign your own name at the end of the letter. Use “Zhang Wei” instead.

Do not write your address. (10 points)

参考范文

Dear my colleague,

Long time no see. Today I'm writing to you to convey my heartfelt thanks to you for your kind reception.

Maybe you've forgotten that rainy day when I got sick because I failed to get accustomed to the weather in America. So many people passed me but nobody turned back to help me. At that moment, you came with an umbrella. I remember clearly that you hurried to rush me to the hospital and then told me, "If you need any help, please let me know." I was comforted by your words. Quickly, I recovered. I am grateful for your assistance.

At last, I hope that you will visit China some day and wish you have a good health.

Yours truly,

Zhang Wei

【参考译文】

亲爱的同事：

好久不见！今天提笔是为了表达我对你衷心的谢意，感谢你对我的盛情款待。

也许你已经忘记了那个雨天，我因不习惯美国的天气而生病了。很多人从我身边经过，但没有人回头帮助我。这时，你带着一把伞来了。我清楚地记得你匆匆把我送到医院，然后告诉我“如果你需要任何帮助，请告诉我”。你的话深深地安慰了我。很快，我康复了。我很感激你的帮助。

最后，我希望有一天你能来中国游玩。祝你身体健康。

你真诚的，

张伟

Part B

Directions:

In this section, you are asked to write an essay based on the following chart. In your writing, you should

1) interpret the chart, and

2) give your comments.

You should write at least 150 words.

Write your essay on ANSWER SHEET 2. (15 points)

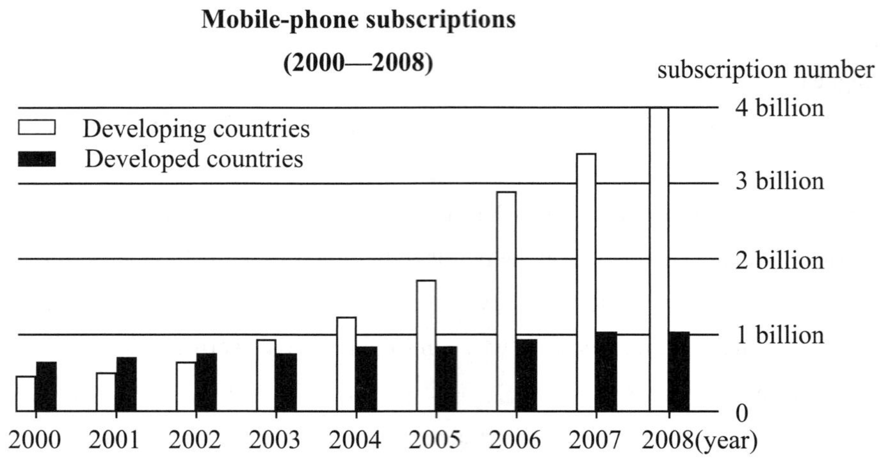

参考范文

What looks beyond dispute in the chart is that the number of mobile-phone subscriptions in developing countries, from the year of 2000 to 2008, jumped by 3.5 billion. In the meantime, the number of those in developed countries grew moderately from about 0.6 billion to about 1 billion. The meaning of the bar chart is quite conspicuous—an increasing number of human beings in developing countries tend to subscribe cellphones.

There exist quite a few elements accounting for the phenomenon. For example, in China, the most essential factor seems to be the favorable policy of nearly forty years. As a result, Chinese economy has been developing rapidly. Under such conditions, the society is becoming more stable and harmonious. People are wealthier and can afford to purchase a cellphone. As a result, more Chinese are inclined to enjoy a convenient life. Another element is that scientific and technological development contributes to the price reduction and good performance of cellphones. With such a cost-effective product, people would ask “why not buy one?”

So can you imagine if the current tendency continues, what will happen in the near future? There, no doubt, will be more communicating tools. What a hopeful matter! However, parents should pay attention to the wide abuse of cellphones by the adolescents.

【参考译文】

图表中非常明显的是，从 2000 年到 2008 年，发展中国家的手机用户数量激增了 35 亿。与此同时，发达国家的手机用户数量缓慢增长，从大约 6 亿增至大约 10 亿。这个图表想要表达的意义相当明显——在发展中国家，越来越多的人会订购手机。

很多原因可以解释这种现象。比如，在中国，最重要的原因是，近四十年的优惠政策使中国经济迅速发展。在这样的情形下，社会变得更加稳定、和谐，人们更加富有，买得起手机了。因此，越来越多的中国人生活趋于便利。另一个因素是，科技的发展导致了手机价格的降低以及性能的提高，有这种划算的产品，人们会扪心自问，为什么不买一个呢？

所以你能想象如果现在的趋势继续下去，在不久的将来会发生什么吗？毫无疑问，将会有更多的通信工具。多好的事情啊！不过父母需要注意青少年过度使用手机的问题。

2. 2011 年写作真题及参考范文

Part A

Directions:

Suppose your cousin Li Ming has just been admitted to a university. Write him/her a letter to

1) congratulate him/her, and

2) give him/her suggestions on how to get prepared for university life.

You should write about 100 words on ANSWER SHEET 2.

Do not sign your own name at the end of the letter. Use “Zhang Wei” instead.

Do not write the address. (10 points)

参考范文

Dear Li Ming,

Congratulations on your success! I am glad to hear that you have been admitted by an esteemed university. Now I am to give you some suggestions to prepare for the coming college life.

You should spend more time on English. The language, as everyone can see, plays a key role in people’s communication, so if you really excel in it, you will be more competitive in the job market while hunting a job. At the same time, in order to prepare for your future career, you should take part in more activities to make more friends and practice your communication skills.

In the end, please bring my best wishes to your families.

Sincerely yours,

Zhang Wei

【参考译文】

亲爱的李明：

祝贺成功哦！听说你被一所名校录取了，在此我给你一些建议，以便让你为即将到来的大学生活做好准备。

你应该在英语上花更多的时间。众所周知，这种语言在人们的交流中起着很大的作用，所以如果你很擅长英语，找工作时，你在就业市场上会更有竞争力。同时，为了为你将来的职业生涯做准备，你应该参加更多的活动，结交更多的朋友，锻炼你的沟通技巧。

最后，把我最好的祝福带给你的家人。

你真诚的，

张伟

Part B

Directions:

Write an essay based on the following chart. In your writing, you should

1) interpret the chart, and

2) give your comments.

You should write at least 150 words.

Write your essay on ANSWER SHEET 2. (15 points)

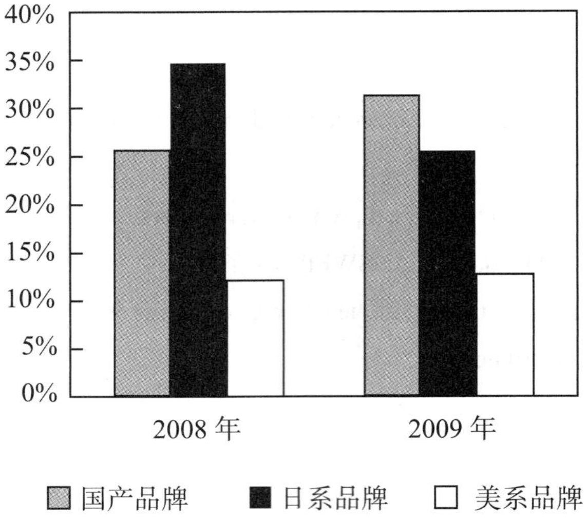

2008 年、2009 年国内轿车市场部分品牌市场份额示意图

参考范文

What can be seen clearly is that the proportion of cars of Japanese brands, from the year of 2008 to 2009, dropped by 10 percent in Chinese market. On the contrary, the share of Chinese cars increased sharply to nearly 33 percent. The bar chart shows the truth that more national products are becoming popular among Chinese customers.

There exist quite a few elements accounting for the phenomenon. To begin with, with the rapid advance of science and technology, not only do Chinese autos become cheaper but also have a higher quality, so why bother to buy more expensive foreign ones? In addition, Chinese government has introduced relevant policies to support national products from which customers can also benefit. At the same time, more customers prefer to lead a convenient life. Under such circumstances, more domestic cars are purchased by Chinese.

If the trend continues, there will be a glorious future in national economy. What a hopeful future! What the public should do is to believe our national industry and support it. Consequently, I just want to say, "Should not the promising trend be worthy of our attention?"

【参考译文】

可以明显看出，从 2008 年到 2009 年，日本品牌汽车在中国市场的销量下降了 10%。相反，国产汽车的比重飙升至近 33%。这个条形图表明了一个事实，那就是更多的国产产品受到中国消费者的欢迎。

有很多原因可以解释这种现象。首先，随着科学技术的飞速发展，中国的汽车不仅变得更便宜，而且质量也更高，那么为什么还要购买更贵的外国汽车呢？此外，中国政府也出台了相关的政策来支持国产产品，消费者也可以从这些政策中获益。同时更多的消费者也倾向于选择过更加便利的生活。在此种情况下，中国人购买了更多的国产汽车。

如果这种趋势继续下去，国民经济将会有一个辉煌的未来。这是一件多么有希望的事情啊！我们所能做的就是相信我们的民族工业并支持它。因此，我只想说："难道这美好的趋势不值得我们关注吗？"

3. 2012 年写作真题及参考范文

Part A

Directions:

Suppose you have found something wrong with the electronic dictionary that you bought from an online store the other day. Write an email to the customer service center to

1) make a complaint, and

2) demand a prompt solution.

You should write about 100 words on ANSWER SHEET 2.

Do not sign your own name at the end of the letter. Use "Zhang Wei" instead.

Do not write the address. (10 points)

参考范文

Dear Sir or Madam,

I am a customer who bought an electronic dictionary from your online store. The purpose of this letter is to express my complaint against your product.

The first problem about the dictionary is that when I opened it, I noticed that the surface of it had been scratched, so I supposed it must have been used. Secondly, I did not find the battery promised in the advertisement posted on the homepage of your online shop, which makes me feel that you have not kept your words.

It really exerts negative influence on my study. Therefore, I strongly request that effective measures should be taken to cope with the problem, such as changing it with a new one or refunding my money. I am looking forward to your reply.

Sincerely yours,

Zhang Wei

【参考译文】

尊敬的先生或女士：

我在贵网店买了一本电子词典。我写这封信的目的是想表达我对贵店产品的不满。

关于词典的第一个问题是，当我打开它的时候，我发现它的表面被刮花了，所以我想它一定是被用过了。其次，我没有找到之前贵网店在首页广告上所承诺的电池，这让我觉得贵店没有遵守承诺。

这真的对我的学习产生了负面影响。因此，我强烈要求采取有效的措施来处理这个问题，比如换一个新的或者把钱退给我。期待您的回复。

您真诚的，

张伟

Part B

Directions:

Write an essay based on the following table. In your writing, you should

1) describe the table, and

2) give your comments.

You should write at least 150 words.

Write your essay on ANSWER SHEET 2. (15 points)

某公司员工工作满意度调查

满意度 年龄组	满意	不清楚	不满意
≤ 40 岁	16.7%	50.0%	33.3%
41~50 岁	0.0%	36.0%	64.0%
＞ 50 岁	40.0%	50.0%	10.0%

参考范文

What is beyond dispute is that in the table, most people of or under 40 are unclear or dissatisfied with their jobs, and 64% of those between 41 and 50 are not satisfied with their jobs. For people over 50, the number of those who are satisfied with their jobs largely exceeds that of the younger groups or under 40, amounting to 40%. The graph, in as obvious a manner as possible, shows that elder people find more pleasure in their jobs compared with the young.

It's not hard to think of some reasons why older people are more satisfied with their jobs. First and foremost, older employees have lower expectations than younger employees, and they can adjust themselves accordingly. Secondly, older employees have higher job satisfaction because they have gone through the process of getting better jobs or more satisfying positions in their careers. Finally, the older they are, the higher their income is, the more likely they are to be satisfied; and the lower their "career expectations" are, the less likely they are to be disappointed.

To sum up, senior citizens enjoy themselves more than the young. In order to improve this situation and make life of those who are between 41 and 50 or younger easier, authorities should adopt some measures to increase salaries and perfect the welfare system. What's more, they themselves should also treat their work with a positive and proper attitude—it's good to have a work to do. They should also spare more time on physical practice after long-hour work. Only by these actions could people at different stages lead a comfortable life.

【参考译文】

不容置疑的是，在表格中，大多数 40 岁以下的人对他们的工作态度是不清楚或不满意的，而在 41 岁到 50 岁之间的人中有 64% 的人不满意。对于 50 岁以上的人来说，满意的人远远超过了 41 岁到 50 岁和 40 岁以下的人，达到了 40%。图表以尽可能明显的方式告诉我们，老年人比年轻人在工作中更能发现快乐。

不难想出一些年长的人对工作满意度更高的原因。首先，年长的员工比年轻的员工期望更低，他们可以相应地调节自己的状态。其次，年长的员工有更高的工作满意度，因为他们在职业生涯中经历了获得更好的工作或更满意的职位的过程。最后，年龄越大，他们的收入越高，他们越有可能得到满足；他们的“职业期望”越低，他们就越不可能失望。

总之，老年人比年轻人更享受生活。为了改善年轻人的状况，让四五十岁的人生活得更容易，当局应该采取一些措施来涨工资并完善福利制度。更重要的是，他们自己也应该以积极和正确的态度对待他们的工作——有工作做是美好的，他们还应在长时间的工作后在体育锻炼上花更多的时间。只有通过这些行动，不同年龄段的人才能都过上舒适的生活。

4. 2013 年写作真题及参考范文

Part A

Directions:

Suppose your class is to hold a charity sale for kids in need of help. Write your classmates an email to

1) inform them about the details, and

2) encourage them to participate.

You should write about 100 words on the ANSWER SHEET.

Do not use your own name. Use “Li Ming” instead.

Do not write your address. (10 points)

参考范文

Dear my classmates,

We will hold a charity sale for children in need of help on the playground on the morning of August 24, 2013.

The kids come from a remote village in Sichuan. They are so poor that they cannot go to school, so our assistance may change their destinies. Besides, all old clothes or books can be collected here. It is English books that are the most welcome, because English, in the modern society, has become so popular that even pupils in extremely poor places are eager to learn it. In the end, some reporters will come and participate in our activity.

So do not hesitate to join us. If you have any problems, please call us at 132 × × × and we are waiting for your coming.

Yours sincerely,

Li Ming

【参考译文】

亲爱的同学们：

我们将于 2013 年 8 月 24 日上午在操场上为需要帮助的儿童举行义卖活动。

这些孩子来自四川的偏远村庄。他们很穷，无法正常上学，所以我们的援助可能会改变他们的命运。此外，这里可以收集所有的旧衣服或书。英语书可能是最受欢迎的，因为在现代社会，英语非常流行，贫困地区的孩子也渴望学好它。最后，会有一些记者来参加我们的活动。

所以赶快加入我们吧。如果你们有任何问题，请拨打 132 × × ×，我们等着你们的到来。

你真诚的，

李明

Part B

Directions:

Write an essay based on the following chart. In your writing, you should

1) interpret the chart, and

2) give your comments.

You should write about 150 words on the ANSWER SHEET. (15 points)

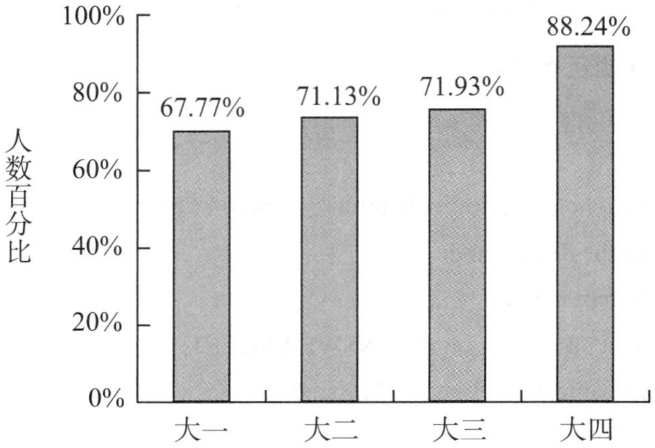

某高校学生兼职情况

参考范文

What can be seen clearly from the chart is that only 67.77 percent of freshmen, in a certain university, have part-time jobs. By contrast, 88.24 percent of seniors have part-time jobs. The meaning of the bar chart is quite obvious—college students especially seniors would like to enrich their experience by taking part-time jobs.

It seems easy to come up with some possible factors to account for this trend. To begin with, although youngsters can master enough knowledge on campus, they need more practical experience once they leave universities. As we all know, students should integrate their knowledge with jobs, so from my perspective, such work opportunities are quite necessary for university students. If a senior fails to put his knowledge into practice, chances are that he will meet a gloomy future after graduation. What is more, to students from underprivileged families, they can make some money through taking part-time jobs, which helps to reduce their families' financial burden.

Thus, this trend may continue for quite a while in the future. For college students, what they must do is to strike a balance between their study and part-time jobs. Only in this way can university youngsters become more suitable for the future career.

【参考译文】

从图表中我们可以清楚地看到，在某高校的大学新生中，只有 67.77% 的人做过兼职工作。相比之下，88.24% 的大四学生做过兼职工作。柱状图的意思很明显——大学生希望通过兼职获得经验，尤其是大四的学生。

提出一些可能的原因来解释这一趋势似乎并不困难。首先，尽管年轻人可以在校园里掌握足够的知识，但是一旦他们离开大学，他们就需要更多的实用经验。我们都知道，学生应该把他们的知识和以后的工作结合起来，所以在我看来，兼职工作对于在校大学生是非常必要的。如果一名大四学生不能把他的知识付诸实践，毕业后他的未来可能会很暗淡。更重要的是，对于贫困家庭的学生来说，他们可以通过兼职赚一些钱，这有助于减轻他们家庭的经济负担。

因此，这一趋势在未来可能会持续相当长的一段时间。对于大学生来说，他们能做的就是在学习和兼职之间取得平衡。只有这样，大学生才更加适合未来的职业。

5. 2014 年写作真题及参考范文

Part A

Directions:

Suppose you are going to study abroad and share an apartment with John, a local student. Write him an email to

1) tell him about your living habits, and

2) ask for advice about living there.

You should write about 100 words on the ANSWER SHEET.

Do not use your own name. Use “Li Ming” instead.

Do not write your address. (10 points)

参考范文

Dear John,

My name is Li Ming. I’m from China and going to be your future roommate. I am writing this letter to share with you my living habits and ask for some suggestions for my future life in America.

Firstly, I am used to reciting some English articles in the morning, so if I bring any inconvenience to your life, please let me know. In addition, I like animals, especially dogs and cats. Would you mind if I keep one in our apartment when I get to America?

At last, could you give me some advice about living there? I will appreciate your suggestions. Best wishes.

Yours sincerely,

Li Ming

【参考译文】

亲爱的约翰：

我的名字叫李明，来自中国，未来将和你成为室友。我写这封信是想和你分享一下我的生活习惯，并为我将来在美国的生活征求一些建议。

首先，我习惯在早上背诵一些英语文章，所以如果我给你的生活带来任何不便，请告诉我。此外，我喜欢动物，尤其是狗和猫。所以如果我到美国后，在公寓里养一只小动物，你会介意吗？

最后，你能给我一些关于在美国生活的建议吗？我将非常感谢你的建议。致以最美好的祝愿。

你真诚的，

李明

Part B

Directions:

Write an essay based on the following chart. In your writing, you should

1) interpret the chart, and

2) give your comments.

You should write about 150 words on the ANSWER SHEET. (15 points)

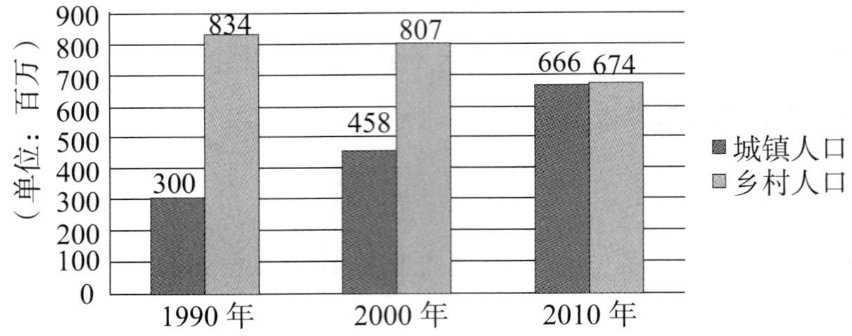

20 年间中国城镇人口、乡村人口变化图

参考范文

What looks beyond dispute is that the population in cities increased at a high speed during the period from 1990 to 2010 while the population in rural regions shrank to a scale which was close to that of cities slightly. We can safely draw a conclusion that with the development of technology and economy, Chinese urbanization is speeding up in contemporary society.

Why does this phenomenon appear? There exist at least three elements accounting for it. The first contributing factor is the substantially fast development of cities in China. Because of such rapid advance, an increasing number of workforces are needed. In addition, farmers can not only earn more money in cities but also make their children enjoy as good education as urban citizens'. In the end, Chinese had been satisfied with the existing state of affairs and reluctant to move forward in the past. However, such situations, years later, become the other way round. More farmers are fond of working in cities.

It is based on the analyses above that we can safely draw the conclusion that the process of urbanization will continue in the years ahead. Children from cities should be educated to respect people from rural areas. At the same time, policies should be introduced in order that farmers can lead a happy and comfortable life. Only in this way can we live a harmonious life together.

【参考译文】

不容置疑的是，从 1990 年到 2010 年，城市人口快速增长，而乡村人口规模有所减少，与城市人口规模略微接近。我们可以有把握地得出一个结论，随着科技和经济的发展，在当代社会，中国的城市化进程正在加速。

为什么会出现这种现象呢？至少有三个原因可以解释这一现象。第一个原因是中国城市发展步伐的整体加快。由于发展如此迅速，所以需要越来越多的劳动力。此外，农民不仅可以在城市赚更多的钱，还可以让他们的孩子和城市居民一样享受好的教育。最后，中国人过去容易满足于现状，不愿改变。然而，多年以后，这种情况反过来了。更多农民喜欢在城市工作。

基于以上分析，我们可以有把握地得出结论，城市化进程将在未来几年继续下去。我们应该教育城市的孩子尊重来自农村的人。同时，政府应当制定政策，让农民过上幸福、舒适的生活。只有这样，我们才能一起过上和谐的生活。

6. 2015 年写作真题及参考范文

Part A

Directions:

Suppose your university is going to host a summer camp for high school students. Write a notice to

1) briefly introduce the camp activities, and

2) call for volunteers.

You should write about 100 words on the ANSWER SHEET.

Do not use your name or the name of your university.

Do not write your address. (10 points)

参考范文

Notice

Do you want to improve your English and make more friends in the coming summer holiday? Then come to join us now.

First of all, the main activity of the summer camp is to share the experience of learning English. A foreign friend will be introduced to you if you like, which is really helpful to your oral English. Besides, volunteers are needed too. If you are sociable and outgoing enough, you are going to be the most suitable one for us.

If you are interested in our activity, please fill in the application form and send it to ×××@163.com before July 10.

Students' Union

【参考译文】

告示

你想在即将来临的暑假里提高你的英语水平、交更多的朋友吗？那现在就来加入我们吧。

首先，夏令营的主要活动是分享学习英语的经验。如果你愿意，我们可以给你介绍一个外国朋友，这对你的英语口语很有帮助。此外，我们也需要志愿者。如果你善于交际，足够外向，你将是我们最适合的人选。

如果你对我们的活动感兴趣，请在 7 月 10 号前填写报名表并发送至邮箱：×××@163.com。

学生会

Part B

Directions:

Write an essay based on the following chart. In your writing, you should

1) interpret the chart, and

2) give your comments.

You should write about 150 words on the ANSWER SHEET. (15 points)

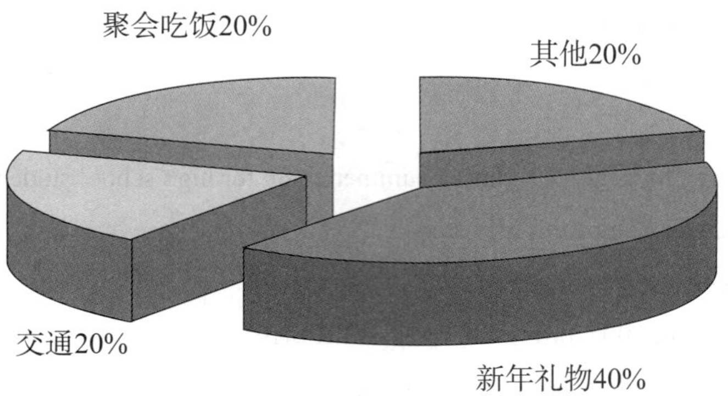

我国某市居民春节假期花销比例

参考范文

What looks quite self-evident is that in the pie chart, the proportion of money, in one city of China, spent on various affairs demonstrates obvious differences during the Spring Festival. The money spent on buying gifts for others takes the lion's share, accounting for 40%, while transportation and dinner party take 20% of the whole proportion respectively.

It is my belief that some reasons can account for such a phenomenon. To begin with, it's a Chinese convention to exchange gifts for good wishes and closer relationships, so most Chinese citizens tend to send gifts to their friends and family. Moreover, with the favorable policy of nearly forty years, Chinese economy has been developing fast. Under such a condition, society is becoming more stable and harmonious. People are richer and can afford presents. As a result, more Chinese are inclined to maintain relationships by sending gifts.

In view of the arguments above, the current phenomenon, from my perspective, is of no surprise. If the trend continues, what will happen in the near future? Chinese consumption level is going to be promoted a lot.

【参考译文】

显而易见，在这个饼状图中，中国某城市居民春节期间在各种事务上的支出比例有明显的不同。花在给别人买礼物上的钱占了支出的绝大部分，为 40%，而交通和聚会吃饭分别占整个比例的 20%。

就我个人而言，我相信一些原因可以解释这种现象。首先，交换礼物是中国的一种习俗，用来表达良好的祝愿，维持密切的关系，所以近一半的中国公民倾向于送礼物给他们的朋友和家人。此外，在近四十年的惠民政策下，中国经济迅速发展。在这种条件下，社会变得更加稳定与和谐，人们富有了，买得起礼物了。因此，越来越多的中国人倾向于通过送礼物来维持他们的关系。

综上所述，我认为目前的现象并不令人惊讶。如果这种趋势继续下去，不久的将来会发生什么？中国的消费水平将会有很大的提高。

7. 2016 年写作真题及参考范文

Part A

Directions:

Suppose you won a translation contest and your friend, Jack, wrote an email to congratulate you and ask for advice on translation. Write him a reply to

1) thank him, and

2) give your advice.

You should write about 100 words on the ANSWER SHEET.

Do not use your own name. Use “Li Ming” instead.

Do not write your address. (10 points)

参考范文

Dear Jack,

I feel grateful to receive your congratulations. I am writing to give you some suggestions on translation.

First and foremost, you should have a solid foundation of English knowledge such as mastering enough words and good grammar, which are fundamental for translation. Then you had better have more communication with foreigners, which guarantees that you have a deep understanding of foreign cultures. In the end, you should take part in more activities to express yourself in public. Only in this way can you have a good mentality.

Thanks for your congratulations again. My suggestions are only for your reference. I wish you good luck. I also hope you make great progress in your future study.

Yours sincerely,

Li Ming

【参考译文】

亲爱的杰克：

我很感激收到你的祝贺。我写这封信是为了给你一些关于翻译的建议。

首先，你应该有扎实的英语知识，如掌握足够的单词和语法，这是翻译的基础。然后，你最好与外国人有更多的交流，这可以保证你对外国文化有深刻的了解。最后，你应该参加更多的活动，在公共场合表达自己。只有这样，你才能有一个好的心态。

再次感谢你的祝贺，建议仅供参考。祝你好运，愿你在未来的学习中取得更大的成功。

你真诚的，

李明

Part B

Directions:

Write an essay based on the chart below. In your writing, you should

1) interpret the chart, and

2) give your comments.

You should write about 150 words on the ANSWER SHEET. (15 points)

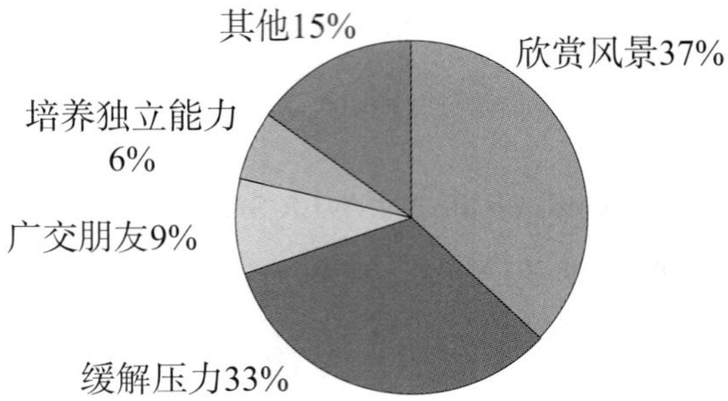

某高校学生旅游目的调查

参考范文

The pie chart shows us the findings of a survey about different travelling purposes of students in a certain university. It looks conspicuous that the purpose of enjoying the beautiful landscape takes a comparatively large share, accounting for 37%, while that of relieving pressure also takes 33% of the whole proportion. The chart has revealed a current social phenomenon that an increasing number of college students would like to travel around with different purposes.

When subjected to analyses, it really has its fundamental reasons. First and foremost, with a strong sense of curiosity about new environments and a desire to learn new things, travelling for enjoying the beautiful landscape still remains the primary purpose. In addition, nowadays, to survive in the competitive society, students need to develop stronger comprehensive abilities and have solid professional knowledge. Therefore, they are faced with a lot of pressure. Travelling is an effective way to release it.

Whatever purpose they may have, such an activity should be inspired. What we must do is to say no to uncivilized behavior and be civilized visitors. This is what we should bear in mind.

【参考译文】

这个饼状图展示了某高校学生不同旅游目的的调查结果。很明显欣赏风景这一目的占了很大的比例，为 37%，同时，缓解压力的目的占了 33%。这个图表很明显地揭示了，越来越多的大学生因为不同目的愿意到处旅游。

认真分析下来，这个问题确实有它的根本原因。首先，大学生对新环境有着很大的好奇心并且渴望学习新东西，所以欣赏美景仍然是（旅游的）主要目的。其次，现如今，为了在这个充满竞争的社会中生存，学生们需要培养更强的综合能力，掌握扎实的专业知识，所以他们面临很大的压力。旅游是缓解压力的有效方法。

不管他们的目的是什么，这样的活动都应该受到鼓励。我们能做的就是对不文明的行为说“不”，做文明的游客。这是我们应当牢记的。

8. 2017 年写作真题及参考范文

Part A

Directions:

Suppose you are invited by Professor Williams to give a presentation about Chinese culture to a group of international students. Write a reply to

1) accept the invitation, and

2) introduce the key points of your presentation.

You should write about 100 words on the ANSWER SHEET.

Do not use your own name. Use "Li Ming" instead.

Do not write your address. (10 points)

参考范文

Dear Professor Williams,

It's my honor to be invited to give a presentation about Chinese culture to the international students of your college. Now I am writing to tell you something important about the presentation.

To begin with, I will introduce some traditional festivals, such as the Spring Festival and the Mid-autumn Day. In the speech, I will introduce the origin and conventions of these festivals. In addition, four greatest inventions in ancient China will also be included in my presentation because they have been the pride of Chinese for thousands of years.

At last, thanks once again for your invitation. I am really looking forward to sharing these with all of the international students.

Yours sincerely,

Li Ming

【参考译文】

亲爱的威廉姆斯教授：

我很荣幸被邀请给贵校的国际学生做一场关于中国文化的演讲。现在我写信是想告诉您一些关于这次演讲的要点。

首先，我将介绍一些传统节日，如春节和中秋节。在演讲中，我将介绍这些节日的起源和习俗。此外，我还会介绍中国古代四大发明，因为它们是中国人几千年来的骄傲。

最后，再次感谢您的邀请。我真的很期待与所有的国际学生分享这些。

您真诚的，

李明

Part B

Directions:

Write an essay based on the chart below. In your writing, you should

1) interpret the chart, and

2) give your comments.

You should write about 150 words on the ANSWER SHEET. (15 points)

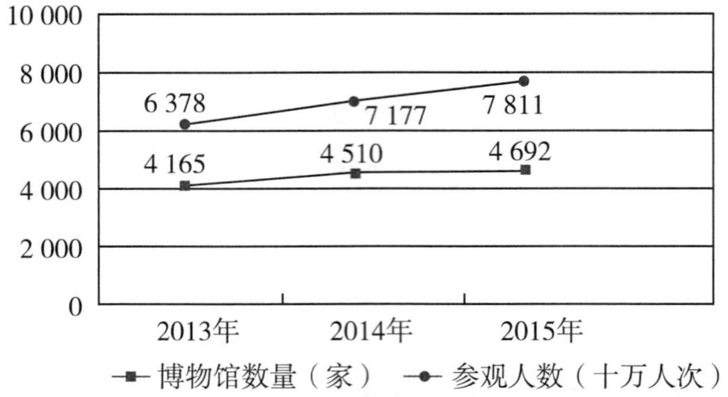

2013—2015 年我国博物馆数量和参观人数

参考范文

As is shown in the graph, the number of museums, during the 3 years from 2013 to 2015, experienced a gradual rise in China. At the same time, the number of visitors ascended gradually from 637.8 million to 781.1 million. The chart does reflect a thought-provoking social phenomenon: more and more citizens are interested in museums.

The following factors, from my perspective, are responsible for this trend. To begin with, there is no denying that the ever-accelerating pace of our life and the improvement of our living standards have come to characterize everyone's living habits, which has in turn led to the increase of the figures in the chart. Moreover, the fact that numerous people have been blessed with academic benefits from museums also conduces to the trend. Still, what cannot be neglected is that the eagerness to explore the unknown also serves as a momentous driving force. That's why we cannot afford to omit this phenomenon.

To put it in a nutshell, the above-mentioned can naturally lead us to the conclusion that the fashion of visiting museums deserves careful analysis from all sides. It is high time we cultivated a better awareness of it and took action in the light of concrete facts. Only bearing the previous points in mind can we make history and culture fuel the fire of hope among young people.

【参考译文】

如图所示，从 2013 年到 2015 年的 3 年间，中国博物馆的数量呈逐渐上升的趋势。与此同时，博物馆参观人数从 6.378 亿人次逐渐上升到 7.811 亿人次。这张图表确实反映了一个发人深省的社会现象：越来越多的公民对博物馆感兴趣。

在我看来，以下因素是这一变化趋势的原因。首先，不可否认，我们生活节奏的不断加快和生活水平的提高反映出每个人生活习惯的特征，而这又导致图表中数字的增加。此外，许多人有幸从博物馆获得了学术上的好处，这也推动了这一趋势。我们依然不可忽视的是，探索未知的渴望也是一个重要驱动力。这就是我们不能忽视这一现象的原因。

总之，以上所提到的内容使我们得出这样的结论：参观博物馆的方式值得从各个方面仔细分析。鉴于具体的情况，是我们该更好地意识到这一点并采取行动的时候了。只有记住前面几点，历史文化才能在年轻人中重燃希望之火。

9. 2018 年写作真题及参考范文

Part A

Directions:

Suppose you have to cancel your travel plan and will not be able to visit Professor Smith. Write him an email to

1) apologize and explain the situation, and

2) suggest a future meeting.

You should write about 100 words on the ANSWER SHEET.

Do not use your own name. Use "Li Ming" instead.

Do not write your address. (10 points)

参考范文

Dear Professor Smith,

I feel regretful to tell you that I have to cancel my travel plan. Thus, I am writing to make an apology.

The major reason is that I ,during the same time, will have to take part in the College English Test Band 6. It is my last chance to take the examination for I will graduate next summer. The certificate of CET6, as we students know, plays an important role in hunting for jobs among undergraduates. So I can not miss the examination and have to pass it.

At last, I am really sorry for any inconvenience. I will certainly pay you a visit later. I am looking forward to your reply at your earliest convenience.

Yours truly,

Li Ming

【参考译文】

亲爱的史密斯教授：

我很遗憾地告诉您，我不得不取消我的行程计划。因此，我写这封信是为了对此道歉。

主要的原因是，正好在这个时期，我必须参加大学英语六级考试。因为明年夏天我就要毕业了，所以这是我参加该考试的最后一次机会了。我们都知道，英语六级证书对于本科学生找工作起着重要作用。所以我不能错过这次考试，并且必须通过它。

最后，给您带来的不便，我深表歉意，以后我一定会去拜访。我期待着您的尽早回复。

敬启，

李明

Part B

Directions:

Write an essay based on the chart below. In your writing, you should

1) interpret the chart, and

2) give your comments.

You should write about 150 words on the ANSWER SHEET. (15 points)

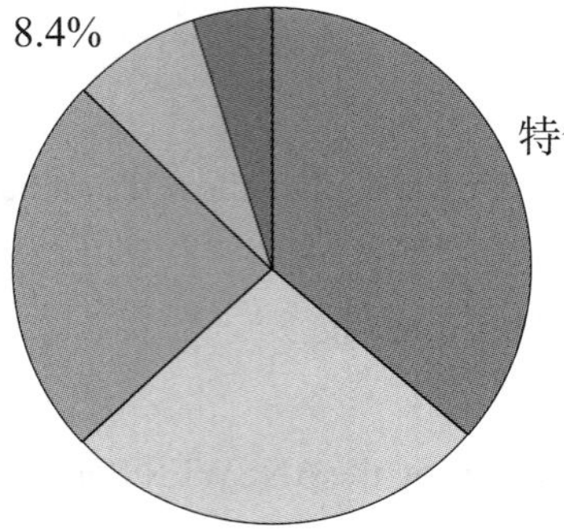

2017 年某市消费者选择餐厅时的关注因素

参考范文

What can be seen clearly in the pie chart is that, 36.3 percent of consumers, when having dinner in restaurants, regard specialties as a matter of prime importance. By contrast, it is surprising that only 8.4 percent of citizens care about the price of their dishes. Apparently, the chart tries to reveal to us that the price is no longer the main concern for quite a few national citizens.

To clarify the phenomenon thoroughly, some factors must be pointed out here. The most essential one seems that with the favorable policy of nearly forty years, Chinese economy has been developing fast. Under such conditions, society is becoming more stable and harmonious. As a result, Chinese citizens become richer and richer, which leads to the situation that the price of products might be ignored by an increasing number of customers. Another element is that there are increasing choices for Chinese consumers because of the fast growing economy. With the fierce competition, the price of food stays low, while other aspects, such as specialties, services and environments are improved, so consumers tend to pay more attention to other elements than to the price of the food.

If the trend continues, more and more people will enjoy a high-quality life. However, it is advisable for the public to consume rationally, avoiding extravagance and waste.

【参考译文】

从饼状图中，我们可以清楚地看到，36.3% 的消费者在餐馆吃饭时，把特色作为一个至关重要的因素。相比之下，只有 8.4% 的市民关心他们饭菜的价格，这是令人惊讶的。显然，该图试图向我们揭示：价格不再是很多国民关心的主要问题。

为了充分阐明这一现象，这里必须指出一些原因。最重要的似乎是，在近四十年来的惠民政策下，中国的经济一直在快速发展，在这样的条件下，社会变得更加稳定与和谐。因此，中国人越来越富有，这就出现了一种情况，即越来越多的中国人倾向于忽视商品的价格。其次，由于经济的迅速发展，消费者的选择也越来越多，因为竞争的加剧，食物的价格也很低。但是其他方面，比如特色、服务和环境，却在提升。所以和价格比起来，消费者更倾向于关注其他因素。

如果这种趋势继续下去，越来越多的人将享受高质量的生活。但是，公众应该合理消费，避免铺张浪费。

10. 2019 年写作真题及参考范文

Part A

Directions:

Suppose Professor Smith asked you to plan a debate on the theme of city traffic. Write him an email to

1) suggest a specific topic with your reasons, and

2) tell him about your arrangements.

You should write about 100 words on the ANSWER SHEET.

Do not use your own name. Use "Li Ming" instead. (10 points)

参考范文

Dear Professor Smith,

I am the chairman of this activity. Now, I feel exceedingly honored to have the opportunity to plan the debate on the theme of city traffic. The subject can be how to relieve air pollution caused by city traffic.

To begin with, the evidence that with the advance of technology, more Chinese tend to make their life convenient indicates that more vehicles will be on the roads. Therefore, we should take effective and environment-friendly measures to cope with it. For example, citizens can take clean-energy vehicles and public transportation. Besides, participants can explore some specific and effective measures to achieve the goal.

I would be grateful to receive your instructions on the issue. I am looking forward to your reply.

Yours faithfully,

Li Ming

【参考译文】

敬爱的史密斯教授:

我是本次活动的主席，非常荣幸有机会来策划这次关于城市交通的辩论赛。我认为，此次辩论赛的主题可以是如何减轻由城市交通带来的空气污染。

首先，随着科技的发展，更多的中国人都想让生活更便捷，这个事实表明街上的汽车将会更多。所以，我们应该采取有效的环保方式去解决这个问题。如市民乘坐节能汽车和公共交通。此外，参赛者可以探索一些具体的、有效的方法以实现环保的目标。

如果您能给出指导，我将不胜感激。期待着您的回信。

您真诚的，

李明

Part B

Directions:

Write an essay based on the chart below. In your writing, you should

1) interpret the chart, and

2) give your comments.

You should write about 150 words on the ANSWER SHEET. (15 points)

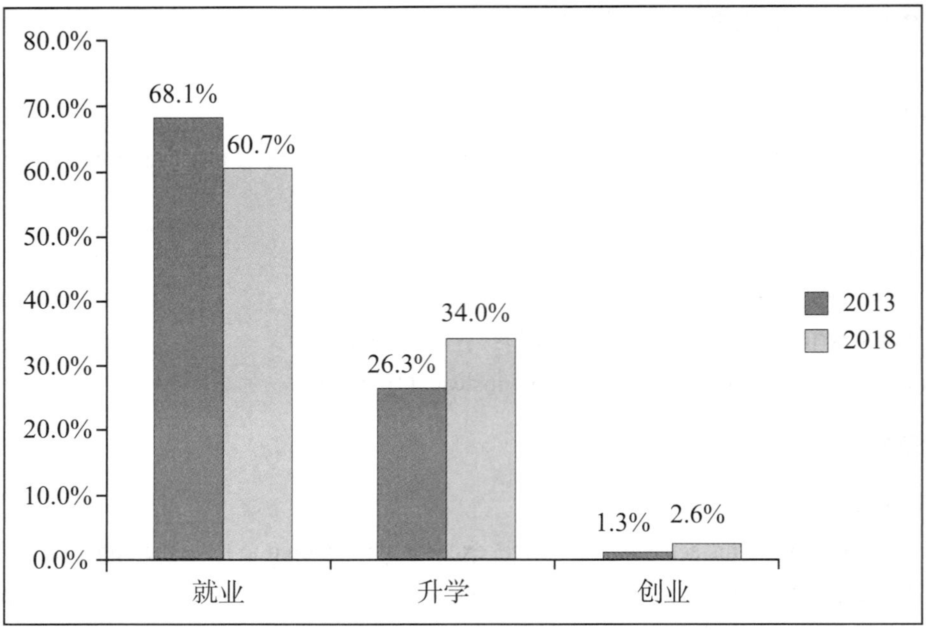

某高校 2013 年和 2018 年本科毕业生去向统计

参考范文

What appears conspicuous in the bar chart is that the percentage of undergraduates who tend to hunt for jobs, from the year of 2013 to 2018, dropped by nearly 8 percent. Comparatively, the percentage of those preferring further study, in the same period, jumped to 34 percent. These figures vividly show that an increasing number of graduates would like to improve themselves after graduation.

What could be responsible for the consequence? The primary element might be that with the rapid advance of science and technology, undergraduates begin to find that their ability fails to satisfy the needs of companies where high salaries could be attained. As a result, if they desire to get high salary, they have to improve their professional skills. Subsequently, more youngsters are admitted by universities year by year, which manifests that a growing number of university graduates flood into the talent market every June. Also, it's extremely exciting to notice that more students chose to start their own businesses.

If the trend continues, there will be a sea of undergraduates who would take the examination of postgraduates. What a surprising matter! The competition would become increasingly fierce on the way to postgraduate degrees. What we could do is to be intent and spare no efforts to realize our dreams.

【参考译文】

从条形图中我们可以清楚地看到，从 2013 年到 2018 年，毕业后直接就业的大学生比例下降了近 8%。对比而言，选择继续深造的大学生比例上升到了 34%。这些数据生动地显示，越来越多的大学生都想要继续深造。

是什么导致了这样的结果呢？最主要的原因可能是随着科技的快速发展，大学生们发现他们的能力已经不足以满足高薪公司的需求。因此，如果他们想要得到更高的工资，就要提升他们的专业技能。除此之外，每年都有更多的年轻人被大学录取，这个事实表明每年六月份都有越来越多的大学毕业生涌入人才市场。另外，看到越来越多的学生选择创业，真是令人欢欣鼓舞。

如果这个趋势继续下去，就会有大量的本科生选择参加研究生入学考试。这是多么令人惊讶的事啊！考研路上的竞争将会更激烈，我们能做的就是专心学习，不留余力地去实现我们的梦想。

11. 2020 年写作真题及参考范文

Part A

Directions:

Suppose you are planning a tour of a historical site for a group of international students. Write an email to

1) tell them about the site, and

2) give them some tips for the tour.

You should write about 100 words on the ANSWER SHEET.

Do not use your own name, use "Li Ming" instead. (10 points)

参考范文

Dear international students,

I am the chairman of the Students' Union in our university. The aim of the letter is to introduce a historical site for you—the Great Wall.

This historical magic, first and foremost, began to be constructed from Western Zhou Dynasty. It was used as military defence and it was the fruit of Chinese laboring people. Therefore, it was viewed as the world cultural heritage in 1987. Subsequently, natives there are so kind and hospitable that you will enjoy staying with them. Besides, there exist a host of delicious snacks popular in Beijing. I believe you will love them.

It is my pleasure to plan this tour for you. Wish you have a pleasant trip.

Yours truly,

Li Ming

【参考译文】

亲爱的留学生们：

我是我们学校学生会的主席。这封信的目的是向你们介绍一个历史景点——长城。

首先，这个历史奇迹从西周开始建造，一直被用作军事防御，它是中国劳动人民的成果。因此，它在 1987 年被列为世界文化遗产。其次，当地人非常友好好客，你们会喜欢和他们待在一起的。此外，那里还有很多在北京很受欢迎的美味小吃，我相信你们会喜欢的。

很高兴为你们计划长城之旅。祝你们旅途愉快。

你真诚的，

李明

Part B

Directions:

Write an essay based on the chart below. In your writing, you should

1) interpret the chart, and

2) give your comments.

You should write about 150 words on the ANSWER SHEET. (15 points)

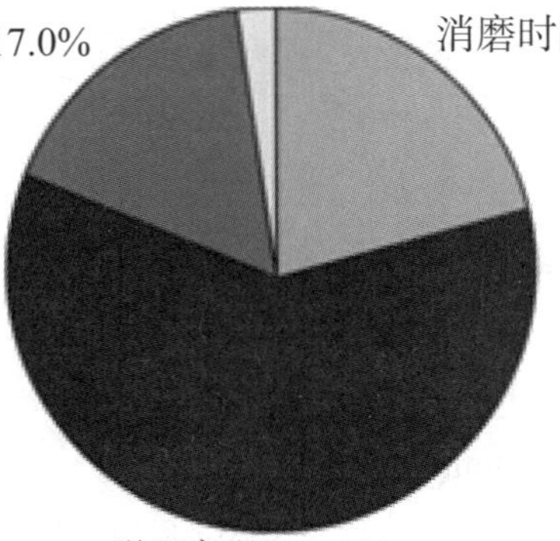

某高校学生手机阅读目的调查

参考范文

It is clearly shown in the chart that 59.5 percent of youngsters of a certain university are applying phones to acquire knowledge. Comparatively, only 21.3 percent of them, as a matter of fact, use cellphones to kill time. Simple as the pie chart seems, it clarifies an unbelievable truth that cellphones become available to students not for entertainment but for studying.

There are a few factors to account for such a phenomenon. The major reason is that the Internet, from the outset, has developed swiftly, beyond the imagination of almost all Chinese citizens. It becomes available in the routine of everyday life such as shopping, entertaining, and seeing doctors. Under such situations, teenagers and youngsters normally have been applying the device in their study. Nevertheless, what should be brought into the limelight is that the abuse of smartphones will do harm to the physical and mental health of teenagers and youngsters because they are too preoccupied by the games and cartoons on the Internet. Thus, it is the very moment to shed light on its shortcomings.

In consequence, smartphone is a two-sided sword. What we can do is to confine its negative impacts and utilize its convenience. Parents, for example, can limit the time when their children play with ipads or cellphones. As a university student, we should realize self-discipline is quite necessary. In the end, just as a well-known writer has put it, "Just talking is not enough; it is important to do it."

【参考译文】

显而易见，图表显示，在某个大学里，有 59.5% 的年轻人用手机获取知识。相比较而言，只有 21.3% 的人用手机消磨时间。尽管饼状图看起来很简单，但它揭示了一个令人难以置信的事实：学生们使用手机不是为了娱乐，而是为了学习。

有几个原因可以解释这种现象。最主要的原因是，互联网从一开始就迅速发展，超出了几乎所有中国公民的想象。它存在于日常生活的各个方面，如购物、娱乐、看医生。在这种情况下，青少年通常也会在他们的学习中使用这种工具。不过，应该引起我们关注的是过度使用手机会危害青少年的身心健康，因为他们太专注于网络中的游戏和漫画了，所以是认清其缺点的时候了。

因此，手机是一把双刃剑。我们所能做的就是限制它的消极影响，利用它的便利性。比如，父母可以限制孩子玩 ipad 或手机的时间。作为一名大学生，我们应该认识到自律是很有必要的。

最后，正如一位著名作家所说："光说还不够，重要的是去做。"

12. 2021 年写作真题及参考范文

Part A

Directions:

Suppose you are organizing an online meeting. Write an email to Jack, an international student

(1) invite him to participate, and

(2) tell him the details.

You should write neatly on the ANSWER SHEET.

Do not sign your own name at the end of the e-mail. Use "Li Ming" instead.

Do not write the address. (10 points)

参考范文

Dear Jack,

I am the president of an online meeting about English learning. I am now writing the letter in order to invite you to participate in our activity and give youngsters some good suggestions on studying English well.

Firstly, the meeting is scheduled to begin at 9 a.m. next Friday. So you have enough time to prepare your materials. In addition, most participants are the representatives from undergraduates in the law school who are not quite good at English but wish to learn it well. So may I ask you to make your presentation as clear as possible and slow down your speaking?

In the end, I hope you can accept my invitation. At the same time, I am looking forward to your reply.

Yours truly,

Li Ming

【参考译文】

亲爱的杰克：

我是一个关于英语学习的在线会议的主席。我写这封信是为了邀请你参加我们的活动，并给年轻人一些关于学好英语的好建议。

首先，会议将在下周五上午 9 点开始。所以你有足够的时间准备你的材料。此外，大多数参与者是法学院本科生的代表，他们不太擅长英语，但希望学好英语。所以，可以请你讲得尽量清楚一些，并放慢语速吗？

最后，我希望你能接受我的邀请。同时，我期待着你的答复。

你真诚的，

李明

Part B

Directions:

Write an essay based on chart below. In your writing, you should

(1) interpret the chart, and

(2) give your comments.

You should write about 150 words on the ANSWER SHEET. (15points)

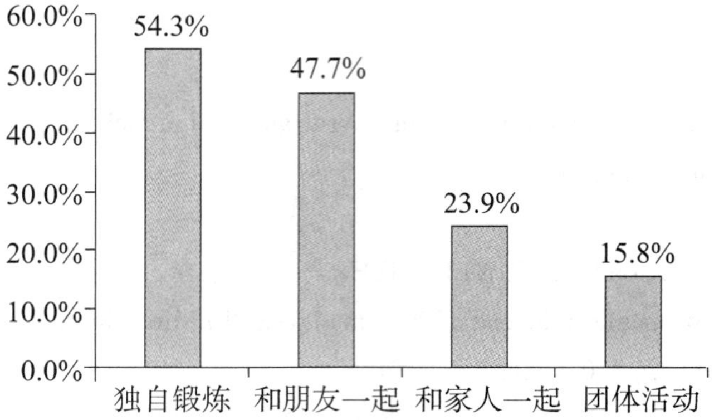

某市居民体育锻炼方式调查

参考范文

It is clearly shown in the bar chart that citizens in some city choose different ways of physical exercise. 54.3 percent of residents prefer exercise alone. On the contrary, 15.8 percent of them would like to work out with a team. The survey clarifies an encouraging truth that with the improvement of their living standards, Chinese have shown great interest in keeping fit.

It is to explain the phenomenon thoroughly that some factors could be pointed out. To begin with, there has been a large population in China, so for a long time, getting enough to eat has been our goal. As a result, with the rapid growth of Chinese economy, we have spent more time and money on foods and drinks, which proves to be harmful to our health. When it is realized, more citizens are fond of making themselves fitter nowadays. What is more, as a saying goes, life lies in movement. If we just eat and sleep, we will have many kinds of diseases, not just obesity. However, if we work out for an hour a day, we will not only keep doctors away but also be in good shape, which is the dream of many youngsters.

So it is really good news that people are paying attention to the importance of workout. It is suggested that the government should improve basic exercise facilities in parks or communities. Then as an undergraduate, I just want to say, "National sports and fitness begin from now on."

【参考译文】

条形图清楚地显示了某城市的公民选择不同的体育锻炼方式。54.3% 的居民更喜欢单独运动。相反，15.8% 的人喜欢参加团体活动。这项调查说明了一个令人鼓舞的事实：随着生活水平的不断提高，中国人对保持健康表现出了极大的兴趣。

可以指出一些原因来充分解释这一现象。首先，中国有大量的人口，所以很长一段时间以来，获得足够的食物一直是我们的目标。因此，随着中国经济的快速发展，我们在食品和饮料上花费了更多的时间和金钱，这对我们的健康有害。当人们意识到这一点时，现在便有越来越多的公民喜欢让自己变得更健康。更重要的是，俗话说，生命在于运动。如果我们只是吃饭睡觉，就会有很多种疾病，而不仅仅是肥胖。然而，如果我们每天锻炼一个小时，我们不仅会让医生远离我们，而且会保持良好的体型，这是许多年轻人的梦想。

因此，人们正在关注锻炼的重要性，这真是个好消息。建议政府完善公园或社区的基础锻炼设施。作为一名本科生，我只想说"全民体育健身，从现在开始。"

13. 2022 年写作真题及参考范文

Part A

Directions:

Suppose you are planning a campus food festival. Write an email to the international students in your university to

1) introduce the food festival, and

2) invite them to participate.

You should write about 100 words on the ANSWER SHEET.

Do not use your own name. Use "Li Ming" instead. (10 points)

参考范文

Dear Friends,

I am the chairman of the Student Union. The purpose of my letter, to be honest, is to introduce an upcoming campus food festival, and hope to invite all of you to attend.

For one thing, it will be held in the Main Dining Room on January 20. There are many delicious foods you can enjoy, including Huimian, a kind of noodles with mutton in it which is popular in Henan province. Apart from this, there is also a kind of soup named Hulatang, which originates from Xihua, a county in Zhoukou. If you come, you will definitely enjoy the activity.

At last, welcome to the party and we are looking forward to your reply.

Sincerely yours,

Li Ming

【参考译文】

亲爱的朋友们：

我是学生会主席。坦率地讲，我写这封信是为了介绍一个即将到来的校园美食节，并希望邀请各位参加。

首先，该美食节将于 1 月 20 日在主餐厅举行。届时各位可以享用许多美味的食物，包括烩面，这是一种放有羊肉的面，在河南省很受欢迎。除此之外，还有一种叫胡辣汤的汤品，它起源于周口市西华县。如果你们来参加，肯定会喜欢这个活动的。

最后，欢迎来参加美食节，期待大家的回复。

你真诚的，

李明

Part B

Directions:

Write an essay based on the chart below. In your writing, you should

1) interpret the chart, and

2) give your comments.

You should write about 150 words on the ANSWER SHEET. (15 points)

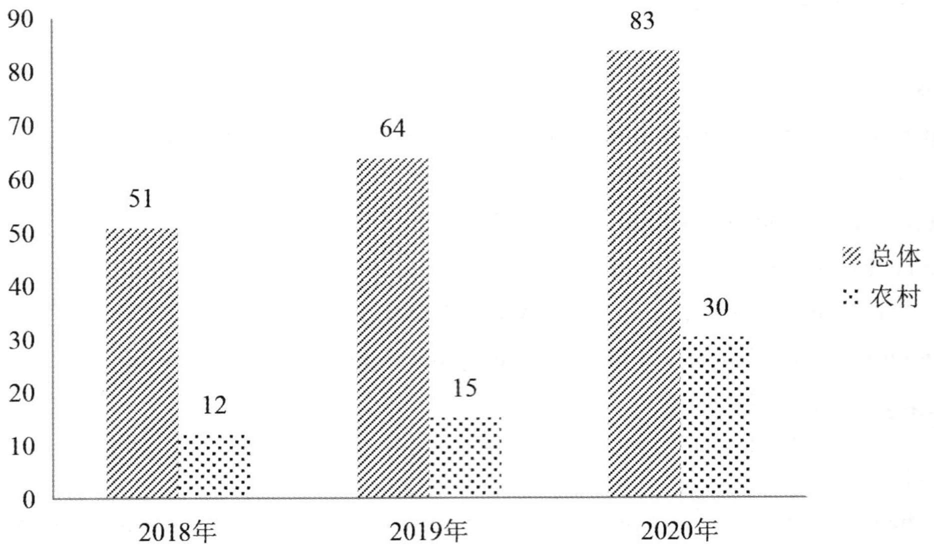

2018–2020 年我国快递业务量变动情况（单位：十亿件）

参考范文

The bar chart shows changes in the volume of parcel delivery based on the whole country as well as rural areas separately over a span of three years. It is clear that whatever the data dimension is, there is a considerably upward trend, increasing from 51 billion pieces to 83 billion pieces around the country, with the figure for rural areas accounting for almost 30% in 2020.

What can be inferred from this chart is that people, including those living outside the city, are increasingly passionate about shopping online. This is attributable to mainly two reasons. On the one hand, a variety of commodities just become more affordable, since people have higher disposable income than ever before. On the other hand, under sound regulations implemented by the government on e-commerce, it is possible for customers to access to a better shopping experience, guaranteeing a rich array of consumer rights, such as after-sale services.

Overall, delivery business has been thriving in these years.

【参考译文】

该柱状图分别显示了三年来我国总体及农村地区的包裹派送量的变化。很明显，各项数据维度都有相当大的上升趋势，全国范围内从 510 亿件包裹上升到 830 亿件，其中 2020 年农村地区的数据占了近 30%。

从这张图中可以推断出，人们越来越热衷于网购，包括那些生活在城市之外的人。这主要有两个原因。一方面，由于人们的可支配收入比以往任何时候都高，各种商品更容易消费得起了。另一方面，政府对电子商务制定了健全的规章制度，消费者可以获得更好的购物体验，一系列消费者权益得到保障，比如售后服务。

总体上来说，这些年来快递业务一直在蓬勃发展。

附　录

写作经典 100 句

建议：请根据以下句子的汉语意思写出英文翻译，再对照参考译文，找到自己的问题所在，然后背诵，默写。

1. 我国如今面临的紧迫问题之一就是如何平衡经济发展和环境保护的关系。

One of the pressing problems our nation faces today is how to strike a balance between economic development and environmental protection.

2. 腐败自古就有。只要了解历史伟人毛泽东主席和周恩来总理是如何为人民服务的，腐败官员就会急剧减少。

Corruption has existed since ancient times. The number of corrupt officials will decrease dramatically as long as they can understand how the great men—Chairman Mao and Premier Zhou, served the people wholeheartedly.

3. 世界上越来越多的人认识到自信的重要性。

There proves a growing worldwide awareness of the importance of self-confidence.

4. 充分的证据使我们合理地得出这样的结论：诚实对于人类来说是最重要的准则。

The ample evidence presented enables us to reasonably conclude that honesty is the most important standard for humans.

5. 很明显，需要立即采取行动禁止过度捕捞，从而维持生态平衡。

Quite obviously, immediate action is needed to forbid overfishing so as to maintain an ecological balance.

6. 认识问题是找到解决办法的第一步，所以我们要在这里分析这种现象可能存在的原因。

Recognizing a problem is the primary step in finding a solution. That's why we want to analyze the possible reasons for the existing phenomenon.

7. 快速解决网络问题的办法仍然很难找到，但是使公众认识到网络的一些弊端仍然是非常必要的。

Immediate solutions for solving network problems remain difficult. However, it is quite necessary that the public should realize some of its disadvantages.

8. 没有人能否认文化交流对中国公民的生活产生了深刻的影响。

No one can doubt that cultural exchanges have had a profound impact on the life of Chinese citizens.

9. 在权衡春晚的利弊时最明显的结论是，它的确不可或缺。

The most obvious conclusion when weighing strong points and weak ones of the Spring Festival

Gala is that it is indispensable indeed.

10. 尽管很多人支持安乐死，但是我仍然不敢苟同。

Although many guys support euthanasia, I still cling to the opposite idea.

11. 最近的一项数据揭示了一个令人满意的事实：绝大多数的大学生仍然坚信怀有梦想是人生所必需的。

A current data revealed a satisfying truth: the vast majority of university students still maintain that a dream is quite necessary in their life.

12. 认识到问题的根源，接下来我们就必须采取行动了。

Having known the roots of the problem, we are to take actions now.

13. 猫是黑色还是白色不重要，重要的是它能不能抓到老鼠。

It really does not matter whether the cat is white or black. What matters is whether it can catch the mouse.

14. 有力的证据表明锻炼对健康至关重要。

There exists strong evidence suggesting that exercise is quite essential to health.

15. 女孩子越充满自信，看起来就越优雅。

The more confident girls are, the more graceful they look.

16. 不幸的是，现有的证据还不能证明沉溺网络和青少年犯罪有直接的关系。

Unfortunately, available evidence fails to establish any direct relation between Internet addiction and juvenile crime.

17. 虽然女人能够在工作中获取高薪，但是她们仍然选择为了家人奉献自己。

Although women can earn a high salary in the workplace, they still sacrifice themselves for their family.

18. 为了找到解决问题的具体办法，我们必须进行以下充分的讨论。

In order to find specific ways to settle the issue, we must have discussions thoroughly as follows.

19. 曾经一个印度著名作家在他的书里写到，自信对于人类就像蓝天对于小鸟一样。

Once, there was a well-known writer in India who stated in his book that confidence was to humans as the blue sky was to little birds.

20. 我一直都坚信，没有积极的心态，一切都会是幻想。

I always believe that everything will be illusion without an active mentality.

21. 不可否认，植物在维持地球生态系统的平衡上起到了关键的作用。

It is an undeniable fact that plants play a vital role in maintaining the balance of the earth's ecological system.

22. 也许当今困扰国家的最危险的现象之一是遍布全国各个领域的污染问题。

Perhaps one of the most dangerous phenomena gripping the nation today is the pollution problem, which is pervasive in all fields of our country.

23. 世界上越来越多的人认识到加强环境保护的必要性。

There is a growing worldwide awareness of the necessity for strengthening environmental protection.

24. 许多专家指出，国际文化交流直接有助于经济的快速发展。

Many experts point out that international cultural exchanges contribute directly to the rapid development of economy.

25. 毋庸置疑，空气污染是一个极其严重的问题。市政府应该采取有力的措施来解决它。

There is no denying that air pollution is an extremely grave problem; the city authorities should take forceful measures to settle it.

26. 根据以上讨论，可以得出结论：网络的优点远大于缺点，并且在现代社会中它仍将发挥重要作用。

From what has been discussed above, a conclusion can be drawn that advantages of the Internet far outweigh its disadvantages and it will still play an important role in modern society.

27. 最近，农民进城打工人数仍呈增长趋势，因此这一问题在世界上大部分城市已引起普遍关注。

There still remains a growing number of migrant workers rushing to the cities to find jobs. Consequently, this problem has caused wide public concern in most cities all over the world.

28. 尽管文化交流对国家的经济发展做出了巨大贡献，但它也不可避免地带来了一些负面影响。

Although cultural exchanges contribute greatly to the economic growth of a nation, it may inevitably bring about some negative impacts.

29. 总之，我们必须理智地考虑这一问题，更加重视大学生的心理健康。任何忽视这一点的政府都将付出巨大的代价。

In conclusion, we must rationally take this problem into account and place more emphases on mental health of university students. Any government that is blind to this point will pay a heavy price.

30. 同时，应该鼓励年轻人自己解决问题，培养他们的独立性，这将帮助他们极大地减少对父母的依赖，而且这对于保持健康的精神状态很有必要。

At the same time, young people should be encouraged to deal with problems by themselves and cultivate their independence, which may help them greatly to reduce dependence on their parents and is essential in the maintenance of mental health.

31. 许多年轻人一提到明星就兴高采烈。他们似乎被明星那迷人的外表以及各种不同款式的时尚服装所吸引。

Multitudes of youngsters always go into raptures at the mere mention of superstars. And they seem to be attracted by their attractive appearance and various styles of fashion clothes.

32. 没有人能否认这一重要事实：最近几年交通问题在全世界受到了普遍关注。越来越多的专家开始相信这种状况将对当地的经济发展产生不利影响。

No one can doubt the essential fact that the traffic problem over recent years has caused wide public concern all over the world. Experts in increasing numbers are beginning to believe that such a situation will produce unfavorable effects on the economic growth of local areas.

33. 众所周知，假冒伪劣商品损害了消费者的利益。

As is widely accepted, fake and inferior commodities harm the interests of consumers.

34. 从上面我所提到的可以清楚地看到，网络暴力对青少年的危害是极大的。

From what I have mentioned above, we can see clearly that the harm of cyber violence to teenagers is enormous.

35. 人们对失败持有不同的态度。面对失败，有人能够经得起考验，从失败中汲取教训，并努力去完成他们下定决心要做的事情。然而，另一些人却丧失信心并退却了。

People differ in their attitudes towards failure. Faced with it, some of them can stand up to it, draw useful lessons from it and try hard to fulfill what they are determined to do. Others, however, lose confidence and give in.

36. 如果一个人要取得成就或实现他的雄心壮志，他必须努力工作、艰苦奋斗、做好准备。否则，机遇来临时他会无法把握。

If one aspires to achieve something or intends to fulfill his ambitions, he must work hard, make efforts and get prepared. Otherwise, he will lose opportunities when they come to visit him.

37. 成功者与失败者的区别在于处理机遇的态度。成功者总是做好充分准备迎接机遇的来临。而失败者工作懒散，眼看机遇悄然而过。

The difference between a man who succeeds and the one who does not is the attitudes with which they treat opportunities. The successful one always makes adequate preparation to meet opportunities as they duly arrive. The unsuccessful person, on the other hand, works little and just waits to see it pass by.

38. 没有一项发明像互联网一样同时受到如此多的赞扬和批评。

No invention has received so much praise and criticism at the same time like the Internet.

39. 每当我听说体育运动能够在国家间建立起友好的感情，以及世界各地的普通人只要能在足球场上相遇就不愿意在战场上相遇之类的话，我总是感到很震惊。

I am always amazed when I heard people saying that sport creates goodwill between nations, and that if the common people around the world can meet one another at the football field, they will have no inclination to meet on the battlefield.

40. 无论是商业领域还是非商业领域，竞争和合作都在社会进步中扮演着很重要的角色。

Both competition and cooperation play vital roles in the advancement of society, both in business and non-business areas.

41. 我们应该持有积极的态度，并且表现出自信。只有这样，我们才能成功地克服我们面临的困难，过上幸福的生活。

We should have positive attitudes and behave confidently. Only in this way can we overcome the difficulties confronting us successfully and lead a happy life.

42. 我们应当始终把“没有付出就没有收获”当作生活和工作中的座右铭。只有那些努力工作、不畏困难的人才最有可能到达成功的顶峰。

“No pains, no gains” should always be our motto in our life and work. Only those who are hard-working and brave enough to encounter difficulties of all sorts are most likely to reach the summit of the mountain.

43. 在生活、工作和学习中，我们肯定会遇到很多挫折。此时，一定要勇于面对，三思而后行。成功是一个过程，需要一步步地去实现。有句谚语说得好，“罗马不是一天建成的”。简言之，努力工作的精神和实事求是的态度是通往成功的关键。

In terms of our life, work and study, we will certainly meet lots of difficulties. At that time, we must always face reality and have a second thought before we make our final decision. Success is a process and needs to be realized step by step. As a proverb goes, "Rome was not built in a day." In short, hard-working spirit and a realistic attitude are the keys to success.

44. 无论在何种环境下我们都应该保持乐观。在生命中，我们必然会经历和面临各种困难，为了实现目标，我们应该积极而不是消极地解决问题。

We should keep optimistic no matter what kinds of circumstance we undergo. In the course of life, we are bound to experience and encounter a variety of difficulties. In order to achieve our goals, we should tackle the obstacles in a positive way rather than in a negative way.

45. 年轻人只有经历更多的逆境，才能磨炼出坚强的个性以及形成未来发展所需要的能力，也只有这样他们才能在这个充满竞争和变化的世界取得最终的胜利。

Only by undergoing more adversity can young people develop strong personality and ability needed in the future, and only in this way can they eventually become winners in the competitive and changing world.

46. 在人生的道路上，我们不能仅仅满足于一两次的成功，只有不断地追求，我们才能取得进步和发展。

On the path of life, we should not focus merely on one or two successes. Only through persistent pursuit can we make progress and improvement.

47. 坚持是我们保持精神向上不可或缺的驱动力，并且能够帮助我们完成自己的学习和工作。

Persistence functions as an indispensable driving force to keep up our spirit and assists us to finish our study and work.

48. 事实上，只有那些努力工作、足够勇敢的人才能克服各种困难，达到成功的顶峰。

In fact, only those who are hard-working and brave enough can overcome obstacles of all sorts and reach the summit of the mountain.

49. 关于机动车使用量增加这一问题，有的人认为应该限制它们的使用。另一些人则持相反意见。也许双方的观点都有一定道理，但是，无论车辆多少，都必须对废气排放进行控制。

When it comes to the increasing use of motor vehicles, some people think that their use should be limited. Others argue that the opposite is right. Perhaps both arguments have strong foundations, but emission controls must be instituted regardless of the number of vehicles.

50. 大多数人认为财富能为所有问题提供解决办法。但是，我认为，尽管财富能够提供物质上的好处，但一个人还是应该放弃物质至上的追求，集中精力追求精神境界，物欲横流并不一定让人幸福，使人真正心满意足。

Most people are of the opinion that wealth provides solutions to all problems. But in spite of the material benefits wealth provides, I believe one should abandon the pursuit of materialism and concentrate on the pursuit of spirit instead. The reason is that the overflow of material desire doesn't definitely mean happiness or genuine contentment.

51. 越来越多的人通过互联网进入了"信息时代"。针对这一现象，一些人认为互联网消除了障碍，为人们提供了与世界即时连接的途径。但是他们有没有意识到迅速发展的信息技术也能导致隐私被侵犯呢?

An increasing number of people are joining the "Information Age" via the Internet. In reaction to the phenomenon, some say the Internet has removed barriers and provided people with immediate access to the world. But do they realize that rapidly advancing information technology can also lead to intrusions of privacy?

52. 越来越多的人开始意识到财富不是幸福的唯一先决条件。

A growing number of people are beginning to realize that wealth is not the sole prerequisite for happiness.

53. 一位著名的思想家曾经写道："人类最大的威胁是人类自身！"如果事实确实如此，那么现状应该促使我们对未来的生存进行思索。毕竟人类命运共同体意味着我们应该迎接一个更好的世界。

A famous thinker once wrote that, "The greatest threat to mankind is mankind itself!" If this is indeed the case, then the current situation should make us ponder our future existence. After all, the common destiny of all human beings means that we should embrace a more wonderful world!

54. 传统的思维方式有了显著的变化。舆论发生了剧变，人们表现出更开放的思想以及决定自己命运的强烈愿望。

Traditional ways of thinking have changed dramatically. The public pendulum has swung and people are exhibiting greater open-mindedness and a burning desire to determine their own destiny.

55. 近年来出现了不良的拜金主义倾向。最近的一项调查表明 65% 的调查对象把致富作为他们的首要目标，相比之下，就在几年前，只有 16% 的人这样想。为什么人们没能意识到财富不一定能带来幸福呢？

There has been an undesirable trend in recent years towards the worship of money. A recent survey showed that 65 percent of respondents ranked getting rich as their top priority, compared to 16 percent only a few years ago. Why do people fail to realize that wealth does not necessarily bring happiness?

56. 不久前的某一天，我的一个朋友死于一场与酒后驾车有关的悲惨车祸。这种事情一点儿也不罕见，这事实上是数以千计案件中的典型案件，这些案件与在酒精作用下开车的人有关。

The other day, a friend of mine was killed in a tragic automobile accident involving drunk driving. The incident was far from rare, and was in fact typical of thousands of cases involving people driving under the influence of alcohol.

57. 简而言之，我们必须勤奋工作，为下一代把世界变成更美好的地方。我们不应该继续做对环境有害的事。比如：让细菌战见鬼去吧！

In short, we must work diligently to make the world a better place for our next generation. We must not persist in pursuits harmful to the environment. For example, hell with germ warfare!

58. 我们必须避免过分放纵和挥霍无度。相反，我们应该继续发扬节俭的优良传统以守护我们新获得的繁荣。

We must avoid over-indulgence and conspicuous consumption. Instead, we must continue to carry forward the convention of thrift in order to protect our newly-found prosperity.

59. 获得成功说起来比做起来容易，坚持不懈才会有好结果。成功人士最重要的特征：一是自信，二是渴望，还有一个是决心。

While achieving success is easier said than done, persistence does in fact pay off. One of the most important traits of a successful person proves self-confidence, another is desire, and still another is determination.

60. 为什么越来越多的中国老年父母不和他们的孩子住在一起？原因之一是年轻一代的上进心增强了。另一个原因是社会给予老年人的机会增加了。然而，主要的原因可能是传统观念发生了巨大变化。

Why are an increasing number of elderly Chinese parents living apart from their children? One reason is the desire to advance of the younger generation. Another is that social opportunities for the elderly are increasing. Perhaps the main reason, however, centers on dramatic changes in traditional concepts.

61. 什么引发了人们对锻炼越来越浓厚的兴趣？一方面，人们更加清楚地意识到身体健康的必要性。另一方面，不断提高的生活水平使中国人能够经常光顾越来越多的娱乐场所。最主要的可能是锻炼带来的身体和心理上的好处。

What has sparked the increasing interest in exercise? For one thing, people have gained a clearer awareness of the necessity of physical fitness. For another, the constantly improving living standards enable Chinese people to patronize an increasing number of recreational venues. The main reason perhaps centers on the physical and psychological benefits brought by exercise.

62. 要找到涉及许多复杂因素的新现象的原因远非一件易事。比如，一些科学家把环境的恶化归因于一些自然因素，而另一些人把责任都推到人类不适当的行为上。

Identifying the reasons for an emerging phenomenon which involves several complicated factors is far from an easy task. For example, some scientists attribute environmental deterioration to a series of natural factors, while others place the blame solely on inappropriate human behavior.

63. 对少年自杀率上升现象的解释涉及很多复杂的因素。有的人把上升的原因归结为过分强调早期的成功，有的人指出是因为同辈人带来的压力不断增加，还有人认为是对不断变化的社会价值感到迷茫造成的。

The explanation for the phenomenon of the rising teenage suicide rate involves many complicated factors. Some attribute the rise to an overemphasis on early success, others to mounting peer pressure, and still others to confusion over ever changing social values.

64. 声称缺少机会不过是用来为失败狡辩的借口。失败最根本的原因通常是个人缺乏动力。

Claiming a lack of opportunities is nothing more than a superficial excuse for justifying failure. The fundamental reason for failure is most often the lack of drive on the part of the individual involved.

65. 虽然全球变暖这一长期问题确实很严重，但考虑到当前诸如环境的迅速恶化和不可再生资源的普遍滥用等问题，它的重要性就有所降低了。

While the long-term problem of global warming is indeed serious, its significance diminishes somewhat when considering current problems such as rapid environmental deterioration and the rampant abuse of non-renewable resources.

66. 与拥有一辆自行车相比，人们更愿意拥有一辆汽车，但拥有后者涉及的问题远远超过前者。原因之一是，汽车昂贵很多，需要更多的维护。原因之二是，汽车污染环境。

Owning a car may be more preferable to owning a bicycle, but the problems associated with the former far outweigh those with the latter. For one thing, automobiles are more expensive and require more maintenance. For another, automobiles pollute the environment.

67. 从成功的角度来说，良好的职业道德与教育同等重要。事实上，成功的确建立在两方面完全融合的基础上。

From the standpoint of success, good work ethics is no less important than education. Success does, in fact, depend on the total integration of both aspects.

68. 无论成功的决心多么坚定，成功的要求多么强烈，一个人永远不能丧失他的道德和社会觉悟。无德无信无义之人禽兽不如。

No matter how firm the determination of success is, and how strong the desire of success is, one can never lose his moral and social consciousness. He who has no virtue, faith or righteousness is worse than a beast.

69. 经济全球化带来的不仅有发展的机遇，也有严峻的挑战，中国传统文化正面临前所未有的冲击。

Economic globalization brings not only opportunities for development but also severe challenges. Chinese traditional culture is now experiencing an unprecedented shock.

70. 锻炼对身体健康的重要性只是生活中人们最常认为理所当然的一个例子。

The importance of exercise to good health is only one example of aspects of life people most often take for granted.

71. 庆幸的是，大量可靠的证据证明抽烟和癌症有直接联系是毫无疑问的。

Fortunately, a mountain of reliable evidence proves the direct link between smoking and cancer is beyond any shadow of the doubt.

72. 数据显示模仿犯罪行为有大幅度的增加，这证明电视暴力是犯罪增加的直接原因。

Television violence has contributed directly to rising crime, as evidenced by statistics showing a dramatic rise in copycat crimes.

73. 尽管许多人认为随着经济的快速发展，使用电视的人数会减少，电视注定会消亡。然而，这几年我收集的信息让我相信电视仍然会继续在现代社会扮演极其重要的角色。

Although many people claim that, along with the rapid economic development, the number of people who use a television is decreasing and it is bound to die out, the information I have collected over the recent years leads me to believe that television will continue to play an extremely important role in modern society.

74. 专家指出，持续增加的污染不仅会导致像全球变暖这样严重的问题，而且还将威胁到人类在这个星球上的生存。

Experts point out that increasing pollution not only causes serious problems such as global warming but will also threaten human's survival on this planet.

75. 考虑到这些严重的状况，我们比以往任何时候都更需要像自行车这样的环保型交通工具。

In view of such serious situations, environmental tools of transportation like bicycles are more needed than any time before.

76. 网络不仅仅是一个虚拟的平台；它也是表达的方法和交流的手段，并因此成为联系他人的有力工具。

The Internet is more than just a virtual platform; it is a means of expression, as well as a vehicle for communication, and as such becomes a powerful tool for reaching others.

77. 环保的路仍然很长，因为在所有人自主地具有环保意识，并在日常生活中去实践之前，环保还需要时间去渗透到生活中。

There is still a long way to go for environmental conservation, since it needs time to sink in life before all people autonomously have the awareness of protecting environment and apply it into routine life.

78. 人们普遍认为现代科技使我们的社会发生了巨大的变化，近几十年来人类在科技方面取得了非凡的进步。

It is commonly thought that our society was dramatically changed by modern science and technology, and humans have made extraordinary progress in science and technology over the recent decades.

79. 现在越来越多的人开始相信学习新的技术和知识能直接帮助他们增加找到好工作或升职的机会。

Now people in growing numbers are beginning to believe that learning new skills and knowledge contributes directly to enhancing their job opportunities or promotion opportunities.

80. 对于那些想过上健康而有意义的生活的人们来说，找时间学习一些新知识是很重要的，正如那句老话："活到老，学到老。"

For people who want to adopt a healthy and meaningful lifestyle, it is important to find time to acquire new knowledge. Just as an old saying goes, "It is never too late to learn."

81. 通过做一份与专业相关的兼职，学生不仅能够提高他们的专业能力，而且能获得从课本上得不到的经验。

By taking a major-related part-time job, students can not only improve their professional skills, but also gain much experience which they will not be able to get from the textbooks.

82. 有关部门需要制定更多的法规，并将其贯彻实施，以惩罚破坏环境的行为。另外，人们应该共同努力，来实现可持续发展。

More regulations should be made and carried out by authorities to punish actions causing environmental damages. In addition, individuals must work in joint efforts to achieve sustainable development.

83. 现在，越来越多的人开始抱怨工作比以前更有压力。许多专家指出这是现代社会发展的必然结果，无法避免。

These days, people in growing numbers are beginning to complain that work is more stressful than before. Many experts point out that, along with the development of modern society, it is an inevitable result and there is no way to avoid it.

84. 人们普遍认为计算机和其他机器已经成为我们社会必不可少的一部分。它们使我们的生活和工作更舒适，并且减少了大量劳动。

It is widely acknowledged that computers and other machines have become an indispensable part of our society, and they make our life and work more comfortable and less laborious.

85. 众所周知，赡养父母不仅是一种应该发扬光大的传统美德，也是法律规定的义务。

It is known to all that taking care of our own parents is not only a traditional virtue which should be cherished and promoted, but also an obligation prescribed by law.

86. 成千上万的人们不得不花费更多的时间和精力学习新的技术和知识，以使他们在就业市场保持优势。

Thousands of people have to spend more time and energy on studying new skills and knowledge so that they can keep a favorable position in job market.

87. 社会公德与传统美德就如同落在我们肩上的阳光，带给我们微笑和力量。不论周围的世界变得多么黑暗，它们都能给我们支持。

Social moralities and traditional virtues, like the sunshine on our shoulders, bring us smile and strength; they can give us support no matter how dark the world around us becomes.

88. 许多人认为国际旅游对经济发展有积极作用，所以应鼓励地方政府促进国际旅游的发展。

Many people believe that international tourism produces positive effects on economic growth and the local government should be encouraged to promote international tourism.

89. 通过以上讨论，我们完全可以得出结论：尽管家长想亲自照看孩子的愿望是可以理解的，但是这样做的缺点远大于优点。

From what have been discussed above, we may safely draw a conclusion that, although the parents' desire to look after children by themselves is understandable, its disadvantages far outweigh the advantages.

90. 通过以上讨论，我们完全可以得出结论：尽管额外学习的确有很多优点，但它的缺点不可忽视，且远大于它的优点。因此，放学后强迫孩子额外学习是不明智的。

From what have been discussed above, we may safely draw the conclusion that although extra studies indeed enjoy many obvious advantages, its disadvantages should not be ignored and they far outweigh its advantages. Thus, it is absurd to force children to take extra studies after school.

91. 拥有健康体魄的人可以精力充沛、充满自信地开展工作，这反过来也有助于他们的健康和幸福。相反，一个生病的人通常缺乏活力和兴趣去完成生活中所扮演的角色，这剥夺了他或她很多成功和幸福的机会。

People with good health can do work with full energy and confidence, and their progress in turn contributes to their health and happiness. On the contrary, a sick one usually lacks the vigor and interest to play his or her role in life, which deprives him or her of many opportunities to become successful and happy.

92. 尽管来自高校和研究所的许多专家坚持认为这是独立生活不可避免的一部分，但是越来越多的家长开始意识到包括教师和教育专家在内的人们应该认真对待这一问题。

Although many experts from universities and institutes consistently maintain that it is an inevitable part of an independent life, parents in growing numbers are starting to realize that people, including teachers and experts in education, should pay considerable attention to this problem.

93. 孩子们正处于身体快速发育时期，缺乏体育锻炼可能会对他们未来的生活造成严重的影响。

Children are undergoing fast physical development; lacking physical exercise may exert disastrous influence on their subsequent life.

94. 很难想象当别的孩子在玩耍的时候，一个学生能集中精力在课本上。

It is hard to imagine a student focusing his energy on textbooks while other children are playing.

95. 通过以上讨论，我们有理由相信在人们的生活和经济发展方面，基础项目能够比艺术文化项目发挥更大的作用。

From what have been discussed above, it is reasonable to believe that basic projects play far more important roles than artistic and cultural projects in people's life and economic growth.

96. 所有家长都应非常重视保持孩子在学习与玩耍之间的平衡，正如那句老话："只学习，不玩耍，聪明的孩子会变傻。"

All parents should place considerable emphasis on their children as to keeping the balance between play and study. As an old saying goes, "All work and no play makes Jack a dull boy."

97. 现在大家都知道，保持一种积极的生活方式在日常生活中至关重要。只有照顾好自己，我们才有可能在工作中、在家庭中、在社会上努力成为自己想要成为的人。

We all know by now that maintaining an active lifestyle should be one of the top priorities in our routine life. Only by taking care of ourselves can we stand a chance of being the kind of person we strive to be in the workplace, in our family and in our communities.

98. 越来越多的假冒伪劣产品严重地阻碍了我国市场经济的发展。消费者必须非常谨慎地购买他们所需的货物或服务，否则他们会落入非法制造商所设的陷阱。

There are more and more fake and inferior products seriously hampering the development of our market economy. Consumers have to be very careful in purchasing goods and services they need; otherwise they will fall into the traps set by the illegal manufacturers who make fakes.

99. 许多人存在这样的误解，他们认为读书浪费时间。显然，他们忽视了书是人类文明的窗户这一基本事实。

A large number of people tend to misunderstand that reading books is a waste of time. Obviously, they fail to take into account the basic fact that books are the eyes of human civilization.

100. 然而，用平板电脑阅读正遭受越来越多的专家的质疑，他们指出，读实体书对读者更有利。

However, reading on the panel computer is now being questioned by more and more experts, who point out that it is more favorable for readers to read physical books.